AMERICAN ART POSTERS OF THE 1890s

in The Metropolitan Museum of Art,

including the Leonard A. Lauder Collection

Catalogue by David W. Kiehl

Essays by Phillip Dennis Cate, Nancy Finlay, and David W. Kiehl

The Metropolitan Museum of Art

DISTRIBUTED BY HARRY N. ABRAMS, INC., NEW YORK

This volume has been published in conjunction with the exhibition *American Art Posters of the 1890s: The Gift of Leonard A. Lauder* held at The Metropolitan Museum of Art, New York, from October 22, 1987, through January 10, 1988.

This publication has been made possible in part by a generous grant from Leonard A. Lauder and The Lauder Foundation, Evelyn and Leonard Lauder Fund.

John P. O'Neill, *Editor in Chief*
Barbara Burn, *Project Supervisor*
Teresa Egan, *Managing Editor*
Rosanne Wasserman, *Editor*
Joseph B. Del Valle, *Designer*
Heidi Haeuser, *Production Associate*

Library of Congress Cataloging-in-Publication Data

Metropolitan Museum of Art (New York, N.Y.)
    American art posters of the 1890s in the Metropolitan Museum of Art, including the Leonard A. Lauder collection.

    Bibliography: p.
    1. Posters, American—Catalogs. 2. Posters—19th century—United States—Catalogs. 3. Decoration and ornament—United States—Art nouveau—Catalogs. 4. Lauder, Leonard A.—Art collections—Catalogs. 5. Posters—Private collections—New York (N.Y.)—Catalogs. 6. Posters—New York (N.Y.)—Catalogs. 7. Metropolitan Museum of Art (New York, N.Y.)—Catalogs.
    I. Kiehl, David W.   II. Cate, Phillip Dennis.
    III. Finlay, Nancy.   IV. Title.
    NC1807.U5M47   1987   741.67′4′097307401471   87-20265
    ISBN 0-87099-501-4
    ISBN 0-8109-1869-2 (Abrams)

All photographs in this volume not otherwise credited were specially taken for this publication by Bobby Hansson.
Title lettering by Wade Hampton
Typeset by Graphic Composition, Inc., Athens, Georgia
Printed and bound by Grafiche Milani, Italy

Jacket: Will H. Bradley. Victor Bicycle, "In Purple and White," 1896. 27
Frontispiece: Edward Penfield. *Harper's,* February 1897. 193

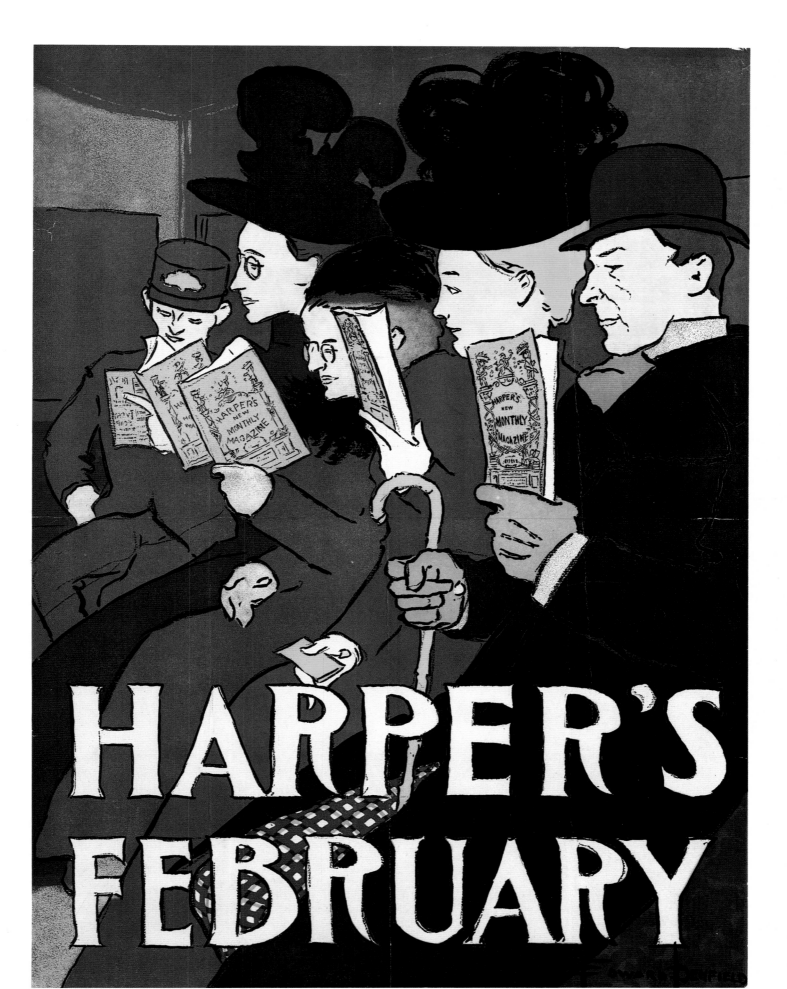

CONTENTS

Colorplates follow pages 20 and 72

FOREWORD

THIS BOOK celebrates the gift of a thoughtful and supportive friend of the Metropolitan Museum. In 1984 Leonard A. Lauder presented to the Department of Prints and Photographs his important collection of 158 American art posters of the 1890s, a collection he had assembled, winnowed, and perfected over a period of seven years. He has since made additional gifts of key works and we are grateful as well for his commitment of funds toward the exhibition and cataloguing of the Museum's entire collection of American art posters of this period. This volume, the first to document such a collection in any American museum, has been made possible by Mr. Lauder's generosity and foresight.

This museum has had a modest collection of American art posters for many years, even as early as the decade in which they were first published, but it began somewhat haphazardly, with items entering the Museum merely as reference material. It was not until 1957 that many of these posters were transferred to the Department of Prints and Photographs, where for the first time posters by such artists as Will H. Bradley, Edward Penfield, J. C. Leyendecker, and Maxfield Parrish were formally accessioned.

Additional donations over the years built up a collection with many strengths, as well as many weaknesses. In 1936 David Silve, a graphic designer long associated with Museum publications, donated thirty-six American posters to the Museum. Included in this gift was an imperfect but extremely rare impression of Will Bradley's large woodcut poster called "The Kiss" (Cat. 30), published in 1896. The Silve gift represented the first group of American art posters to enter the Museum officially as works of art.

A particularly strong and early collection of American and French posters of the 1890s, which was formed by the painter Robert Vonnoh, was presented to the Museum in 1941 by Vonnoh's widow, the sculptress Bessie Potter Vonnoh. These posters, including more than 125 by American artists, date from 1893 to 1896; many still bear numbered stickers and mounting pinholes from an 1896 exhibition of posters held at the Pennsylvania Academy of the Fine Arts that was organized by Vonnoh and Maxfield Parrish. Some of the posters are quite rare, having been made by lesser-known illustrators, while others are by well-known artists, such as the poster especially designed for the Philadelphia exhibition by Maxfield Parrish (Cat. 133).

One other important donation to our holdings was made in 1952 by Fern Bradley Dufner, Will Bradley's daughter. Bradley designed some of the most sophisticated early posters, many for *The Chap-Book*. Included in the Dufner gift were rare trial proofs, preliminary drawings, and impressions of some of his posters.

In the years to come, selections from the Lauder collection will continue to be displayed on a rotating basis in the American Wing. It is our hope that this inaugural exhibition and catalogue, so splendidly supported by Leonard A. Lauder and carefully assembled by David W. Kiehl, Associate Curator in the Museum's Department of Prints and Photographs, will help acquaint the public with a lively and illuminating aspect of American art.

PHILIPPE DE MONTEBELLO
Director

INTRODUCTION

ASK ANY COLLECTOR how it all began, and you may hear wonderful stories about childhood collections ranging from bottle caps to baseball cards. I started to collect in earnest at the age of ten. It was in 1943, during World War II, that I acquired my first American poster. The Office of War Information (OWI) issued a series of patriotic posters. "Loose Lips Sink Ships," "Remember Pearl Harbor," and other slogans were incorporated into beautiful, vibrant images that captured my imagination. My goal was to collect every war poster published by the OWI. Riding subways and buses often for hours to the outlying boroughs, I trudged to every OWI office in New York City in search of the missing numbers in the series. Even at that age, I had the compulsion to collect. Over the years my interests and tastes have changed, but the drive to collect and the thrill of forming a collection have stayed with me.

My childhood fascination with posters lay dormant until 1977. That year, the Whitney Museum of American Art mounted an exhibition, *Turn-of-the-Century America*, brilliantly curated by Patricia Hills. Tucked away in a corner was a group of art posters of the 1890s. They reflected a self-confident, seemingly problem-free America, conveying the freshness, innocence, and excitement of the period. The spirit of these lively images captivated me. Once again my enthusiasm for the American poster was sparked. I decided then to assemble a collection of these works, which from the start I intended for donation to a museum.

Before embarking on my search, I had a lot to learn. I read endlessly on the subject. It was with this knowledge that I began to outline how the collection would look. The works included would be chosen for their quality, composition, and historic value. I identified the images that I felt were essential, as well as the overall "feel" I wanted to achieve in the completed collection. I am often asked which was the first poster to enter the collection. It is impossible to remember. By the time I bought the first poster, I had already shaped the collection so carefully in my mind that each addition was like fitting a piece into a jigsaw puzzle. Each acquisition gave me enormous pleasure, as it filled an already identified gap. This is not to say, however, that as the collection grew there were not many wonderful surprises. There was nothing more exciting than finding an entirely undocumented or unique poster.

The collection was not intended to be encyclopedic. Selectivity always plays a major part in forming a unified collection. There is as much significance in the works rejected as in those included. These decisions reflect the collector's personal vision but also demand an extraordinary amount of time and looking. I did not collect in a blitz; each acquisition came in slowly and carefully, and each was savored.

The bulk of the collection consists of works by the major poster artists of the period. Will H. Bradley and Edward Penfield, the leaders of the movement, are well represented but certainly not exclusively. I have tended to be less interested in artists such as Maxfield Parrish, whose roots were more firmly established in magazine illustration than in the production of the art poster. According to Penfield, "a design that needs study is not a poster no matter how well it is executed." I have taken these words to heart. The most successful poster is one that elicits an immediate response. The concise wording and simplified forms employed by these artists work together to create a narrative with strong impact.

Most of the posters in the collection are not advertising posters as we know them today. Certainly during this period, there were numerous examples of quite ordinary posters, hawking circuses, theatrical productions, and patent medicines. Often made by apprentices rather than by the lithographers themselves, these works lack power in both composition and color. The posters I have chosen may promote bicycles and literary magazines, yet the artists have elevated their subjects beyond the realm of mere commercial art.

That these posters have survived at all is a small miracle. For more than seventy years they were considered mere ephemera. Not surprisingly, many were found badly damaged, having been folded, tacked up on walls, taped, or trimmed. In the course of my search, I had to pass up key images due to their poor condition. With time, a pristine example would emerge. In the context of my collection, I could insure that these high-quality examples would be preserved indefinitely.

As the collection took form, Bonnie Clearwater, my curator at the time, and I turned our attention to finding a home for the works. Since I am a New Yorker and the city has nurtured my cultural interests, a New York institution seemed desirable. But most importantly, I wanted a place where the cohesiveness of the collection could work to its best advantage. The Metropolitan Museum of Art proved to be the ideal place.

The Metropolitan Museum already had a significant number of American turn-of-the-century posters. Happily, my collection was abundant in the areas where theirs was lacking. By joining forces with me, the Metropolitan Museum now has one of the strongest collections of American art posters of the 1890s. I worked closely with Colta Ives, Curator of the Department of Prints and Photographs, and David Kiehl, Associate Curator, and we were able to come to agreements concerning both the acceptance of the donation and the display of selected works over a period of years. Their enthusiasm for the collection, as well as for the publication of this catalogue and for the concurrent exhibition, has been infectious.

My thanks go not only to Colta Ives and David Kiehl of The Metropolitan Museum of Art, but also to Bonnie Clearwater and her successor, Julia Blaut. I am also indebted to my art-dealer associates, Jack Banning, Susan Reinhold and Bob Brown of the Reinhold Brown Gallery, and Deborah Glusker-Lebrave, my "French connection." My deepest gratitude, however, is to my family. They endured my absences on evenings and weekends and remained patient while living with piles of posters in the closets and under the bed. The forming of a collection is not a one-person job, and it is to all of these people that I am grateful.

LEONARD A. LAUDER
New York
November 1986

AMERICAN ART POSTERS OF THE 1890s

David W. Kiehl

I N APRIL 1893 something new was spotted in the shops of American news vendors and booksellers. Amid the handbills and letterpress notices of topical interest, there was a small poster that pictured a man in a green overcoat and a hunter's cap, intently reading a magazine and heedless of the falling rain. The only lettering on the poster was "HARPER'S FOR APRIL." The magazine that captured the man's undivided attention was *Harper's Monthly Magazine.*

This was unprecedented. There was no listing of contents, no headline stressing an important story or new serialized novel. Moreover, nothing in the image made any reference to a holiday season. It was just April. The poster was bold in its simplicity: the singular, isolated figure of the man; the magazine; a mere suggestion of the weather proverbially associated with the month; and bold lettering carefully integrated into the design. The implication was quite clear. *Harper's Monthly Magazine* was worth a walk to the news vendor even in the pouring rain.

The next month, Harper and Brothers sent a new placard to replace the man in the green coat. For May—and again the presentation was simple—a young girl in a white frock, a floral wreath on her head, held up a copy of *Harper's* (Cat. 139, Fig. 1). As in the April poster, the lettering, "HARPER'S for MAY," was carefully integrated with the design. In each succeeding month, a new poster appeared, carefully designed. Some made discreet references to adages characterizing the month, others to seasonal activities. The regularity of appearance and the singularity of design attracted the attention of the literate public and, moreover, of editors of rival periodicals intended for the same middle- and upper-class readership. By the end of 1893, Charles Scribner's Sons, J. B. Lippincott Company, The Century Company, and other publishers had plans for or were distributing their own posters in competition with those of Harper and Brothers. The race had begun and, with the added encouragement of collectors, the enthusiastic interest in the poster already rampant in Paris accelerated across the United States during the rest of the decade.

There are no records of the deliberations preceding the decision of the editors of Harper and Brothers to inaugurate this experimental advertising campaign. Some of these men undoubtedly were familiar with the posters by Jules Chéret, Théophile-Alexandre Steinlen, Eugène Grasset, and Henri de Toulouse-Lautrec, which covered Paris hoardings and kiosks

Fig. 1 Edward Penfield. *Harper's*, May 1893. 139

and were first exhibited in New York at the Grolier Club in 1890.[1] In part, though, their decision was also influenced by the success of the cover commissioned from the French artist Grasset for the Christmas 1892 issue of *Harper's*. Special holiday covers and art supplements had become a routine feature of American magazines in the last quarter of the century; these holiday supplements succeeded in increasing readership. Some Christmas covers in the early 1890s were specially printed as placards for the use of news vendors. On the other hand, during nonholiday months, covers were comparatively dull—a masthead, a listing of contents, and sometimes a wood-engraved illustration of topical interest. Could a monthly poster unrelated to a special holiday issue attract enough attention to encourage the purchase of *Harper's*?

The poster, as a medium for advertising, was not at all new to the American public. In the eighteenth century, letterpress and woodcut handbills were posted regularly in taverns, inns, and shops. Nineteenth-century revolutionary advances in color printing by means of lithography were quickly marshaled: by businessmen and merchants for household products and other goods; by theatrical producers and circus owners; and by political organizations for elections and other issues. To meet the growing demand, many of the larger lithographic firms in New York, Boston, Chicago, Philadelphia, San Francisco, Buffalo, and Cincinnati employed skilled artists to produce a continual flow of images suitable for the advertising needs of their clients. Few records survive for these large firms, and even less information is known about the artists they employed. Yet the surviving posters are testaments to the imaginative skill and quality of the products of commercial printing firms. These posters were ubiquitous across the United States and even in Europe, where American circus posters may have had an influence on Chéret.

Harper and Brothers chose not to employ the services of one of these large lithographic firms. They wanted a poster that would attract attention because it was completely different from its fellows. Also, they chose not to commission a well-known French artist; not only was there an impending deadline, but also they feared that the exuberant young ladies so frequently found in French posters might offend their potential readership. Instead, the editors turned to the head of their art department, the young Edward Penfield. He had run the art department for Harper and Brothers since 1891, after his studies at the Art Students League. Amid the hectic duties of overseeing the artistic needs of this important publishing firm—supervising staff and contractual illustrators; planning layouts of books and magazines and designs of covers; and working with printers—Penfield had little time to devote to his new assignment. His first poster was reportedly the product of an overnight spurt of creative activity. The achievement clearly illustrated his understanding of an effective poster, its simplicity and good composition, which he coupled with subtle humor most often expressed by visual references to the proverbial qualities of the seasons and by quiet comments on the lifestyles of the more leisured classes of American society. These qualities insured the attention of the desired readership, of other publishing houses, and of the artistic community.

In a recently discovered letter of December 7, 1895, to John Hilliard, editor of *The Union and Advertiser*, a Rochester, New York, newspaper, Penfield looked back at his early posters and his impact on American design.

My original intention was to be an illustrator, and I followed that branch for several years, making drawings in pen and ink and wash for various purposes. Lately, I have given my attention to decorative work, such as posters, bookcovers, &c. as I find it interests me most. My first decorative poster was done for Harper & Brothers for their April "Magazine," 1893. It was only an experiment and was done long before I ever heard of Lautrec or Steinlen as poster designers. To be sure I was familiar with Steinlen, but only as a caricaturist. Later on, Richard Harding Davis asked me to make a poster for his book "Our English Cousins" [Cat. 158, issued 1894], and showed me about a dozen French posters, which were the first I had seen. I think the American Poster has opened a new school whose aim is simplicity and good composition. One can see its effects in all directions, especially in our daily papers. . . .[2]

From the beginning, American art posters of the 1890s were distinguished by their acknowledgment of the creative personality responsible for a poster's artistic statement. Penfield started the tradition, signing his first *Harper's* poster with his initials, the second with his full name, and succeeding posters with either initials, signature, or his logo, a bull's head. In France, posters were signed regularly since the artist often held the copyright to an image. This had not been the practice in America. Prior to Penfield and his posters for *Harper's*, poster images rarely carried any mention of the artist's name. Instead, the name of the lithography or printing firm was often prominently printed, proudly advertising the quality of the printing job itself. Artistic quality was of tertiary or at most secondary importance. The primary function of a poster advertising a circus or a stove was to succeed in getting the product sold and to exhibit the quality and reputation of the printing firm. Since manufacturers depended on the printer to provide the best quality in a poster to sell products effectively, artistic issues were the concern of the printing firm.

But the art poster in America was mainly a product of the publishing trade. From past experience editors and publishers knew that a well-known or popular illustrator or artist could enhance the sales of illustrated books and magazines. Charles Dana Gibson, Edwin Austin Abbey, and Frederic Remington, among others, received large commissions for their illustrations. It was common practice in publishing to acknowledge artistic contributions; the illustrator sometimes received more attention on title and contents pages than an author. And, as noted earlier, editors vied to have the best artists provide covers, art supplements, and illustrations for special holiday issues, especially Christmas numbers. Among publishers, then, the tradition of acknowledging the artist was firmly in place before the appearance of Penfield's first poster for Harper and Brothers.

By the end of 1893, the poster became an accepted extension of a publisher's normal activity. Most posters for publishing houses were signed by the artist or designer; and unlike the posters created for theatrical events, food or tobacco products, and so forth, they seldom carry the name of the printer. Presumably, many posters for books and magazines were printed on the presses of the publishers themselves. Although some posters were contracted to outside commercial lithography and engraving firms, the name was frequently omitted in these cases also. Perhaps, since quality printing was such an inherent part of a publishing house's image in the marketplace, the name of the printer was not considered essential.

The April 1893 *Harper's* poster was an experiment, but it had been a successful gamble, and Penfield continued his monthly series until July 1899. While Harper and Brothers used Penfield exclusively for their posters, The Century Company, Charles Scribner's Sons, and others used many different artists for posters; some publishers issued posters only for holiday numbers or special editions, others for each new issue. J. B. Lippincott Company first contracted with Will Carqueville for a twelve-poster series for their monthly magazine to begin in December 1894. When Carqueville decided to continue his artistic studies in Paris, the firm commissioned Joseph J. Gould, Jr., to continue the series until mid-1897.

The Century Company employed many American artists to provide covers for their several magazine titles. However, the posters to accompany a popular serialized history of the life of Napoleon in *The Century Magazine* came from France, not America. Grasset designed the poster that announced the first installment in the November 1894 issue of the magazine.[3] In 1895, a competition for Napoleon posters was opened in France. The Century Company circulated the top entries across the United States. The competition for a poster for the 1896 midsummer fiction number of *The Century* may have been organized in response to criticism engendered by the Napoleon poster contest. The artist Joseph Christian Leyendecker won the midsummer fiction contest with his well-known Art Nouveau design of a young woman surrounded by poppies (Cat. 112, colorplate 12). Maxfield Parrish received the second prize because, it is said, his design would require four colors to produce instead of the three encouraged by the contest rules. Parrish's design was issued as a poster for the 1897 midsummer fiction number (Cat. 134, colorplate 13). The design submitted by Henry M. Rosenberg received an honorable mention and was used for the September 1896 poster for *The Century* (Cat. 272).

The rules for *The Century* midsummer fiction poster contest were announced by March 1896, when *The Poster* printed the following:

The Century Co. offers three prizes of $125, $75 and $50 for the best designs for a poster advertising the Midsummer Number of *The Century Magazine*. The offer is open to everyone, whether professional artist or amateur. Designs must be submitted on or before the 30th day of April, 1896, at the office of The Century Co., Union Square, New York. Neither name nor initials should appear upon the sketch, but a small device should be drawn in the margin, and the full name and address of the artist placed in a sealed envelope bearing the same device and sent with the sketch. The judges will be three well-known artists whose names will be announced later. [The judges were the painters Elihu Vedder and F. Hopkinson Smith and the architect Henry J. Hardenbergh.] They will be asked to consider the effectiveness of the posters from the advertising standpoint, and the ease and cheapness with which they can be reproduced.[4]

The Century Company received seven hundred entries, and the judges gave twelve honorable mentions in addition to the three prizes.[5]

Seven hundred entrants in The Century Company's contest seems a huge number, but by 1896 the art poster was all the rage with collectors and publishers. The benefits to be derived from a well-designed, artistic poster were understood by publishers not only of major magazines but also of the many so-called little magazines that blossomed throughout the decade. Posters were frequently presented as a premium for subscribing; for example, Will H. Bradley designed two posters (Cat. 19, 29), as did John Sloan (Cat. 277), for the *Echo* of Chicago and later New York; Sloan again for *Moods* of Philadelphia (Cat. 276); Arthur Wesley Dow for *Modern Art* of Prang and Company, Boston (Cat. 66, colorplate 4); Elisha Brown Bird for *The Red Letter* of New York and Boston (Cat. 10); and Ethel Reed for *Time and the Hour* of Boston (Cat. 246, colorplate 23); among many others. The eight posters designed by Bruce Porter and Florence Lundborg for a San Francisco humor and literary magazine, *The Lark*, were among the few printed from wood blocks, confirming an interest among California artists in this technique and other arts of Japan.

The most influential of the little magazines was *The Chap-Book*, the house organ of the Chicago and Cambridge firm of Stone and Kimball, American publishers of *The Yellow Book*. The firm was noted for fine printing and fine graphic design, seen in the first poster for *The Chap-Book*, May 1894, as well as in their other posters issued periodically throughout the decade. One of their posters was commissioned from Lautrec and issued in 1895. However, the placards of the artist and graphic designer Bradley brought the magazine lasting fame. Bradley developed a style quite similar to that of Aubrey Beardsley. He was also interested in the goals favored by the English Arts and Crafts movement, to introduce good design and taste into everyday life. He was a superb designer, and his designs, such as the first *Chap-Book* poster, known as "The Twins" (Cat. 13, Fig. 2), lacked the archness of Beardsley's work. For his second poster for the magazine, "The Blue Lady" (Cat. 14, colorplate 3), Bradley juxtaposed planes of flat color separated by an unprinted white line. Bradley was well versed in the printing arts and achieved "The Blue Lady" with only two colors. Later, Frank Hazenplug continued the *Chap-Book* lady series with a "Red Lady" (Cat. 97, colorplate 10), a "Black Lady" (Cat. 99), and a "Green Lady" (Cat. 100).

By the time that Bradley's last *Chap-Book* poster was announced, he had left Chicago for Springfield, Massachusetts, and had founded his own graphic-design firm, The Wayside Press at the Sign of the Dandelion. In April 1896, he issued a prospectus for a new periodical, *Bradley: His Book*, dedicated to the promotion of fine typography, design, paper, and printing. In the May issue, Bradley advertised a magazine poster, which, due to printing difficulties, was not available for distribution until November. The poster embodied Bradley's assimilation of Pre-Raphaelite ideals. A maiden in aesthetic garb succumbs to temptation in the guise of a peacock. The undated poster became known as "The Kiss" (Cat. 30, colorplate 2). Other

Fig. 2 Will H. Bradley. *The Chap-Book*. "The Twins," May 1894. 13

posters were issued for the magazine for the remaining months of 1896 (Cat. 31–34). The magazine contained a number of Bradley-designed advertisements for printing-ink and paper companies, many located in the Springfield area. One of the most notable of these designs, a poster for Whiting Paper Company, was known as "The Acorns" (Cat. 26). The small poster had nothing to do with paper in the literal sense; it showed only an Art Nouveau design of a woman with poppies within a border of oak leaves and acorns. But it implied that the fine quality of Whiting paper was essential for fine printing. Bradley designed a second poster for Whiting known as "The Shield." Some poster exhibitions of the decade listed advertisements designed by Bradley for the ink firm of Ault and Wiborg among his posters. However, these images were most likely special supplements in such trade periodicals as *The Inland Printer.*

The Inland Printer was an influential journal for the printing trade, with numerous articles on advances in presses, type fonts, inks, and so forth. *The Inland Printer* also issued posters. Some of Bradley's striking cover designs were adapted as such with additional typescript noting that the issue was "now ready" and "for sale here." In 1897, the publishers of the magazine commissioned a series of designs from Leyendecker for use as covers and posters. These designs had descriptive subtitles, such as "The Spring Poet" for March, "The Sun" for August (Cat. 113, colorplate 36), and "The Chase" for October. Like the posters associated with other periodicals, the *Inland Printer* posters had little to do with printing presses. Instead, the subject was the quality of the printing itself. Another journal associated with the publishing and printing trades, *The Bookman*, also used the same designs for covers and posters: for example, George Frederick Scotson-Clark's design of a medieval abbot reading in his cell and Louis Rhead's design for Christmas 1896 of an eighteenth-century reader browsing in a bookshop.

Publishers of magazines and periodicals were not alone in realizing the commercial potential of the art poster. Many of these firms, such as The Century Company, Stone and Kimball, Harper and Brothers, and Charles Scribner's Sons, also published books. By 1894, artist-designed placards in bookstores enticed customers to purchase the latest volumes from a number of different publishing houses. Penfield, as was to be expected, designed many of the Harper and Brothers book posters, often for books by the popular novelist Richard Harding Davis. Bradley designed a curvilinear, Beardsleyesque poster printed in vermilion and green for Tom Hall's *When Hearts Are Trumps* (Cat. 15). This poster, issued by Stone and Kimball, is one of the masterpieces of Art Nouveau style in America. The same firm adapted Charles Dana Gibson's illustrations for two different placards for Chatfield-Taylor's *Two Women and a Fool* (for one, see Cat. 75). Frederick A. Stokes, a New York publisher of novels, relied on the talents of A. W. B. Lincoln to design a series of striking placards, small but with eye-catching images and enigmatic yet sensational titles—*The Phantom Death, A White Baby* (Cat. 115), and *A Dead Man's Court* (Cat. 114). For Robert Buchanan's *Diana Hunting* of 1895, Lincoln based his figure of the Greek huntress on Augustus Saint-Gaudens's monumental sculpture crowning the newly erected Madison Square Garden. In Boston, the talents of Ethel Reed were employed by Copeland and Day and by Lamson, Wolffe, and Company. Her posters, such as that for the novel *Miss Träumerei* (Cat. 235, Fig. 3), received critical acclaim in Europe and in America. The success of such posters as these presaged developments in the book trade familiar to contemporary readers—the dust jacket and the attention-getting covers of mass-market paperbacks.

Newspaper editors quickly turned to the art poster as an effective means of attracting an even larger readership. Placards and broadsides had long been the traditional and most effective means of advertising the sensational news of the day. To increase readership, editors began adding features—expanded Sunday editions with literary and fashion supplements, holiday editions with artistic supplements printed in color, seasonal fashion editions, and special women's editions. Artist-designed posters announced these features from the walls of news vendors and from hoardings. Two New York papers, the *Sun* and the *Journal*, commissioned designs from Rhead for large posters, sometimes needing two sheets. There were no headlines on these posters; they were intended to advertise the newspaper itself, not particular stories. Rhead supervised the printing of the *Sun* and *Journal* posters, but such involvement was rare. More commonly, the design was printed on the same presses used for the daily editions. Little care was spent in aligning colors or correcting printing errors. For example, Rhead only provided the designs for the Easter 1896 (Cat. 263) and the Christmas 1896 (Cat. 268) issues of the *New York Herald*. Both posters were printed with poor registration of color and design. Many newspaper posters have a naive, lively, and spontaneous quality not found in other posters. Quite typical are the many weekly posters issued by the *New York World* (Cat. 4, Fig. 4), which combine a sprightly design printed in one or two colors with a listing of contents to entice the reader.

Fig. 3 Ethel Reed. *Miss Träumerei*, 1895. 235

Fig. 4 Anonymous. *The Sunday New York World*, January 19, 1896. 4

There was a conscious effort among many of the more popular periodicals and newspapers to increase their appeal to the American middle and upper classes. Since the periodicals were relatively expensive, the prospective reader needed not only money to purchase the magazine but also the time for reading. Leisure was an important part of this life. Many of the people depicted in Penfield's *Harper's* posters, when not reading, were swimming, going out to the tennis court or football stadium, fishing, playing golf, or visiting the horse show. Several new magazines in the 1890s were devoted to leisure activities, among these *Outing*, *Recreation*, and *Bearings*. Distinctive posters were issued to advertise the latest issue with seasonal reference to a particular sport or related activity.

The bicycle in particular symbolized the new time for leisure. Bicycles were expensive. *Bearings* was a magazine for bicycle enthusiasts. Charles A. Cox designed many of its posters, making bicycles an integral part of his designs (Cat. 60, Fig. 5). Bicycle manufacturers were among the few companies actively recruiting free-lance artists to design posters, in preference to relying on printing-house designers. These posters were large, intended for hoardings and the walls of shops. Designs usually provided space for the addition of a local merchant's name

Fig. 5 Charles A. Cox. *Bearings*, 1896. 60

and address. Penfield created designs for several bicycles: the Waltham Manufacturing Company's Orient (Cat. 174, colorplate 15); Stearns Manufacturing Company's Stearns bicycle (Cat. 190, colorplate 16); and Northampton Cycle Company's the Northampton (Cat. 225, colorplate 53). These three posters, while distinctively by Penfield, show a knowledge of his French contemporaries, especially Steinlen. Bradley produced at least four posters for the Overman Wheel Company's Victor bicycle, all in a marked Art Nouveau style. Only one, "In Purple and White" (Cat. 27, colorplate 32), is without an elaborate foliated border. Bradley also designed posters for the Springfield Bicycle Club's annual tournaments in 1895 (Cat. 21) and 1896.

In 1896, the Pope Manufacturing Company of Hartford, Connecticut, announced a competition for a poster to advertise their Columbia bicycle. The winning designs became the property of the company. The three prize winners each received a Columbia bicycle, valued at $100, and cash awards: first prize, $250; second prize, $100; and third prize, $50.[6] About one thousand entries were received, and the successful competitors were Maxfield Parrish, first; O. Rohn of Montclair, New Jersey, second; and A. Romez of New York, third. The editor of *The Poster* noted that "the fault in the majority of the designs, seeing that they were wanted for advertising purposes, was that the lettering was confused, or was not conspicuous enough at first sight."[7]

Large lithography firms kept their monopoly on posters for commercial purposes throughout the decade. However, competitions such as those sponsored by the Pope Manufacturing Company and The Century Company were an indication that this monopoly on the design of product advertising was weakening. Advertising was increasingly vital to the survival of both old and especially new products, whether it was *Scribner's Magazine*, a bicycle, or a camera, all of which competed in an expanding market.

Although the art poster of the 1890s was associated primarily with the publishing world, its effects on the commercial world in general have continued to the present day. Increasingly in the new century artists were hired to provide suitable images for posters and other advertisements for a growing range of products. The pioneering efforts of such artists as Penfield, Reed, Bradley, and McManus thus foreshadowed the burgeoning activity of the modern advertising agencies of Madison Avenue.

NOTES

1. Grolier Club, *Catalogue of an Exhibition of Illustrated Bill-Posters* (New York, 1890).

2. David L. Holmes, *Autographs*, catalogue 16, Philadelphia, October 1986, item 68.

3. See the introduction to the Napoleon posters in *The Century and Echo Poster Show: Catalogue of Artistic Posters*, Chicago, 1895, n.p.

4. *The Poster* 1.3 (March 1896), p. 32.

5. *The Poster* 1.5 (May 1896), p. 60.

6. *The Poster* 1.2 (February 1896), p. 16.

7. *The Poster* 1.3 (March 1896), p. 39.

1 Elisha Brown Bird. *The Poster*, 1896. 9

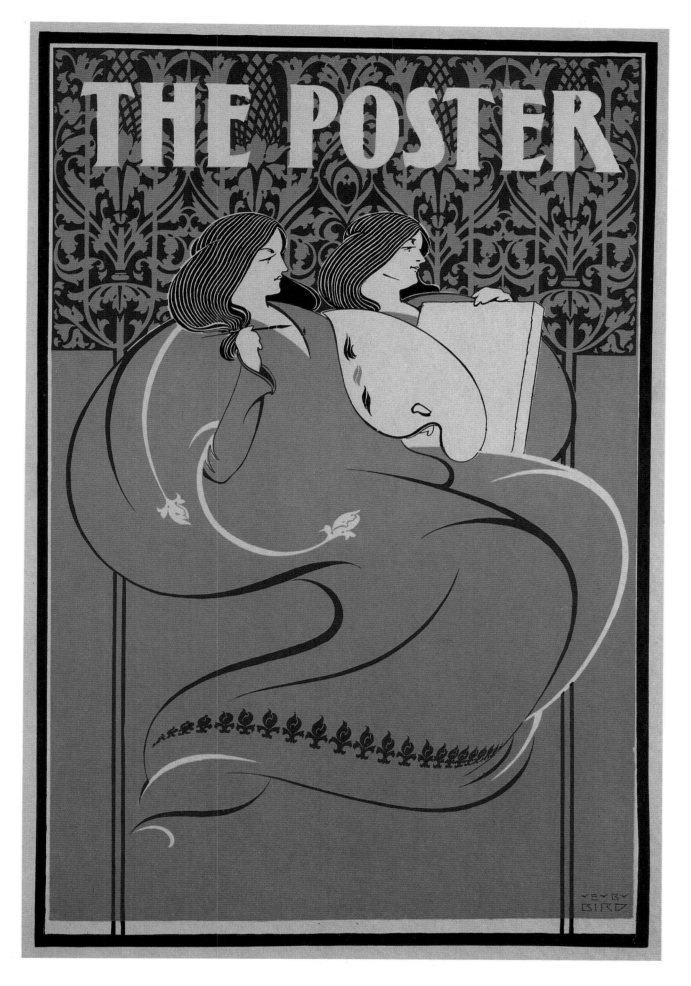

2 Will H. Bradley. *Bradley: His Book*, "The Kiss," 1896. 30

22

3 Will H. Bradley. *The Chap-Book*, "Blue Lady," 1894. 14

4 Arthur Wesley Dow. *Modern Art*, 1895. 66

5 Florence Lundborg. *The Lark*, November 1895. 118

6 William L. Carqueville. *Lippincott's*, February 1895. 45

7 William L. Carqueville. *Lippincott's*, August 1895. **52**

8 Joseph J. Gould, Jr. *Lippincott's*, February 1897. 89

9 Joseph J. Gould, Jr. *Lippincott's*, December 1896. 87

10 Frank Hazenplug. *The Chap-Book*, "Red Lady," 1895. 97

11 Blanche McManus. *The Adventures of Captain Horn*, 1895. 125

12 Joseph Christian Leyendecker. *The Century*, August 1896. 112

13 Maxfield Parrish. *The Century*, August 1897 (1896). **134**   14 Maxfield Parrish. *Scribner's*, August 1897. **135**

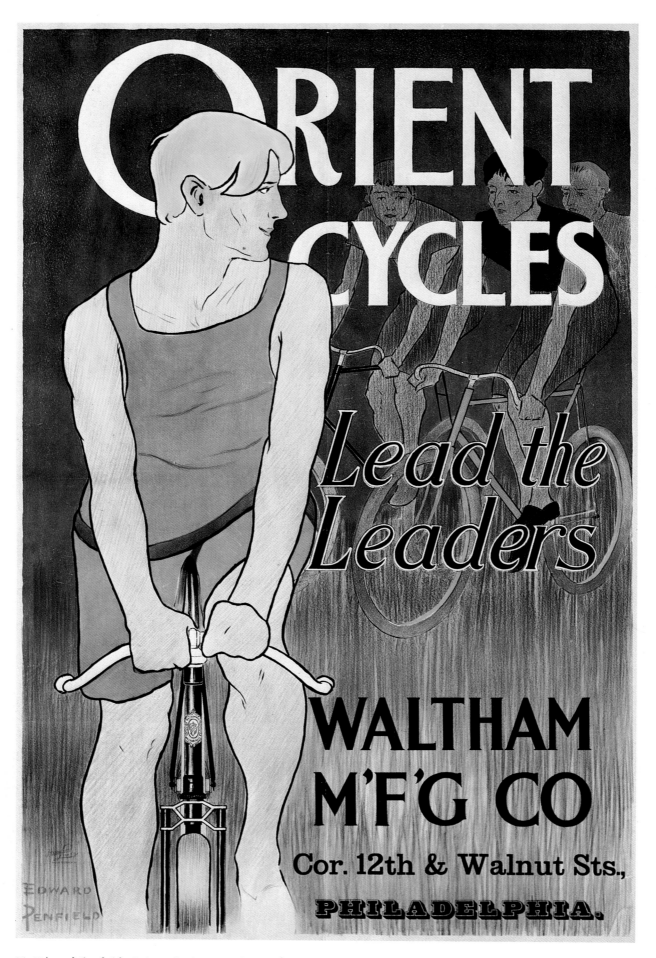

15 Edward Penfield. Orient Cycles, ca. 1895–96. 174

16 Edward Penfield. Stearns Bicycle, 1896. 190

17 Edward Penfield. *Harper's*, June 1893. 140

18 Edward Penfield. *Harper's*, September 1894. 153

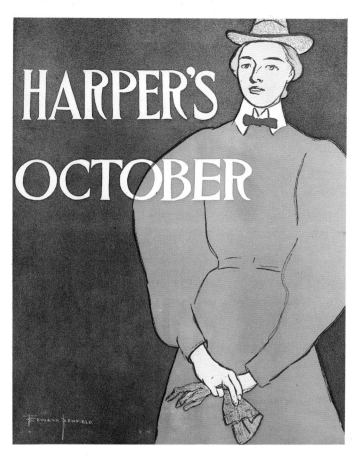

19 Edward Penfield. *Harper's*, October 1896. **185**

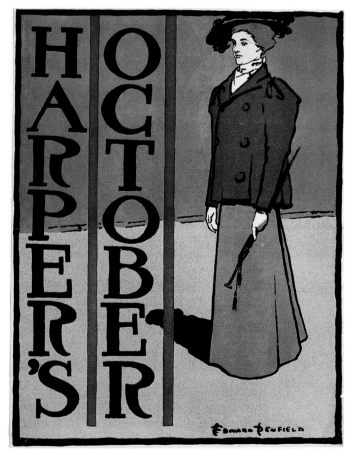

20 Edward Penfield. *Harper's*, October 1897. **201**

21 E. Pickert. *The New York Times*, 1895. 226

22 Louis John Rhead. *The Sun*, 1895. 261

23 Ethel Reed. *Time and the Hour*, 1896. 246

In Childhood's Country ❧ By Louise Chandler Moulton ❧❧❧ Pictured by Ethel Reed ❧❧

Boston: Copeland and Day ❧❧ Price $2.00

24 Ethel Reed. *In Childhood's Country*, 1896. 245

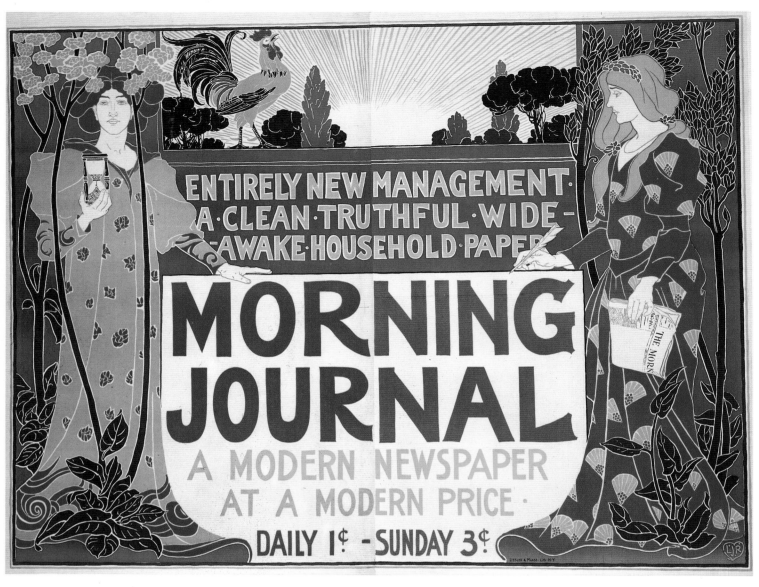

25 Louis John Rhead. *Morning Journal*, 1895. 257

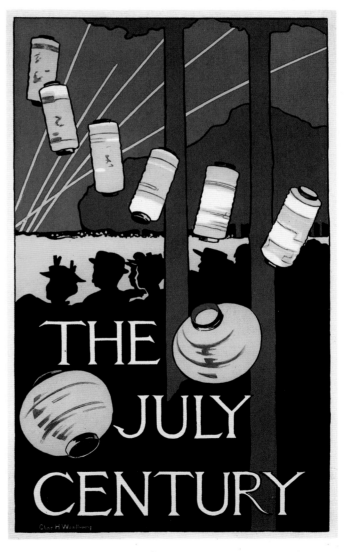

26 Louis John Rhead. *Meadow-Grass*, 1895. **252**

27 Charles H. Woodbury. *The Century*, July 1895. **288**

AMERICAN POSTERS AND PUBLISHING IN THE 1890s

Nancy Finlay

I N ANY STUDY of American posters of the 1890s, book and magazine posters occupy a predominant place for their sheer numbers as well as for their unquestionable quality. The American poster period began with Edward Penfield's monthly posters for *Harper's Magazine* in 1893. It ended in the last years of the decade, as book and magazine publishers turned their attention to other forms of advertising. From beginning to end, the relationship between poster artists and publishers was remarkably close. Many of them shared an admiration for contemporary French and British designers, so that publishers, unlike manufacturers of soap or shoe polish, were prepared to accept radical and avant-garde styles of poster design. This was especially true of publishers of modern fiction and poetry, such as Copeland and Day in Boston and Stone and Kimball in Chicago, but even the more conservative older firms showed remarkably advanced taste. In New York, Scribner's, Harper and Brothers, and The Century Company all commissioned important poster designs from a variety of artists. In Boston, Houghton Mifflin and Company and Joseph Knight Company commissioned a few designs that were as startling in their originality as anything issued by the younger firms.

This ready acceptance of the poster style by publishers was surely one reason for the predominance of book and magazine posters in the 1890s, but it was not the only reason and probably not the most important one. Advances in color printing and photomechanical reproduction also contributed to the blossoming of the poster movement, and publishers and printers were among the best informed of these changes in technology. Most American poster artists were draftsmen rather than printmakers, and few of them had any training in the traditional printmaking processes. John Sloan has recorded the excitement felt by young artists at the opportunities for the mass production of "original drawings" through photomechanical methods,[1] and many of the best early posters, including Penfield's *Harper's* posters, were essentially facsimile drawings reproduced on a large scale. Although the best American poster artists, such as Edward Penfield and Will H. Bradley, had a clear understanding of the limits and capabilities of the new technology, others knew next to nothing of the means used to reproduce their work. Furthermore, whether they understood the processes or not, most artists sold their drawings outright to the publishers, who then assumed full responsibility for their reproduction. While Penfield presumably had considerable control over the printing of his *Harper's* posters, in other cases it was the publisher and not the artist who saw the

28 Elisha Brown Bird. *The Captured Cunarder*, 1896. 8

designs through the press. For some Copeland and Day books, the publisher Fred Holland Day dealt directly with the printer and made key decisions regarding the scale of the poster, the color of the paper, and the color of the ink.[2] Inevitably, such a situation gave book and magazine publishers a distinct advantage over other manufacturers, who lacked the publishers' knowledge of the technical processes and their contacts with the printing industry. One outstanding exception to this pattern was provided by Bradley, who was a printer as well as a designer. Because he was in control of all stages of production from the original design through the actual printing of the advertisement, he was able to offer his services to a wide variety of clients, including bicycle firms, drug companies, and paper manufacturers, as well as publishers. Bradley's Wayside Press, established in Springfield, Massachusetts, in 1896, was one of the earliest advertising agencies, as well as one of the most distinguished small presses of the 1890s.[3]

Although publisher and poster artist enjoyed a special relationship throughout the 1890s, the relationship between the poster itself and the book or magazine it advertised was somewhat uneasy. While originally book and magazine posters were intended primarily as advertisements, they quickly came to be considered and collected as independent works of art. There is no generic correspondence between most manufacturers' posters and the products that they advertise—a poster has nothing in common with a bicycle or a bottle of "Extra Tivoli." But posters, books, and magazines are all printed objects combining lettering with illustration. Stylistically they could be at least potentially related to one another. At the beginning of the period there was usually little resemblance between poster and book cover, or book cover and illustrations. As the period progressed, the interconnections became far more complicated. The rapid evolution of book covers, book jackets, and magazine covers in the 1890s was largely a reaction to the poster craze.

The typical trade book of the 1890s was a small volume bound in brightly colored cloth.[4] Books intended for popular consumption, such as fiction, poetry, and collections of essays, usually had a decorative design stamped on one or both covers in gold (or occasionally silver) and/or colors. Such decoration was widely popular for so-called gift books, issued by publishers for the holidays. By 1890, the design of these cover decorations had become a well-established specialty. Although well-known artists in other fields, such as Elihu Vedder and Stanford White, were responsible for a few cover designs, many more were the products of specialists such as Margaret Armstrong, who produced hundreds of designs, chiefly for Scribner's, and Sarah Wyman Whitman, who created what was virtually a house style for Houghton Mifflin and Company.[5]

A primary characteristic of these designs is that they were nonfigurative, stressing the structure of the book as object. Many of Whitman's designs imitate the metal clasps and hinges of early bookbindings. While most of Armstrong's designs utilize floral motifs, these are never naturalistically treated but rather form discrete borders and panels echoing the shape of the book. Although Armstrong in particular was influenced by the sinuous forms of Art Nouveau, the development of this style of book-cover design in America was entirely independent of the rise of the poster. Because these stamped designs were relatively fragile and the cloth-covered boards were subject to wear, many books with decorated covers came protected by a slipcase or jacket.[6] Book jackets were known much earlier, but it seems to have been only in the 1890s that they became common. Most were made of glassine or plain unprinted paper and were obviously intended only to protect the book during shipping and handling in the bookstores. Printed jackets occasionally reproduced the cover design, though more commonly they only listed title, author, and publisher.

Fig. 1 Margaret Armstrong. Cover design for *The Adventures of Captain Horn* by Frank R. Stockton (New York: Charles Scribner's Sons, 1895). The Houghton Library, Harvard University

The inside of the typical nineties trade book had very little to do with its outside. Although there are a few examples of gift books with endpapers, title pages, or decorative borders by Armstrong and other decorative designers, usually the contribution of these artists was limited to the cover design. Illustrations, if present, were halftones or photo-linecuts after such artists as E. W. Kemble, C. H. Russell, and Charles Dana Gibson. These great illustrators enjoyed tremendous prestige and their work was extremely popular. The realist style of their illustrations seldom related to either cover or poster design, however, though enlargements of illustrations with added lettering were occasionally used as posters by some publishers. In such cases the artist probably had little control over the manner in which an illustration was adapted as a poster design. That the illustrations often sold the book or magazine is quite clear from the prominent mention that the illustrator received in many contemporary posters. A *Scribner's* poster by William Sargeant Kendall (Cat. 109) consisted of a full-length portrait of Gibson accompanied by an announcement that Gibson was "One of the Illustrators in this Month's Scribner's." Two best-selling novels by Frank R. Stockton, published by Scribner's in 1895 and 1896, exemplify the total lack of visual relationship among book cover, illustrations, and poster typical of the period. Armstrong designed both books' decorative covers featuring nautical motifs (Fig. 1), but both have striking and totally unrelated posters by other artists. The poster for *The Adventures of Captain Horn* (Cat. 125, colorplate 11), with its rather ominous lurking figure and startling colors, is the work of Blanche McManus; the more modest sailing ship on the poster for *Mrs. Cliff's Yacht* was designed by E. B. Wells (Cat. 284). *The Adventures of Captain Horn* was unillustrated, but its sequel, *Mrs. Cliff's Yacht*, had eight full-page halftone illustrations of a distinctly melodramatic character, after drawings by A. Forestier. Surprisingly, a magazine advertisement for the earlier of the two books featured the central motif from Armstrong's cover design rather than McManus's poster.[7] A possible explanation is that the *Captain Horn* poster relies heavily upon the use of color for its effect, and in 1895, magazine advertisements were invariably printed in black and white. The smaller scale of the book decorations and their direct relationship to the product advertised may have been additional factors, since in general the book advertisements in magazines tended to reproduce cover designs rather than posters.

Magazine covers, like book covers, remained the province of the decorative designer well into the decade. Most magazines were issued with the same standard covers month after month, a practice that continues for many scholarly journals to the present day. The dignified but basically uninteresting standard covers of *Harper's* and *Lippincott's* figure in many a spritely advertising poster by Penfield and Will Carqueville. At a time when The Century Company was publishing more book and magazine posters than any other American firm, its house organ, *The Century*, appeared monthly in staid standard wrappers designed by Stanford White. The breakthrough came in 1894, when Bradley was asked to design a standard cover for *The Inland Printer*, a Chicago printing journal. Instead of designing one permanent cover, Bradley convinced the publishers to change the cover with every issue.[8] Although it appears that Bradley had not yet designed any posters himself, the covers that he contributed to *The Inland Printer* reveal a close study of the work of European poster artists, including Aubrey Beardsley and Eugène Grasset. In fact, it seems likely that the changing covers of *The Inland Printer* were inspired by Beardsley's changing covers for the controversial *Yellow Book*. The innovation of changing covers was quickly adopted by a host of little magazines with names like *The Red Letter* and *Miss Blue Stocking*, and Bradley continued it in his own short-lived but influential periodical, *Bradley: His Book*. Most mass magazines, however, clung persistently to their old standard covers, and even some of the more progressive periodicals proved re-

markably resistant to the new idea. Stone and Kimball's *Chap-Book*, which advertised itself in a marvelously varied sequence of posters by Bradley, Frank Hazenplug, Elisha Brown Bird, J. C. Leyendecker, and Claude Fayette Bragdon, appeared semimonthly in standard covers in a conservative style.[9] J. M. Bowles's *Modern Art* never adopted the innovation of changing covers either, but its standard cover design, drawn by Bruce Rogers, was featured on a poster advertising the magazine. Many *Inland Printer* covers, notably a series designed by Leyendecker in 1897, also did double duty as poster designs (see Cat. 113, colorplate 36).

Book covers, like magazine covers, soon began to reflect the influence of the poster style. Again, a probable source for this innovation was the figural cloth covers of the British *Yellow Book*. A second source was the lithographed paper wrappers typical of contemporary French books. Many of these jackets were designed by Henri de Toulouse-Lautrec, Pierre Bonnard, and Théophile-Alexandre Steinlen. All were closely related to the artist's poster style; in a few cases, extra copies of the wrappers themselves were used as posters.[10] American paperbacks, unlike their more respectable clothbound counterparts, had never entirely abandoned figurative covers and were among the first books to adopt the poster style. Examples are Sloan's cover for *The Lady and Her Tree* (Vortex Co., 1895; Cat. 275) and Leyendecker's for *One Fair Daughter* (E. A. Weeks, 1895), both of which echo the poster designs for the books. Cheap sensational novels were typical of the paperbacks of the period, though most publishers regularly issued a line of paperback books for summer reading.[11] Many children's books were also issued with paper covers or paper-covered boards.

Paper-covered boards were a compromise solution adopted by several publishers. Although these bindings were more fragile than cloth covers, they were much easier to produce. As early as 1894, Copeland and Day used paper-covered boards printed with a smaller version of the poster design for *Songs from Vagabondia*, a popular book of poetry by Bliss Carman and Richard Hovey. The design incorporated portraits of the two poets and the artist, Thomas Buford Meteyard. Bird's design for *The Captured Cunarder* (Cat. 8, colorplate 28), another Copeland and Day book (1896), was also used for both poster and book cover (Fig. 2). The fine detail of Bird's drawing would probably have been distorted or lost had it been printed on coarse-grained cloth. As it is, reproduced on both front and back covers in black and red on blue-gray paper, it is one of the most dramatic and effective designs of the period. The title appears only on the spine of the book. The added lettering on the poster may not be by Bird, since similar lettering appears on Sloan's poster for *Cinder-Path Tales* (Copeland and Day, 1896; Cat. 278, colorplate 54) and many Copeland and Day posters by different artists share nearly identical lettering.[12] Other books with paper-covered boards include two with covers by the Impressionist painter J. H. Twachtman, *W. V. Her Book* and *The Invisible Playmate*, both written by William Canton and published by Stone and Kimball in 1896. A strong French influence is evident in the lithographed designs. In both cases Twachtman was responsible only for the cover designs. Francis Berkeley Smith's poster for *W. V. Her Book* was totally unrelated to Twachtman's cover, and there was no poster issued for *The Invisible Playmate*. Twachtman's only poster was for Harold Frederic's best-selling novel *The Damnation of Theron Ware* (Cat. 282), which was issued in 1896 by Stone and Kimball in plain undecorated green cloth.[13] A French influence is also discernible in Peter S. Newell's cover for *A Shadow Show* (Century Co., 1896), which, like some French paper wrappers, also served as the poster for the book (Fig. 3). Such identity of book cover and poster was extremely rare in America.

The poster style also had an impact on the decoration of clothbound books. One early and fairly unusual example is Meteyard's design for *The Ebb Tide*, by Robert Louis Stevenson and Lloyd Osborne (Stone and Kimball, 1894). Meteyard's stylized tropical-island landscape

Fig. 2 Elisha Brown Bird. Cover design for *The Captured Cunarder* by W. H. Rideing (Boston: Copeland and Day, 1896). Harvard College Library

was featured not only on the poster for the book but also on the green cloth cover and, exceptionally, on the paper jacket. Decorated jackets were still extremely rare at this date; *The Ebb Tide* is the only Stone and Kimball book known to have been issued with such a jacket.[14] Figurative, posterlike designs appeared on the cloth covers of a number of books published by Copeland and Day in the 1890s, although Scribner's and Houghton Mifflin continued throughout the period to favor the nonfigurative designs of Armstrong, Whitman, and their imitators. Even at the height of the poster movement, posterlike covers remained the exception rather than the rule. Stone and Kimball and Copeland and Day both issued many books with perfectly plain cloth covers (such as *The Damnation of Theron Ware*, cited above) or with simple, nonfigurative decorative designs. Only toward the end of the decade were figurative cover designs widely adopted both by some publishing firms and by the mass magazines. This development appears to have been inextricably related to the simultaneous decline of the poster.

To understand the poster's rise and fall in popularity requires some knowledge of how book and magazine posters were distributed and collected, a phenomenon that has never been adequately studied. Most book and magazine posters were never intended to be posted at all, in the most literal sense. They were not displayed on the streets, randomly stuck to walls or billboards. Occasionally a book poster was designed as a streetcar ad—examples are Sloan's poster for *The Lady and Her Tree* and a poster by George Wharton Edwards for Funk and Wagnalls's *Standard Dictionary*—but contemporary commentary suggests that such use was rare and considered undignified.[15] Most of the familiar book and magazine posters of the nineties were originally intended for display at bookstores and newsstands. Although some, at least, were also intended as collectors' items, their primary function was always as advertisements to promote the sale of books and magazines. From the beginning, however, they seem to have been rather unsuccessful as advertising. Many book dealers simply did not know what to do with them: they were so large and soon so numerous that it was impossible to display them all. One early poster collector described finding a cache of American book and magazine posters in a midwestern bookshop about 1896:

> The little man who talked to me said yes, he had a few posters that he received occasionally from the American News Company in bundles with his papers and periodicals, and from eastern publishers. He had no use for them, but thinking them too pretty to throw away, he put them as they came into a large drawer under the counter.[16]

This group of eighty-three posters included the *Century* Napoleon posters, the first three *Chap-Book* posters, and all but two of Penfield's *Harper's* designs. Many canny booksellers never displayed publishers' posters at all, saving them in mint condition for favorite customers.

Of course the publishers were not unaware that their posters were being collected; many of them were poster collectors themselves. Besides sending them to bookstores and newsstands, most publishers also sold their posters directly to individual collectors. Stone and Kimball advertised back posters for sale in *The Chap-Book*, and *The Century* issued a list with prices. Lamson, Wolffe, and Company, a Boston publisher, made a special sideline of "fine-art" book posters, produced in "a most artistic and expensive style." This line of fine-art posters included McManus's striking advertisement for *The True Mother Goose* (Cat. 127) and all of Ethel Reed's posters for the firm. Small posters, such as *Trilby the Fairy of Argyle* and *The House of Trees*, were priced at twenty-five cents. Large ones, such as *Fairy Tales* (Cat. 238), sold for one dollar. The large and showy poster for *Behind the Arras* (Cat. 236) was offered in two

Fig. 3 Peter S. Newell. Poster for his book *A Shadow Show* (New York: The Century Company, 1896). Department of Printing and Graphic Arts, The Houghton Library, Harvard University

versions: an ordinary trade edition for fifty cents, and a limited edition on imported paper for one dollar. A special set of Reed posters, limited to fifty copies signed and numbered by the artist, was also offered for sale by the publisher.[17] Since signed and numbered limited editions were by no means the rule in 1896 even for fine prints, these Lamson, Wolffe posters were clearly regarded by their publishers as works of art, not just as advertisements. On the basis of their artistic and technical quality, such an opinion is not unjustified. Nevertheless, Frederic Thoreau Singleton complained in *Poster Lore*, a Kansas City journal devoted to poster collecting, that it was "un-American" for publishers to charge for their advertising matter.[18] Though most publishers did just that, a few less pretentious posters continued to be offered free as come-ons to potential book and magazine buyers. A typical 1896 advertisement promised subscribers

> A Bradley poster free. The Echo . . . will be sent three months for 50 cents, with a poster by Bradley, Nankivell or Sloan free.[19]

With the poster craze at its height, poster magazines proliferated and poster dealers sprang up in the cities. Posters quickly became big business, but still they were not very successful as advertisements. Highly sought after themselves, they did little to promote the sale of the books and magazines they were supposed to advertise. As early as 1896, Frederic Singleton commented:

> Because I have to pay for my posters I cannot buy so many books. I purchase the poster now when once I would [have] purchase[d] the book and I do not think my publishers profit thereby.[20]

Looking back on the collecting craze from 1901, another writer recalled that

> Three or four years ago these posters would not have been up ten minutes before some steady customer would demand them [of the newsdealer]. They did not think of buying the magazine advertised; they only wanted the poster.[21]

Fig. 4 Edward Penfield. Cover design for *Collier's Illustrated Weekly* (June 7, 1902). Harvard College Library

Because collectors of the 1890s were more interested in acquiring posters than in buying books, the movement was doomed from the beginning. As soon as it became clear that poster collectors were not necessarily book buyers, the publishers' interest in posters as advertising began to flag. Significantly, this was also the moment when posterlike designs began to appear in great numbers on book covers and jackets, and on the covers of mass magazines.

The advertising value of eye-catching book and magazine covers has long been recognized. An early historian of the poster movement, Charles Matlack Price, described how "a bookshop has often attracted one across the street by reason of the strength of design in certain bookcovers." He went on to argue that "since many magazines present covers of considerable surface area, and since these are hung conspicuously on newsstands with a view to attracting attention, they differ in no essential features from posters proper."[22] In his book *Poster Design*, Price drew no distinction between the posters of the 1890s and the magazine covers of the early 1900s, treating both as aspects of the same phenomenon. Many of the artists who had designed posters in the nineties went on to successful careers as cover designers after 1900. Penfield, Bradley, and Leyendecker designed covers for *Collier's* (Fig. 4), *Judge*, *Metropolitan Magazine*, and *The Saturday Evening Post*. Parrish designed covers for numerous Harper publications, including *Harper's Weekly* and *Harper's Young People*, as well as for *Collier's* and other magazines. Parrish always referred to his advertising designs as "posters" no matter if they were reproduced as magazine covers, window cards, or twenty-four-sheet billboard advertisements.[23]

Although this shift from poster design to magazine covers and other forms of advertising is sometimes considered the artist's deliberate choice, the real initiative clearly lay with the publishers. If the eye-catching design was on the cover itself rather than on a separate poster, the customer who wished to acquire the design would be obliged to buy the magazine. Many early magazine covers are stylistically so close to posters that it is sometimes difficult to tell poster from cover in a small reproduction. Posterlike book covers also became much more common in the last years of the 1890s. Although the series of brightly colored figurative covers designed by Amy Sacker for L. C. Page and Company beginning about 1897 were clearly influenced by the poster style, few, if any, of her designs were ever reproduced as posters.[24] Likewise, the cover designs of the New York firm known as the Decorative Designers reflect the impact of the poster style without being directly related to any actual posters.[25] Although such covers suggest a new design direction about 1900, parallel to contemporary developments in magazine cover design, the days of the decorated binding were numbered. The printed book jacket was soon to display much greater advertising potential than the cloth book cover. One of the earliest posterlike book jackets was based on a dramatic design by Leyendecker. It protected the decorated covers of *Ionia* by Alexander Craig (Fig. 5), published in 1898 by the E. A. Weeks Company, the same Chicago publisher for whom Leyendecker had designed his first poster three years earlier. The front cover shows a woman in classical garb reading before a Greek temple, juxtaposed against a resolute workingman and a despairing woman in an industrial landscape on the back. The black-and-white reproduction on the jacket is even more effective than the full-color cloth cover.

Paper book jackets were also an ideal surface for printed advertisements. The practice of advertising other titles on the flaps of a book jacket began in the 1890s; the use of brief quotations from reviews and of specially written blurbs became increasingly prevalent around the turn of the century. Gelett Burgess's 1906 satire of a blurb on the jacket of *Are You a Bromide?* ("YES, this is a 'BLURB!' All the Other Publishers commit them. Why Shouldn't We?") suggests that the practice was well established by this time.[26] Neither poster nor printed cover could adequately perform this function, and the fact that advertisements are still printed on book jackets is surely a measure of their success. Printed and decorated jackets

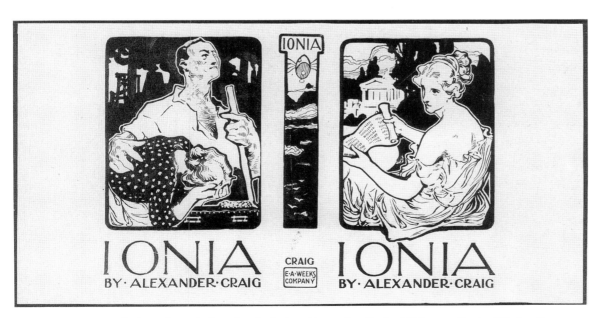

Fig. 5 J. C. Leyendecker. Dust jacket for *Ionia* by Alexander Craig (Chicago: E. A. Weeks Company, 1898). The Houghton Library, Harvard University

became increasingly common after 1900; by 1910 they were practically universal, replacing decorated bindings in all but a few cases.

Magazine covers, book covers, and ultimately jackets were evolving rapidly at the turn of the century. At the same time, the artistic poster was beginning to decline. Copeland and Day, and Lamson, Wolffe and Company, small publishers who made a specialty of artistic posters, both went out of business in 1899. Stone and Kimball dissolved their partnership in 1897. The larger publishing companies continued to issue some book and magazine posters after 1900, but these were slicker, more commercial productions and were not collected as obsessively as the posters of the nineties. The tensions between art and advertising that persisted throughout the 1890s seemed finally resolved in favor of advertising. Poster artists and decorative designers began to evolve into modern commercial artists as advertising proliferated. Color printing, at first reserved for posters and cover designs, began to appear in magazines both for illustrations and for full-page advertisements, opening a new field not only for designers but also for the manufacturers who had been slow to adopt the new poster styles in the nineties. While the most typical advertisements of the 1890s are the book and magazine posters of Bradley and Penfield, after 1900 ads for manufacturers' products play an increasingly prominent role. The most memorable ads of the opening years of the new century would include Parrish's designs for Fisk tires and Leyendecker's for Arrow shirts. Advertisements for such products, including posters, were mass produced on a scale previously undreamed of. The early twentieth century would also see the development of the travel poster, the entertainment poster, and, in 1917–18, the war poster. Although book and magazine posters were not entirely unknown after 1900, they would never again assume the leading role that they had played in the 1890s.

NOTES

1. *American Art Nouveau: The Poster Period of John Sloan*, ed. Helen Farr Sloan (Lock Haven, Penn.: Hammermill Paper Co., 1967), n.p.: "So the new photo-mechanical methods of reproducing original drawings were part of the industrial revolution, as it affected art. There was a kind of excitement in the air for those of us who were interested in drawing as a means of communicating ideas, when these new opportunities for mass production through publishing were opening up."

2. See, e.g., Nancy Finlay, *Artists of the Book in Boston, 1890–1910* (Cambridge, Mass.: Harvard College Library, 1985), p. 26. The work in question is Rhead's design (Cat. 252) for *Meadow-Grass* (Boston: Copeland and Day, 1895). Letters in the Houghton Mifflin Archives at the Houghton Library, Harvard University, indicate that both Henry Oscar Houghton and George Mifflin exercised a high degree of aesthetic control over the appearance of their firm's books.

3. On the work of Bradley, see Roberta Waddell Wong, *Will H. Bradley, American Artist and Craftsman (1868–1962)* (New York: The Metropolitan Museum of Art, 1972). A large collection of Bradley's advertising designs is preserved in the Massachusetts Historical Society, Boston.

4. The best general reference on decorated bindings is Charles Gullans and John Espey, "American Trade Bindings and Their Designers, 1880–1915," *Collectible Books, Some New Paths* (London and New York: R. R. Bowker, 1979), pp. 32–33. Useful also is Laurie W. Crichton, *Book Decoration in America, 1890–1910: A Guide to an Exhibition* (Williamstown, Mass.: Williams College, 1979). Finlay concentrates on designers active in the Boston area.

5. On Armstrong, see Gullans and Espey, *A Checklist of Trade Bindings Designed by Margaret Armstrong* (Los Angeles: University of California Library, 1968). Gullans is currently preparing a bibliography of Whitman's work.

6. On the early history of the book jacket, see Charles Rosner, *The Art of the Book Jacket* (London: Victoria and Albert Museum, 1949) and *The Growth of the Book Jacket* (Cambridge, Mass.: Sylvan, 1954). G. Thomas Tanselle, *Book-Jackets, Blurbs and Bibliographers* (London: Bibliographical Society, 1971), contains an excellent discussion of early book jackets, chiefly from a bibliographical point of view.

7. *Publishers' Weekly*, no. 1222 (June 29, 1895), p. 1040.

8. See Victor Margolin, *American Poster Renaissance* (New York: Watson-Guptill, 1975), p. 26.

9. *The Chap-Book* did use decorative cover designs occasionally beginning October 1, 1895.

10. See Peter A. Wick, *Toulouse-Lautrec: Book Covers and Brochures* (Cambridge, Mass.: Harvard College Library, 1972), and Phillip Dennis Cate and Susan Gill, *Théophile-Alexandre Steinlen* (Salt Lake City: Gibbs M. Smith, 1982), for bookwork by these artists.

11. Brander Matthews, "Books in Paper Covers," *The Century* 50 (1895), pp. 354–361. Matthews quotes Charles Dudley Warner on "summer novels . . . in light paper covers, ornamental, attractive in colors and fanciful designs, as welcome and grateful as the girls in muslin . . ." (p. 360). Matthews does not clearly distinguish between paper wrappers and paper-covered boards; he also discusses contemporary magazine covers.

12. E.g., Reed's poster for *Jacques Damour* (1895, Cat. 243) and the poster based on Parrish's cover design for *Free to Serve* (1897, Cat. 136). Although the artists who drew the pictorial designs probably had nothing to do with the poster layouts, all are homogeneous compositions suggesting the hand of a master designer. It is tempting to ascribe the composition of such posters to Bertram Grosvenor Goodhue, who was closely associated with Copeland and Day at this period. On Copeland and Day, see Joe W. Kraus, *Messrs. Copeland and Day, 69 Cornhill, Boston 1893–1899* (Philadelphia: George S. McManus, 1979). For biographical background on Fred Holland Day, see Estelle Jussim, *Slave to Beauty: The Eccentric Life and Controversial Career of F. Holland Day, Photographer, Publisher, Aesthete* (Boston: David R. Godine, 1981).

13. Sidney Kramer, *A History of Stone and Kimball and Herbert S. Stone and Co., with a Bibliography of their Publications 1893–1905* (Chicago: University of Chicago Press, 1940), pp. 236–238, 247. *The Damnation of Theron Ware* was entered for copyright on March 6. *W. V. Her Book* was copyright May 21; *The Invisible Playmate* (no record of copyright) carries the date October 1896 in its colophon; their paper-covered boards with Twachtman's design were used only for the first printings. The second printings were bound in red cloth.

14. See Richard E. Oinonen, *Oinonen Book Auctions*, Sunderland, Mass., Sale Number 71 (Sunday, June 10, 1984), no. 279. The jacket is described as repeating the book design (i.e., the cover design) in black. Kramer (p. 214, no. 24) was apparently unaware that the book was issued with a jacket, for he makes no mention of it.

15. *Publishers' Weekly*, no. 1295 (November 21, 1896), p. 853: "The gracefully-robed muse of philology or orthography [in Edwards's poster] . . . seems rather out of place sandwiched between skirt-binding and baking powder." The ad itself is reproduced in *Publishers' Weekly*'s "Christmas Bookshelf for 1896," p. 208.

16. Theodore Adams, "A Few Words about the Beginnings of a Collection," *Poster Lore* 1.1 (January 1896), p. 16.

17. This special set of Reed posters was advertised in a brochure of current publications, Lamson, Wolffe and Company, 1896. *Publishers' Weekly* noted that Lamson, Wolffe and Company were making a specialty of posters (July 18, 1896, p. 133).

18. *Poster Lore* 1.4 (July 1896), p. 121.

19. *Poster Lore* 1.2 (February 1896), p. 62.

20. *Poster Lore* 1.4 (July 1896), p. 121.

21. "A Fad That Has Passed Away," *New York Tribune*, August 18, 1901.

22. *Poster Design* (New York: George W. Bricka, 1922), pp. 6, 299. As early as 1895, the preface to *An Exhibition of Posters—Mostly American—at the Cosmos Club* (Washington, D.C., 1895) noted that "Book-covers are nearly allied to posters in their purpose." Some poster exhibitions in the 1890s also included book covers.

23. Coy Ludwig, *Maxfield Parrish* (New York: Watson-Guptill, 1973), p. 106. On the later work of Leyendecker, see Michael Schau, *J. C. Leyendecker* (New York: Watson-Guptill, 1974). On the later work of Penfield and other artists, see Price, pp. 215 ff.

24. See Finlay, pp. 103–104.

25. On the work of the Decorative Designers, see Gullans and Espey, *The Decorative Designers 1896–1932* (Los Angeles: University of California Library, 1970).

26. Tanselle, pp. 102–103, discusses the history of advertising on book jackets.

Fig. 1 Charles Martin. Installation of 1889 poster exhibition at the Galerie Préaubert, Nantes, France. At far left is Chéret's *La Terre* and at far right is Grasset's *Librairie romantique.* The Jane Voorhees Zimmerli Art Museum, Rutgers University, David A. and Mildred H. Morse Art Acquisition Fund

THE FRENCH POSTER
1868–1900

Phillip Dennis Cate

IN NOVEMBER 1890, the first exhibition of French posters to be held in the United States took place in New York at the Grolier Club, founded in 1884 for collectors of rare books and prints, and by 1890 located at 29 East 32nd Street. The exhibition presented a fascinating new visual experience for Americans and as its catalogue preface suggests offered a new field of collecting:

The illustrated artistic poster (*affiche*) is, relatively, a new-comer in the domain of the collector.

It belongs to what may be called ephemeral or fugitive art, and, but for the collector, would only for a short time decorate our streets and avenues, and then disappear forever. That it has at last conquered its right to stay, is shown by the fact that there have been within the last two years two successful exhibitions; one in Paris and another in Nantes, exclusively of illustrated posters. This collection is not as large as either the Paris or Nantes exhibit, but it contains many of the best specimens of each, and a few samples of the art in this country.

The modern illustrated poster first appeared about 1830, and artists such as RAFLET [*sic*], GRANDVILLE, DAUMIER and others contributed largely to its artistic success. Since then, the progress has been marvelous, and, to-day, the works of CHERET, GRASSET, LEVY, CHOUBRAC, etc., are, many of them, masterpieces of high artistic merit and taste.[1]

Only six years earlier, in 1884, the first poster exhibition actually occurred in Paris, on the Right Bank at the Palais Vivienne. Of greater consequence, however, were the two major shows at Paris and Nantes, the first in 1889 at the Paris Universal Exposition, the second at the Galerie Préaubert. Photographs of the Nantes show (Figs. 1, 2) suggest the contents of the 1889 Paris exhibition and that at the Grolier Club; they also reveal the very practical clothespin system of displaying the posters border to border. Essentially the exhibitions summed up an era of poster art in which Jules Chéret was the dominant figure.

The year after the Grolier Club show, 1891, the work of Pierre Bonnard and Henri de Toulouse-Lautrec appeared, as well as a new stylistic rapture with posters of the past half-century. The decade of the nineties is particularly significant for the influence French posters exerted on American graphic artists, as well as for the degree of respectability that poster art assumed among the young avant-garde, who saw it as a means of self-expression.

By 1890, Jules Chéret had already been creating color lithographic posters for more than twenty years. He was universally recognized as the master of the medium for his ability to combine craftsmanship and artistry in invention of printing techniques and in design. In 1869, three years after establishing his lithographic shop in Paris, Chéret invented an inexpensive means of printing posters with several colors (Fig. 3). Henri Beraldi described this system in 1886:

> In principle, the posters of Chéret are made by three superimposed impressions. One, in black, establishes the drawing, strongly indicated and skillfully composed in order to receive in certain places the energetic red coloration, which is the most violent color to attract the eye. Another impression gives this "red touch." The third harmonizes the brutal note of the red by means of a gradated background [*fond gradué*]: the cool tones,

Fig. 2 Charles Martin. 1889 poster exhibition. At center is Choubrac's *Robert Macaire.* The Jane Voorhees Zimmerli Art Museum, Rutgers University, David A. and Mildred H. Morse Art Acquisition Fund

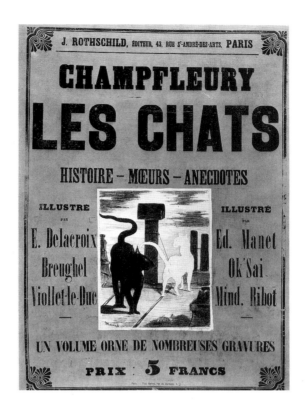

Fig. 3 Jules Chéret. *Valentino*, 1869.
Jane Voorhees Zimmerli Art Museum,
Rutgers University

Fig. 4 Edouard Manet. *Cats' Rendezvous*, 1868.
Bibliothèque Nationale, Paris

blues or greens, placed at the top half of the poster; the warm tones, yellow or orange,
placed at the bottom.

The gradated background was already employed for drawing-papers; but it is
Chéret, I believe, who first had the idea of applying it to posters. This triple impression
became the normal, classic process for Chéret's posters. In exceptional cases, he added a
fourth impression for yellow. Even sometimes, but very rarely, a fifth.[2]

The application of a *fond gradué* allowed Chéret to integrate color dramatically within his
poster image and thus to go far beyond the limited effects obtained by the two- or three-color
lithographic posters produced up to that time.

The year before Chéret invented the *fond gradué*, Edouard Manet created *Cats' Rendezvous*
(Fig. 4), a black-and-white lithograph used for the poster advertising Champfleury's book *Les
Chats*.[3] Manet did not conceive the image as fully integrated with the text of the poster. It is
instead an independent lithograph pasted onto a large sheet of violet paper on which the
words had been typographically printed beforehand. The combination of black type and violet
paper is startling, and it is made even more impressive by Manet's dynamic composition. The
unmodeled, silhouetted black and white cats, with their serpentine tails, and the boldly
and simply drawn smokestacks impart a strong decorative quality that parallels the two-
dimensionality of the solid lettering.

An emphasis on the decorative and the two-dimensional is especially important in the
art of the 1890s. It is significant, yet not unexpected, that we find its genesis in the late
1860s, with *Cats' Rendezvous*, the only poster by Manet. He, like the next generation of

artists—Lautrec, Bonnard, and others—explored a variety of new aesthetic concepts. Indeed, Manet's emphasis on depicting aspects of modern life in a direct painterly fashion made him a precursor of and a hero to the young avant-garde of the nineties. However, more than twenty years elapsed between Manet's poster and the accomplishments of the end of the century. Chéret's activities during the interim prepared the way technically and in many ways aesthetically for the next generation to build upon the accomplishments of Manet.

There is no documented evidence of Chéret's contact with Manet, but Chéret must have known the highly publicized cat poster as well as Manet's paintings. In 1876, Chéret created his own version of two cats on a roof for the poster *Duo des Chats*,[4] strongly reminiscent of Manet's composition, though less decorative. The same year that Manet created his only color lithograph, *Le Polichinelle* of 1874, Chéret, the master of color lithography, produced a large poster advertising a masked ball at the dance hall Frascati (Fig. 5). The foreground of Chéret's deep perspective of the hall contains a figure dressed as a polichinelle. While this character is often associated with costume balls, it is striking that the two artists created the same subject, in the same medium, at the same time. In *Masked Ball at the Opéra*, painted toward the end of 1873 and the beginning of 1874, Manet again included the figure of a polichinelle.

This shared content in the work of Manet and Chéret implies that Chéret actively responded to contemporary tendencies, and not only to art of the past, especially the eighteenth-century Rococo to which his work is often compared. In his later career Chéret often associated closely with younger, more radical colleagues in exhibitions, print publications, and mural decorations.

Fig. 5 Jules Chéret. Frascati, 1874. The Jane Voorhees Zimmerli Art Museum, Rutgers University, Class of 1937 Purchase Fund

Fig. 6 Jules Chéret. *Les Girard*, 1877.
Bibliothèque Nationale, Paris

During the seventies and early eighties, the *fond gradué* color system continued to play an important part in Chéret's work. Yet, as in the Frascati poster, Chéret also explored rich multiple color schemes, eliminating the *fond gradué* in favor of a more painterly effect. While creating complicated designs using traditional perspective systems and modeling, he produced a number of simplified compositions, such as *Les Girard* of 1877 (Fig. 6). In this, Chéret's most successful attempt at combining image and text, the background is neutralized and the bodies of the dancers rhythmically intertwine with the words. In the tradition of Manet's *Cats*, *Les Girard* is a powerful precursor of the decorative concerns of Art Nouveau. By 1884, Chéret had probably created nearly a thousand poster designs, advertising for a great variety of clients.[5] By the end of the decade these included operas, theaters, cafés-concerts, dance halls, circuses, novels, journals, art exhibitions, department stores, and a multitude of personal commodities.

An early trademark of Chéret's designs was the "Chéret woman"—a beautiful, dreamy, flimsily clad, floating female. Though modest in comparison to the figures on turn-of-the-century posters by Chéret and others, she proved that sexually appealing images were an effective means of selling almost any product. In the nineties, as posters became more daring, it was perfectly acceptable to depict a bare-breasted woman if she served as an allegorical figure, such as the muse of art in Mucha's *Salon des Cent* of 1896 (Fig. 7). However, when in 1899 Steinlen portrayed a contemporary woman similarly exposed, in a poster advertising a novel on white slavery, it was censored and he was required to redo the design by covering her with a chemise.

Fig. 7 Alphonse Mucha. *Salon des Cent*, 1896. The Jane Voorhees Zimmerli Art Museum, Rutgers University, Gift of Harold and Barbara Kaplan

By 1890, the time of his first one-man exhibition, Chéret had mastered all the technical possibilities of color lithography that would be available to himself and his followers until 1900. Especially important to Chéret for the creation of an atmospheric effect was *crachis*, a spattered-ink technique, used in combination with lithographic crayon or with the flat application of tusche (lithographic ink). His palette varied from three colors to more than six, and he utilized both larger formats for posters like *La Terre*, 1889 (97 by 34 in.), and more standard sizes, 49 by 33 inches (the double colombier) or 23½ by 31 inches (the colombier). Often, reduced lithographic versions of his posters were made for interior display or as a supplement to such journals as the *Courrier français*. In 1891, Chéret created four decorative color lithographic panels, "les estampes murales": *La Pantomime*, *La Musique*, *La Danse*, and *La Comédie*.[6] These panels, as large as posters but void of lettering, were meant to be framed and hung indoors. Chéret's large nonposter color lithographs are the predecessors of an entire genre of printmaking developed in the 1890s, sometimes called "panneaux décoratifs" or "estampes décoratives." They essentially supplied large colorful works of art to the public at a cost lower than that of paintings. Artists including Steinlen, Mucha, Rivière, and Bonnard were commissioned to design these murals by several publishers—Charles and Eugène Verneau, Champenois, and Molines among them.

As early as 1818, Alöys Senefelder, the inventor of lithography, experimented with printing on zinc plates in place of the usual Bavarian limestone; however, zinc as a practical

Fig. 8 Eugène Grasset. *Encre L. Marquet*, 1892. The Jane Voorhees Zimmerli Art Museum, Rutgers University, David A. and Mildred H. Morse Art Acquisition Fund

surface for planographic printing was not perfected until 1874. Because of its lightness, pliability, and relatively low cost, zinc quickly replaced the litho stone in many commercial shops. Chéret's firm, nevertheless, apparently preferred stone to zinc.

In 1850, Firmin Gillot invented a process, called gillotage, that allowed lithographic and intaglio (etching) images to be transferred onto a zinc plate and placed in relief in order to be printed from a typographical press (letterpress).[7] Prior to gillotage, books or journals illustrated with lithographs or etchings were by necessity involved in two printing processes: one for the image; and a second, relief system of printing—letterpress—for the text. Gillotage allowed a far more economical combination of processes, so that image and text could be printed simultaneously on the letterpress.

By 1875, Charles Gillot, Firmin's son, converted his father's invention to photography, permitting a photographic negative of a line drawing to be exposed to light over a photosensitized zinc plate. The exposed areas of the photo emulsion paralleled the drawing, then were hardened and made acid-resistant by the light. The unexposed areas washed away, and the entire plate was placed into an acid bath. The action of the acid etched the bare zinc, leaving the protected line drawing in relief, ready for printing from a letterpress. This new photorelief printing process was soon adapted to and revolutionized the production of illustrated books and journals. Although photo color separation was not yet commercially possible, by using the initial photorelief plate of the drawing as a guide, craftsmen could produce

Fig. 9 Pierre Bonnard. *France-Champagne*, 1891. The Jane Voorhees Zimmerli Art Museum, Rutgers University, Gift of Ralph and Barbara Voorhees

additional relief color plates nonphotomechanically, in order to create a multicolor image. By the end of the 1880s, Steinlen and Grasset had created posters with this new process (Fig. 8). During the nineties, concurrently with their work in color lithography, it became common practice for French and American artists, without compromising their art, to create poster designs that would be printed from photorelief plates.

Poster mania was already in full swing in France by the time of the 1889 Paris Universal Exposition, although posters were a new interest in 1890 in the United States. Gustave Fustier's 1884 article "La Littérature murale," and two books of 1886, Ernest Maindron's *Les Affiches illustrées* and Beraldi's *Les Graveurs du XIX siècle*, evaluated, categorized, and catalogued the posters by Chéret and several of his colleagues.[8] The print and rare-book dealer Edmond Sagot had by 1886 begun to sell posters to the public, specializing in Chéret to such a degree that in 1890 he was publishing limited editions of the artist's works on special paper for connoisseurs.

In 1881, a new Freedom of the Press law offered greater toleration to posters in regard to censorship. The law restricted the locations where posters could be placed, but also protected them from avid collectors by fining individuals who peeled posters off the walls. By the end of the decade, as the quantity of posters and collectors rapidly increased, these two aspects of the law were no longer respected to any great degree by the "afficheurs" or by collectors.

Other notable artists creating posters prior to the nineties included Léon and Alfred Choubrac, Adolphe Willette, and Eugène Grasset. But there is little work of distinction by artists other than Chéret. Rather, in contrast to the colorful and often evocative posters by Chéret and a few others, the 1870s and 1880s saw an abundant category of posters, mostly in black-and-white lithography, stylistically akin to academic painting of the period and in content appealing to the taste of the bourgeoisie for melodrama and sentimentality. Chéret's accomplishments and his contributions to poster art of the 1890s are all the more outstanding when weighed against the quantity of these minor productions.

As the photographs of the Nantes exhibition generally attest, many of the posters of the 1880s, including some by Chéret, are visually complicated by too many words and by an anecdotal quality. Most superimpose text awkwardly on a realistically depicted scene or on a group of realistic vignettes. Very rarely was this successful, and few posters reached the simplicity and unity of Choubrac's *Robert Macaire*, Grasset's *Librairie romantique*, Chéret's *La Terre*,

Fig. 10 Henri de Toulouse-Lautrec. *Moulin Rouge, La Goulue*, 1891. Mr. and Mrs. Herbert D. Schimmel

Fig. 11 Jules Chéret. *Bal du Moulin Rouge*, 1889. The Jane Voorhees Zimmerli Art Museum, Rutgers University

Fig. 12 Henri de Toulouse-Lautrec. *May Milton*,
1895. Mr. and Mrs. Herbert D. Schimmel

or Willette's *Nouveau Cirque.* The accommodation of the poster image to the two-dimensional
text was the essential issue facing poster artists at the beginning of the 1890s. Chéret had
struggled with the problem for years; while he came close to success with *Les Girards*, his
tastes and times precluded decorative extremes and abstractions.

The great achievement of the artists of the 1890s was to evolve not one but several
formulas of poster art that successfully merged the decorative, symbolist, and realist tendencies of the decade. The breakthrough came in 1891 with *France-Champagne* by Bonnard (Fig.
9) and with *Moulin Rouge, La Goulue* by Lautrec (Fig. 10). The two posters differ widely in
mood and content yet adhere to the same essential design principle: all compositional elements emphasize the two-dimensionality of the picture. If one compares these works to Chéret's 1889 poster for the Moulin Rouge (Fig. 11), the innovations of Bonnard and Lautrec
may be better understood.

In Chéret's four-color poster, colors overlap to create modeling and shadowing that suggest solid figures based on academic methods, as with the haunches of the donkey in the
foreground and with the women's dresses. The figures are placed within a three-dimensional,
illusionistic environment reemphasized by the letters at the top, placed in relief by the blue

shadows behind them. Although Bonnard's poster borrows Chéret's familiar young woman in a low-cut dress, and thus superficially takes on the gaiety and frivolity of Chéret's work, the two posters are otherwise worlds apart. *France-Champagne* simply incorporates three colors: yellow, black, and red, which creates orange when laid over the yellow. Most importantly, the white of the paper functions in its compositional role as boldly as the three blending pigments. All modeling and shadowing are eliminated from Bonnard's poster; except for the slight suggestion of the woman's cleavage, there is no traditional hint of three dimensions. The background is neutral; decorative black contours play over it, interlocking the planes of color and emphasizing its two-dimensionality. The zigzag contours of the woman's left hand mimic the decorative flutter of her hair and shoulder strap, while the calligraphic contours of her boneless body rhythmically repeat the letters in the bold two-word title of the poster. The white of the paper serves as the champagne bubbling from the glass, while linear shapes, abbreviated like Bonnard's simple monogram at the top right, suggest a mouth, a glass, a hand, and so forth. Bonnard's lyrical design unifies text and subject on the frontal plane and evokes an intoxicating euphoria.

Fig. 13 Maurice Denis. *La Dépêche de Toulouse*, 1892. The Jane Voorhees Zimmerli Art Museum, Rutgers University, Alvin and Joyce Glasgold Purchase Fund

Lautrec's *Moulin Rouge, La Goulue* uses the three primary colors, red, blue, and yellow, plus black, and also emphasizes the two-dimensional design by eliminating modeling and shadow. The floor lines—tilted up rather than receding—the bold contours, and the interlocking flat areas of color continually reassert the supremacy of a frontal plane upon which words, performers, spectators, and lights are parallel. Unlike Chéret's exuberant fairyland rendition of look-alike young women riding donkeys in the Moulin Rouge garden, Lautrec depicted two individuals, La Goulue and her partner Valentin le Déssosé, performing inside the dance hall illuminated by electric lights and surrounded by spectators, some of whom are also identifiable. The vigor, intensity, and decadence characteristic of late-night performances at the Moulin Rouge are implied in Lautrec's poster.

The muscular contortions of Valentin le Déssosé ("the boneless one") are contrasted to the high-kicking steps of the *chahut*, or cancan, performed by La Goulue. It is a taut dance of individuals who appear each to be in a solitary stylized performance, but whose distinct facial profiles are connected by a line drawn by La Goulue's arm and leg. There is strong psychological and sexual tension between the two as La Goulue unabashedly entices her partner and us with her dress pulled up and her legs spread apart. Valentin's hand, silhouetted against her white undergarments, seemingly waves her on, while the large globes of yellow light emphasize the heat of their encounter. The silhouetted spectators are voyeurs of this vulgar, erotic dance. The poster reflects an implicit and explicit sexuality for which La Goulue and her dance were well noted.[9]

With the work of Bonnard and Lautrec, the poster became a powerful art of suggestion. It titillates the senses so that the viewer imagines the effects of a drink, the thrill and intensity of a dance hall, or the ecstasy derived from a performer. The compositional devices and the abstract simplicity of these first works were exaggerated further by Bonnard and Lautrec (Fig. 12) and within the next year were to inspire the first posters of Maurice Denis (Fig. 13) and Henri-Gabriel Ibels. The real importance, however, of Bonnard's and Lautrec's early works is that they revealed to many artists the great potential for poster design of the decorative qualities of line, shape, and color. These two-dimensional elements were exploited throughout the decade in unique styles by the great masters of the medium: Grasset, Mucha, Cappiello, and countless other Europeans and Americans who often went to great extremes of abstraction.

However far the abstraction was to go, the pictorial content of the posters was always recognizable. After all, the function of a poster is to advertise, and while the poster medium allowed artists to produce some of the most artistically daring work of the period, its intrinsic function precluded pure abstraction. It is therefore not surprising that, concurrent with radical decorative poster designs, some artists chose to maintain a more naturalistic style by effectively combining decorative elements with naturalism. Steinlen epitomizes this school. His *La Rue* of 1896 (Fig. 14) realistically depicts men, women, and children from a variety of social strata, walking along the street but narrowly confined in a friezelike arrangement. Each person is a portrait of a particular Parisian type—the laundress, nursemaid, laborer, businessman, bourgeois wife, and so on. The poster, indeed, is an inventory of the Parisians whom Steinlen depicted over and over in his prints and illustrations for journals and books. The work does not advertise a product but, rather, the services of Charles Verneau, a publisher and printer of posters. Therefore, the poster demonstrates all the firm's technical skills and qualities, including color, lettering, and a tour-de-force size. The immense poster, 92⅝ by 120⅝ inches, was printed in sections on six pieces of paper, three vertical and three horizontal, which were then pasted together. It is a virtuoso accomplishment of design, color registration, and printing. *La Rue* is a lifesize paper "fresco" meant to be displayed on the street, creating somewhat of a trompe-l'oeil effect. The lettering successfully merges with the realistic scene by appearing on a placard on the very wall that the pedestrians nonchalantly pass. In addition, the decorative qualities of the lettering are subtly echoed in the sway of the women's dresses and in their spit curls and elaborate bonnets.

Cazals's poster advertising the seventh exhibition of the Salon des Cent (Fig. 15), sponsored by the journal *La Plume*, also places part of its text on the wall of a realistic exhibition hall, with the letter "S" in the word "Salon" decoratively replaced by a swan. Words become a natural part of the interior setting and function as the sign entitling the exhibition. As in *La Rue*, this kind of pictorial trick was a convenient system of integrating text and image. It allowed realistic depictions to appear on attractive posters without the design clash that early poster artists encountered.

Cazals's *Salon des Cent* also illustrates the tendency of some French artists at the end of the century to make personal puns within their works and to include depictions of friends and colleagues.[10] This is particularly true of Lautrec, who recorded in his posters a world reflecting his own social milieu. Among the silhouetted figures in *La Goulue* are his cousin Gabriel Tapié de Céleyran (far left), Jane Avril (third from left), and William Tom Warrener (fifth from left). In Lautrec's poster for the Divan Japonais cabaret, the two spectators viewing a stage performance of Yvette Guilbert are the dancer Jane Avril and the poet and art critic Edouard Dujardin. Cazals's poster depicts his two friends, the poets Paul Verlaine and Jean Moréas, inspecting the works in the fourth exhibition of the Salon des Cent, in August 1894. Verlaine, in the foreground, admires a portrait of himself by Cazals.

Posters of the period also expressed artistic and political ideology. Carloz Schwabe's poster for the 1892 Salon de la Rose + Croix not only announces the exhibition but pictorially expostulates the pseudoreligious symbolist philosophy of the group.[11] Steinlen's 1899 poster for the journal *Le Petit Sou* dramatically and symbolically states the socialist view that the oppressors of the working class and of liberty are the capitalists, the church, and the military. Both works go far beyond functioning as mere placards of information, endeavoring to artfully reveal universal truths to a large public via a new visual vocabulary and a revitalized expressive medium, the poster.

The 1890s were the golden age of French and American posters; however, the achievements of the United States artists could not have existed without those of the French. Clearly, French posters offered a great variety of subjects and aesthetics with an extraordinary amount of serendipitous information about the artists' world in particular and French society in general. These qualities defiantly belie the term "ephemera" that is even today inappropriately applied to the great art of posters.

NOTES

1. Grolier Club, *Catalogue of an Exhibition of Illustrated Bill-Posters* (New York, 1890), pp. 3–4.

2. Henri Beraldi, *Les Graveurs du XIX siècle* 4 (Paris, 1886), p. 171.

3. *Manet*, exhibition catalogue (New York: The Metropolitan Museum of Art, 1983), see entry no. 114 by Juliet Wilson Bareau, pp. 299–300.

4. Lucy Broido, *The Posters of Jules Chéret* (New York: Dover, 1980), no. 146.

5. See Gustave Fustier, "La Littérature murale," *Le Livre* (November 10, 1884), pp. 337–356.

6. See Phillip Dennis Cate and Sinclair Hamilton Hitchings, *The Color Revolution: Color Lithography in France 1890–1900* (Santa Barbara and Salt Lake City: Peregrine Smith; New Brunswick, N.J.: Rutgers University Art Gallery, 1978), p. 29.

7. For gillotage and the photo process, see Cate, "Printing in France, 1850–1900: The Artist and the New

Fig. 14 T.–A. Steinlen. *La Rue*, 1896. The Metropolitan Museum of Art, Harris Brisbane Dick Fund, 1932. 32.88.18

Fig. 15 Frédéric-Auguste Cazals. *Salon des Cent*, 1894. The Jane Voorhees Zimmerli Art Museum, Rutgers University, David A. and Mildred H. Morse Art Acquisition Fund

Technologies," *Gazette of the Grolier Club*, n.s. 5.28–29 (June–Dec. 1978), pp. 57–73.

8. Fustier; Ernest Maindron, *Les Affiches illustrées* (Paris: H. Launette, 1886); Beraldi.

9. Maurice Delsol, *Paris-Cythère* (Paris: [1895?]), pp. 151–152.

10. See Phillip Dennis Cate and Patricia Eckert Boyer, *The Circle of Toulouse-Lautrec: An Exhibition of the Work of the Artist and of His Close Associates*, exhibition catalogue, The Jane Voorhees Zimmerli Art Museum, Rutgers, The State University of New Jersey, November 17– February 2, 1986.

11. See Marla H. Hand, "Carloz Schwabe's Poster for the Salon de la Rose + Croix: A Herald of the Ideal in Art," *Art Journal* 44.1 (Spring 1984), pp. 40–45.

29 Will H. Bradley. *Bradley: His Book*, June 1896. **32**

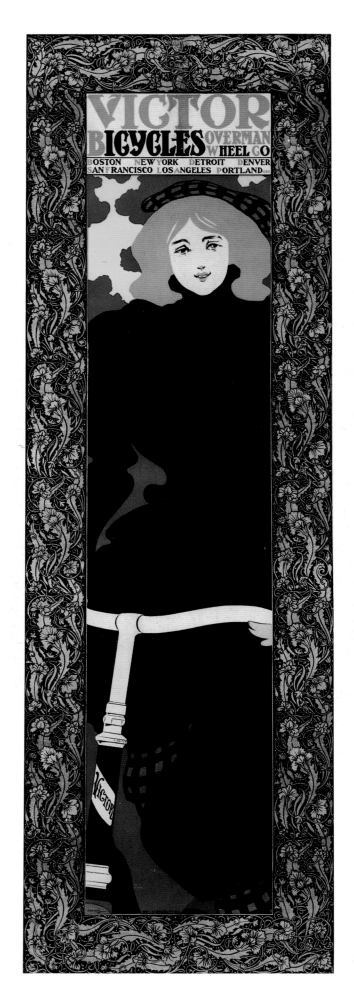

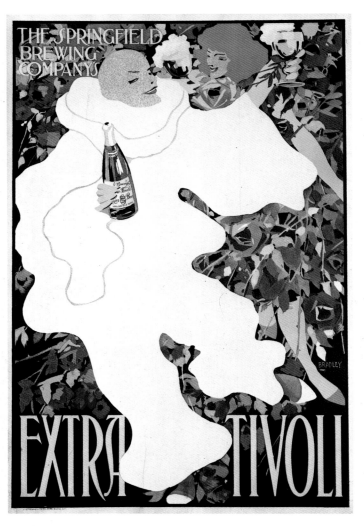

31 Will H. Bradley. Extra Tivoli, 1896. **28**

30 Will H. Bradley. Victor Bicycles, "The Knickerbockers,"
1895. **24**

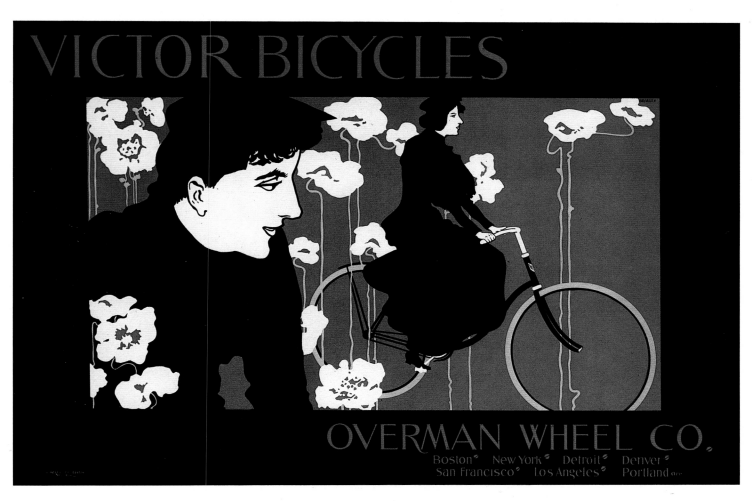

32 Will H. Bradley. Victor Bicycles, "In Purple and White," 1896. 27

33 Will H. Bradley. *The Chap-Book*, Thanksgiving Number, 1895. 23

34 Alice Russell Glenny. *Buffalo Courier*,
Womens Edition, 1895. 78

35 William L. Carqueville. *International*, April 1897. 57

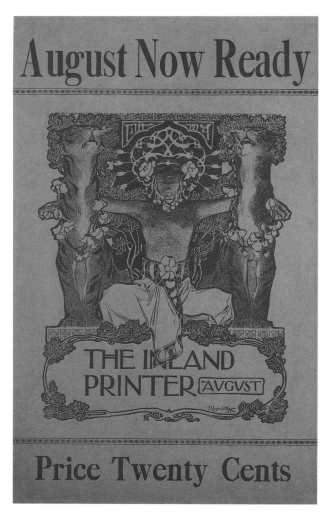

36 Joseph Christian Leyendecker. *The Inland Printer*, August 1897. 113

37 Florence Lundborg. *The Lark*, November 1896. 122

38 Ernest Haskell. *Truth*, Christmas 1896. 96

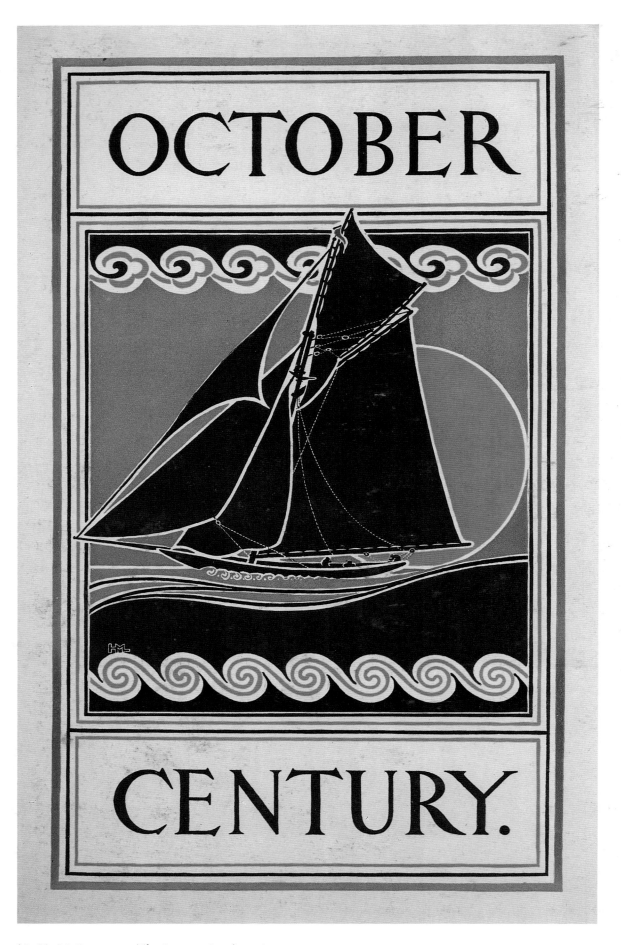

39 H. M. Lawrence. *The Century*, October 1895. 111

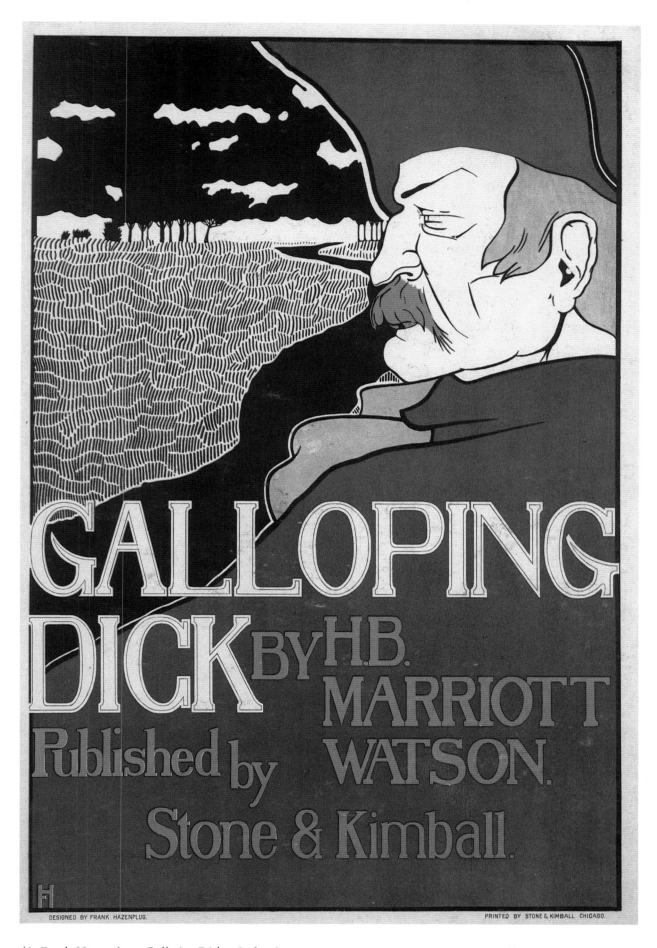

GALLOPING DICK BY H.B. MARRIOTT WATSON Published by Stone & Kimball.

40 Frank Hazenplug. *Galloping Dick*, 1896. 98

41 Blanche McManus. *Captains Courageous*, 1897. **128**

THREE GRINGOS IN CENTRAL
AMERICA AND VENEZUELA
BY RICHARD HARDING DAVIS
ILLUSTRATED
HARPER & BROTHERS · N · Y ·

42 Edward Penfield. *Three Gringos*, 1896. **188**

43 Edward Penfield. *Harper's*, May 1896. 180

UNIVERSITY OF Nebraska Lincoln

‖‖‖‖‖‖‖‖‖‖‖‖‖‖‖‖‖‖‖‖‖‖‖‖‖‖‖‖‖‖‖

ILL: 113305300

Thank you for loaning us the following item:

Title: American art posters of the 1890s in the Metropolitan Museum of Art, including the Leonard A. Lauder collection /
Author:

OCLC#: 16227191

UNL ILLiad Tn #: 807758 ‖‖‖‖‖‖‖‖‖‖‖‖‖‖‖‖‖‖‖‖‖‖‖‖‖

Pieces: 1
Special Instr:
Lending Library's Due Date: 05/28/14

This item is being returned to: **UPM**

PENNSYLVANIA STATE University
Libraries, Interlibrary Loan
127 Paterno Libr. Curtin Rd.
University Park, PA 16802

If there are any questions about this item, please give us a call at
402-472-2522 or e-mail us at ill1@unl.edu.

UNIVERSITY OF Nebraska Lincoln
Interlibrary Loan – University Libraries
221 Love Library, 13th & R Strs
PO Box 884103
Lincoln NE 68588-4103

LIBRARY MAIL

To:
PENNSYLVANIA STATE University
Libraries, Interlibrary Loan
127 Paterno Libr. Curtin Rd.
University Park, PA 16802

UPM   IL.: 113305300   Special Instr: Due: 05/28/14

44 Edward Penfield. Poster Calendar for 1897, 1896. 191A

45 Ethel Reed. *Is Polite Society Polite*, 1895. 240

46 Louis John Rhead. *The Century*, Midsummer Holiday Number, 1894. **249**

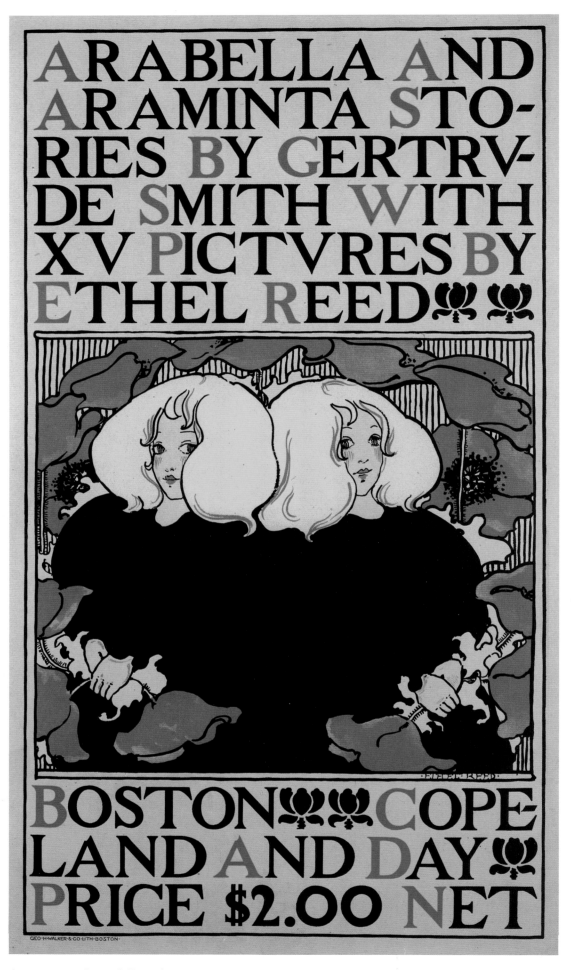

47 Ethel Reed. *Arabella and Araminta*, 1895. 234

48 Louis John Rhead. "His Lordship," 1896. **264**

49 Louis John Rhead. Poster Calendar for 1897 (1896). **267A**

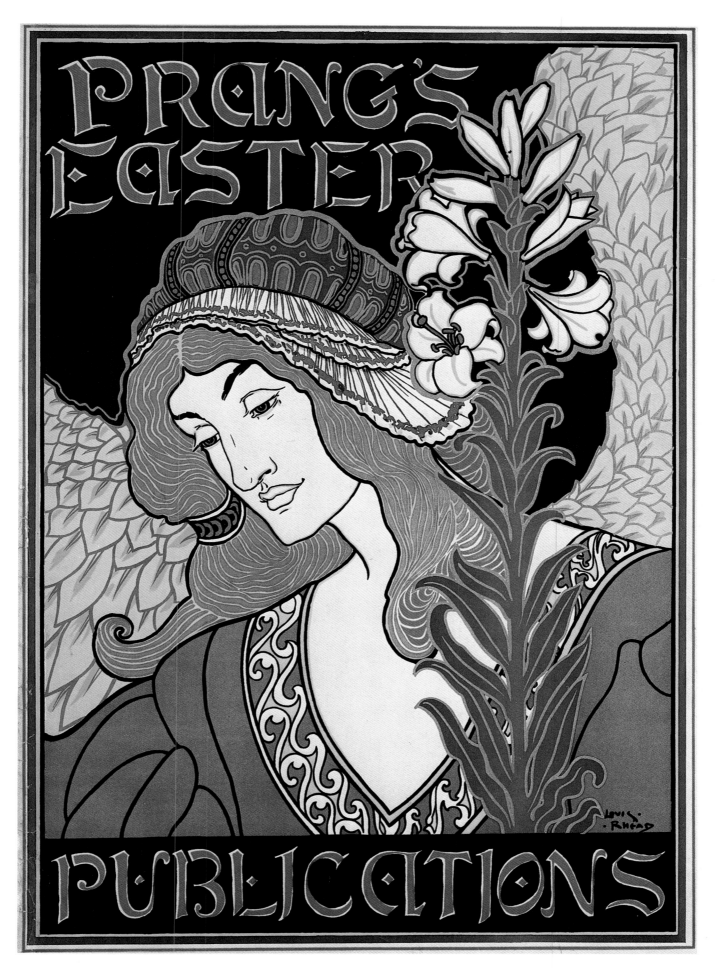

50 Louis John Rhead. Prang's Easter, 1895. **258**

51 Louis John Rhead. *Salon des Cent*, 1897. 269

52 Louis John Rhead. *Scribner's*, Christmas 1895. **260**

53 Edward Penfield. Northampton Cycle, ca. 1899. **225**

54 John Sloan. *Cinder-Path Tales*, 1896. 278

55 Charles Herbert Woodbury. *Trolley Trips*, 1897. 289

A CATALOGUE OF AMERICAN ART POSTERS OF THE 1890s IN THE METROPOLITAN MUSEUM OF ART

David W. Kiehl

J UST AFTER the publication of his abbreviated catalogue of American posters in 1895, Wilbur Cherrier Whitehead wrote to Frederic Thoreau Singleton, editor of *Poster Lore*:

I have not felt that I cared to undertake to compile a list of all the posters that have been put out. I thought it would do to catalogue my collection, which I verily believe is as complete, if not more so, than any other collection of American posters in existence. I have about 1500 American posters; of the 1500 there is quite a number, say one or two hundred, that I hardly think I will catalogue; quite a number more will be dismissed with a mention. The balance will be catalogued and described. . . . [*Poster Lore* 2.1 (September 1896), pp. 30, 31]

Whitehead's plans for a complete catalogue of posters by American artists of the 1890s never came to fruition. His comments raise two issues—first, the need for a serious catalogue even during that decade of creation; and second, the number of posters actually designed and produced at the time.

The only legacy of Whitehead's project is his brief catalogue. Almost eighty years later, in 1973, the first scholarly catalogue of American posters of the 1890s appeared. The first volume of a three-volume survey of early posters (mainly 1870–1910) bore the series title *Das frühe Plakat in Europa und den USA* (DFP). The volume was devoted to the posters of Britain and the United States. The compilers relied on the holdings of a consortium of German museums and libraries, and their work remains a major reference. *American Art Posters* upgrades and enhances the information in DFP using the holdings of The Metropolitan Museum of Art, now so greatly enriched by the generosity of Leonard A. Lauder. The Metropolitan Museum by no means owns all the posters described in the earlier catalogue, but its collection includes others not found in the German institutions.

This raises Whitehead's second point: over fifteen hundred American posters were produced during that decade. Where are they now? Needless to say, many may lie forgotten in the recesses of libraries and museums across the country. Others may be recorded only by a reference in a contemporary exhibition catalogue. During the course of my research, I began taking extensive notes on 1890s posters in other public collections, and those named in contemporary literature and in catalogues of poster exhibits in America. These notes are by no means complete, but already there are indications for close to nine hundred different poster titles. And there are many more public collections to be seen. It is my wish that this catalogue will encourage a greater appreciation of this part of our American cultural history, as well as other cataloguing efforts. Maybe, in the near future, Whitehead's dream of a thorough catalogue of American art posters of the 1890s will become a reality.

Artists used signatures, initials, monograms, and logos to sign their posters. How the artist signed his or her work is noted in the catalogue list following, with an indication of the position on the poster. In two cases, unsigned posters are attributed on the basis of other information found on the poster. Two posters in the collection are listed as anonymous. Both were shown in the 1896 exhibition at the Pennsylvania Academy of the Fine Arts and listed in the accompanying catalogue under "Anonymous"; one has a monogram that has defied deciphering.

Texts are given as found on the posters. Capitalized words are presented as such. Slashes indicate the end of a line on the original. Listings of contents have been abbreviated.

Dates have been derived by a variety of means: as printed on the poster either in the text or in a copyright line; from contemporary notations added by public and private collectors; from descriptions found in contemporary exhibition catalogues, articles, and other publications; and from bibliographical data found in the *National Union Catalogue*.

The last quarter of the nineteenth century witnessed many changes in the methods of reproducing images. These changes corresponded to the technical advancements in the world of printing itself. The pages of new publications, such as *The Inland Printer*, were filled with descriptions of new inventions, modifications, and other developments in the industry. In 1892, the print department of the Museum of Fine Arts, Boston, sponsored an exhibition "illustrating the technical methods of the reproductive arts from the XV century to the present time, with special reference to the photo-mechanical processes." The catalogue of this show is not illustrated, and it is difficult to distinguish between one inventor's process and another's. Most poster catalogues have avoided this issue simply by not referring to the printing process used. The compilers of DFP went into some detail on technique, noting if a poster was produced by lithography with a stone or a zinc plate; whether it was a photoengraving or a photolithograph; whether letterpress was used or not; and so on. The question of technique is a source of much disagreement. First, the Babel of information in the 1892 Boston catalogue has not been sorted out. Second, differences in ink viscosity can cause one process to resemble another superficially. Third, many posters use multiple techniques, as yet unidentified. Clear answers are not always available. For this reason, I have simplified the description of technique in most instances to "commercial relief process" or "commercial lithography."

Previous catalogues and books on American posters have simply noted that a poster was printed in color. If the authors described the color, they tended to list the colors as seen and not those of the inks used in printing. The cataloguers for DFP used an elaborate system of color description that sometimes noted the colors of the finished product and sometimes the colors of the printing inks. Color is subjective: what is vermilion to one viewer may be orange to another. In the present catalogue, the colors noted have been simplified to basic descriptions of those inks used to print the poster and listed in the probable order of printing. For some posters, especially those printed by Louis Prang and Company, nine or more inks were used. Even after lengthy and thorough examination, there may be future disagreement over the number of ink colors and the order of their use.

Measurements are given with height followed by width, inches followed by centimeters. When the image does not extend to the edge of the sheet of paper, the image dimensions are listed first. Sheet size is that of the poster impression illustrated.

The names of publishers frequently appear in the text of the poster itself—noted here as "Published by." On some posters the date of copyright appears with the publisher's name. In such cases, it is noted as printed with an indication of location on the poster. Not all book posters have the publisher's name as part of the text; in such cases, this information comes from the *National Union Catalogue*. If the name of the printer appears on the poster, it is also noted as printed, with an indication of location.

The catalogues issued during some of the poster exhibitions of the 1890s have proved to be most useful for identifying artists, ascribing dates, and determining an approximate order of appearance for posters by a given artist within a particular year. If a poster appears in *Das frühe Plakat*, the DFP number is listed first; other references follow in the order of issue. DFP notes the appearance of a given image in contemporary poster literature. If a catalogue raisonné or any contemporary listing of an artist's work exists, a reference appears in proper sequence. Abbreviations are as follows:

Bolton	Bolton, Charles Knowles. *A Descriptive Catalogue of Posters, Chiefly American, in the Collection of Charles Knowles Bolton with Biographical Notes and a Bibliography May MDCCCXCV.* Boston: Winthrop B. Jones, 1895.
Bradley	*Catalogue: Being a List of Some Few Posters and Various Other Sketches by Will Bradley . . .* Springfield, Massachusetts: The Wayside Press, [January] 1896.
Century and Echo	*The Century and Echo Poster Show: Catalogue of Artistic Posters.* Chicago: *The Echo* [December], 1895.
DFP	Malhotra, Ruth; Christina Thom; et al. *Das frühe Plakat in Europa und den USA.* Vol. I: *Grossbritannien und Vereinigte Staaten von Nordamerika.* Berlin: Gebr. Mann, 1973.
Flood	Quadrangle Club. *Catalogue of an Exhibition of American, French, English, Dutch, and Japanese Posters from the Collection of Mr. Ned Arden Flood.* Chicago, [May] 1897.
Ludwig	Ludwig, Coy. *Maxfield Parrish.* New York: Watson-Guptill, 1973.
Mass. Mech.	Massachusetts Charitable Mechanic Association. *Exhibition of Posters: October 2 to November 30 MDCCCXCV.* Boston, 1895.
Morse	Morse, Peter. *John Sloan's Prints: A Catalogue Raisonné of the Etchings, Lithographs, and Posters.* New Haven: Yale University Press, 1969.
PAFA	Pennsylvania Academy of the Fine Arts. *Exhibition of Posters.* Philadelphia, [March] 1896.
Poster-NY	"A Complete List of Posters Designed by Louis J. Rhead to January 20, 1896." *The Poster* 1.3 [March 1896], pp. 30, 31.
Quincy	*Art Poster Exhibit in Aid of the Quincy City Hospital . . . May 7 to 10. . . .* Quincy, Mass., 1895.
Reims	Henriot, Alexandre. *Catalogue de l'exposition d'affiches artistiques, françaises et étrangères, modernes et rétrospectives.* Reims, [November] 1896; repr., Paris: Union Centrale des Arts Décoratifs, 1980.

Richmond	*A List of French, English and American Posters . . . the Poster Show Benefit Old Dominion Hospital. . . .* Richmond, Virginia, [June] 1896.
Union League	*Some Modern Posters Shown at the Union League Club, February 14–15–16 1895.* New York, 1895.
White	White, Gleeson. "The Posters of Louis Rhead." *The Studio* 8.41 [August 1896], pp. 156–161.
Whitehead	Whitehead, Wilbur Cherrier. *A Memorandum Catalogue and Check List of American Posters in the Collection of Wilbur Cherrier Whitehead.* Cleveland, [December] 1895.
Wong	Wong, Roberta Waddell. *Will H. Bradley: American Artist and Craftsman (1868–1962).* New York: The Metropolitan Museum of Art, 1972.

If there is more than one impression of a poster title in the holdings of the Department of Prints and Photographs, all accession numbers are listed. The first number is that of the poster illustrated and described in the entry. The sources of these posters, either by gift or by purchase, are listed below in order of accession number.

36.23	Gift of David Silve, 1936
41.12	Gift of Bessie Potter Vonnoh, 1941
44.36	Gift of Helen L. Card, 1944
52.625	Gift of Fern Bradley Dufner, 1952
54.582	Gift of Fern Bradley Dufner, 1954
57.627	Museum Accession; Transferred from the Library, 1957
65.658	The Elisha Whittelsey Collection, The Elisha Whittelsey Fund, 1965
1972.687	The Elisha Whittelsey Collection, The Elisha Whittelsey Fund, 1972
1984.1029	Gift of Mr. and Mrs. Dave H. Williams, 1984
1984.1202	Leonard A. Lauder Collection of American Posters, Gift of Leonard A. Lauder, 1984
1985.1051	Purchase, The Lauder Foundation, Leonard and Evelyn Lauder Fund Gift, 1985
1985.1123	Gift of Weston J. Naef, 1985
1985.1129	Purchase, The Lauder Foundation, Leonard and Evelyn Lauder Fund Gift, 1985
1985.1132	Purchase, The Lauder Foundation, Leonard and Evelyn Lauder Fund Gift, 1985
1985.1152	Purchase, The Lauder Foundation, Leonard and Evelyn Lauder Fund Gift, 1985
1986.1005	Purchase, The Lauder Foundation, Leonard and Evelyn Lauder Fund Gift, 1986
1986.1207	Gift of Leonard A. Lauder, 1986
1987.1010	Purchase, The Lauder Foundation, Leonard and Evelyn Lauder Fund Gift, 1987

Edwin Austin Abbey

1   THE/QUEST/OF THE/HOLY/GRAIL/EDWIN/A./ABBEY/
PUBLISHED/BY/R. H. RUSSELL/& SON/NEW YORK

1895
Image 21 × 16 in. (53.3 × 40.6 cm.); *sheet* 22¾ × 16⅜ in. (57.9 × 41.6 cm.)
Commercial relief process; red and black
Signature E. A. Abbey/1895 (*lower right corner*); Copyright 1895 by Edwin A. Abbey. (*lower center*)
Published by R. H. Russell and Son, New York

References Mass. Mech. 1; Whitehead, p. 4; Century and Echo 130; PAFA 151; Richmond 1; Reims 1682; R. H. Russell and Son cat. (1897)
41.12.221 [Vonnoh]

Note: Edwin Austin Abbey, *The Quest of the Holy Grail* (New York: R. H. Russell and Son, 1895).

V. S. Vanderbilt Allen

2   HARPER'S/WEEKLY

1894
Sheet 16¹⁄₁₆ × 12⁵⁄₁₆ in. (40.9 × 31.3 cm.)
Commercial relief process; tan, red, green, and black
Signature allen (*middle left*)
Published by Harper and Brothers, New York
References DFP 146; Bolton, p. 3; Mass. Mech. 3; Whitehead, p. 4

41.12.145 [Vonnoh]

Note: The subject of the November 12 issue of *Harper's Weekly* was the National Horse Show at Madison Square Garden; hence this humorous scene of formally dressed rider, fallen horse, and broken fence.

Anonymous

3   THE/NEW YORK/SUNDAY WORLD. 1895–6/SUNDAY./
DEC. 29TH/GREAT/NEW/YEAR'S/NUMBER./More
Features than any THREE MAGAZINES./More Humor Than/
PUCK or JUDGE./Notify Your Newsdealer NOW or You
Won't be Able to Get It.

1895
Sheet 17⅞ × 12 in. (45.4 × 36.5 cm.)
Commercial relief process; black, yellow, and red

Published by New York World
Reference PAFA 492
41.12.184 [Vonnoh]

Anonymous

4   THE SUNDAY/NEW YORK WORLD/JAN. 19TH./THE
GREATEST/IN Notable Achievements!/IN Number of Pages!/
IN Public Service!/IN Influence!/IN Circulation!/IN Endless
Variety!/IN Famous Contributions!/Order a Copy from your
Newsdealer and You will Read this Paper the rest of your Life.

1896
Sheet 18⁵⁄₁₆ × 12¹⁄₁₆ in. (46.6 × 30.7 cm.)
Commercial relief process; blue, yellow, and red

Unidentified monogram (*center*)
Published by New York World
Reference PAFA 507
41.12.192 [Vonnoh]

Barnes

5 TO DATE'S/NEW/STORY/5¢/The/FEMALE/REBELLION/
JUST OUT.

1895
Image 12½ × 10⁷⁄₁₆ in. (31.7 × 26.5
cm.); *sheet* 12⁷⁄₈ × 10¹³⁄₁₆ in. (32.7
× 27.4 cm.)
Commercial lithography; yellow,
red, blue, and black
Signature Barnes (*lower left*)
Published by To Date
References Whitehead, p. 4;
PAFA 242

41.12.183 [Vonnoh]

Note: Barnes also designed a poster
advertising the conclusion of "The
Female Rebellion" in the
latter November issue of *To Date*.

Elisha Brown Bird

6 POSTER/EXHIBIT/MECHAN-/ICS FAIR/THE 19TH EX-/
HIBITION/A.D. 1895

1895
Image 19⅛ × 12¼ in. (48.6 × 31.1
cm.); *sheet* 21¹⁄₁₆ × 13⁵⁄₁₆ in. (53.6
× 35.5 cm.)
Commercial relief process; black on
gray paper
Signature BIRD (*lower right corner*)
Published by Massachusetts
Charitable Mechanic Association,
Boston

Printer ENGRAVED BY THE
SUFFOLK ENGRAVING CO
BOSTON. (*lower left*)
References Whitehead, p. 6; Century
and Echo 166; Flood 6
1984.1202.1 [Lauder]

7 THE CENTURY/FOR/MARCH/[contents]/Sold here. Price
35 cents./Published by THE CENTURY CO. NEW YORK.

1896
Image 19¾ × 12⅞ in. (50.2 × 32.6
cm.); *sheet* 20½ × 13½ in. (52.2 ×
34.3 cm.)
Commercial lithography; yellow,
blue, brown, and black
Signature E. B. BIRD (*lower right
corner*)
Published by The Century Co., New
York

Printer H. A. THOMAS & WYLIE,
LITH. CO. N.Y. (*lower right
corner*)
References DFP 148; PAFA 244;
Richmond 8; Reims 1131; Flood 3
41.12.180 [Vonnoh]; 57.627.10 (20)

8 THE CAPTURED CUNARDER/BY WILLIAM H.
RIDEING. 75¢/BOSTON: COPELAND AND DAY

1896
Image 18⅛ × 10¹⁵⁄₁₆ in. (46 × 27.8
cm.); *sheet* 23¹⁄₁₆ × 12½ in. (58.6
× 31.7 cm.)
Commercial lithography; black and
vermilion on blue paper
Signature BIRD (*lower right*)
Published by Copeland and Day,
Boston
Printer GEO. H. WALKER & CO.
BOSTON. (*lower center*)
References DFP 149; Flood 2

1984.1202.2 [Lauder]

Note: William H. Rideing, *The
Captured Cunarder: An Episode of the
Atlantic* (Boston: Copeland and
Day, 1896). This poster is
identical to the design printed on
the book's front cover and appears
in reverse on the back cover.
Colorplate 28

9   THE POSTER

1896
Image 16½ × 10¾ in. (42 × 27.4
cm.); *sheet* 19¹⁄₁₆ × 12⅝ in. (48.4
× 32.1 cm.)
Commercial lithography; black and
vermilion
Signature E. B. / BIRD (*lower right
corner*)
Published by William H. Clemens,
New York
Reference Richmond 9
1984.1202.5 [Lauder]

Note: "The Poster," commissioned by
William Clemens as the first poster
for his magazine of the same name,
was also called "Miss Art and Miss
Litho." Collectors could order a
copy for fifty cents post-free (*The
Poster* 1.3 [March 1896], p. 40).
The same design was printed in
different colors for the covers of
the March, April, and May issues.
Colorplate 1

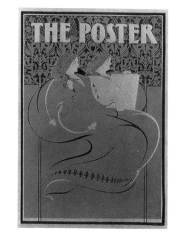

10   THE RED/LETTER

1896
Image 23 × 15³⁄₁₆ in. (58.4 × 38.6
cm.); *sheet* 25¹⁵⁄₁₆ × 17¹⁵⁄₁₆ in.
(65.8 × 45.5 cm.)
Commercial lithography; black and
red
Signature BIRD (*lower center*)
Published by Barta, Badger, and
Bird, Boston
Printer LITHOGRAPHED BY . . .
FORBES CO. BOSTON. (*lower left
and right corners*)

1984.1202.3 [Lauder]

Note: This first poster for *The Red
Letter* was titled "In the Library"
and was available either with a
subscription or for twenty-five
cents (*The Red Letter* 1.1 [August
1896], inside cover).

11   TOWN AND/COUNTRY/FOR SALE HERE

1896
Image 32⁷⁄₁₆ × 17¼ in. (82.3 × 43.9
cm.); *sheet* 33¼ × 17¹⁵⁄₁₆ in. (84.5
× 45.6 cm.)
Commercial lithography; green and
brown
Signature BIRD (*within leaf, lower
right corner*)

Publisher COPYRIGHT 1896 BY
W[. . .] (*lower right corner;
partially missing*)
Printer [. . .]S & CO. BOSTON.
(*lower left corner; partially missing*)
1985.1152 [Lauder]

12   R. H. RUSSELL'S/PUBLICATIONS/BOOKS/R. H. RUSSELL, NEW YORK/FOR SALE HERE

ca. 1897
Image 26¹⁵⁄₁₆ × 14⁷⁄₁₆ in. (68.5 ×
36.7 cm.); *sheet* 27½ × 14¹⁵⁄₁₆ in.
(69.9 × 38 cm.)
Commercial lithography; gray-
brown, yellow, and red

Unsigned
Published by R. H. Russell and Son,
New York
1984.1202.4 [Lauder]

Will H. Bradley

13 The Chap-Book

1894

Image 19 × 13 in. (48.2 × 33.1 cm.); *sheet* 20 × 14 in. (50.7 × 35.6 cm.)

Commercial lithography; red and dark green

Signature WILL H/BRADLEY/'94 (*lower left corner*)

Published by Stone and Kimball, Chicago

References DFP 152; Union League 8; Bolton, p. 4; Mass. Mech. 23; Whitehead, p. 8; Century and Echo 152; Bradley 20, PAFA 20, 183; Reims 1139; Wong 1

1984.1202.8 [Lauder]; 57.627.4(12)

Note: The first in a series of posters for *The Chap-Book*, this design was

called "The Twins." A critic in *The American Printer* of December 1894 (see Wong 1) pointed out some of its difficulties:

. . . the very funniest thing out is the "Chap-Book" poster. No mortal man can possibly tell without deliberately investigating, what it means or what it represents. Ten feet away one would be willing to make an oath that it was a very, very red turkey gobbler very poorly represented. On closer inspection it seems to have been intended for two human beings, one at least being in a red gown very short at both ends. The remaining characteristics are very lightly outlined, hence the turkey gobbler aspect when seen a few feet away.

14 THE/CHAP-/BOOK

1894

Image 18⁵⁄₁₆ × 12⁷⁄₁₆ in. (46.5 × 31.6 cm.); *sheet* 19¹⁵⁄₁₆ × 13¹⁵⁄₁₆ in. (50.6 × 35.4 cm.)

Commercial lithography; vermilion and blue

Signature BRADLEY (*lower right corner*)

Published by Stone and Kimball, Chicago

References DFP 157; Union League 9; Bolton, p. 4; Mass. Mech. 24;

Whitehead, p. 8; Century and Echo 153; Bradley 21, see 21A,B; PAFA 21, 180, see 21A,B; Richmond 12; Reims 1136; Wong 3

36.23.20 [Silve]; 57.627.4(10)

Note: Bradley's second poster for *The Chap-Book*, "The Blue Lady." Colorplate 3

15 WHEN HEARTS/ARE TRUMPS/BY TOM HALL

1894

Image 16³⁄₈ × 13⁷⁄₁₆ in. (41.7 × 34.1 cm.); *sheet* 17³⁄₁₆ × 14⅛ in. (43.5 × 36 cm.)

Commercial lithography; vermilion and green

Signature WILL H BRADLEY (*middle left*)

Published by Stone and Kimball, Chicago

References DFP 150; Union League 11; see Bolton, p. 4; Quincy 12; Mass. Mech. 22; Whitehead, p. 8;

Century and Echo 151; Bradley 27, see 27A; PAFA 27, 159; Richmond 18; Reims 1150; Wong 22

1984.1202.6 [Lauder]; 36.23.21 (cut, picture only) [Silve]

Note: Thomas Winthrop Hall, *When Hearts Are Trump* (Cambridge and Chicago: Stone and Kimball, 1894).

16   The Chap-Book/Being a MISCELLANY of Curious and
      Interesting Songs,/Ballads, Tales, Histories, &c.; adorned with
      a variety/of pictures and very delightful to read; newly/
      composed by MANY CELEBRATED WRITERS; To/which are
      annex'd a LARGE COLLECTION of No-/tices of BOOKS.

1895
Image 19½ × 12⅜ in. (49.5 × 31.6   10; Bolton, p. 4; Mass. Mech. 25;
   cm.); *sheet* 20⅞ × 13¹³⁄₁₆ in. (53.2   Whitehead, p. 8; Century and
   × 35.4 cm.)   Echo 154; Bradley 22; PAFA 22,
Commercial lithography; black   173; Richmond 13; Reims 1135;
Signature WILL H BRADLEY 1895   Wong 5
   (*lower right corner*)   41.12.91 [Vonnoh]; 52.625.151
Published by Stone and Kimball,   [Dufner]
   Chicago   *Note:* The third *Chap-Book* poster,
References DFP 155; Union League   issued January, "Poet and His Lady."

17   NARCOTI-/CURE PRICE $5.00/BOOK OF/PARTICULARS
      FREE/CURES THE TOBACCO HABIT IN FROM 4 TO 10
      DAYS/THE NARCOTI CHEMICAL CO. SPRINGFIELD,/
      MASS.

1895
Image 19¹³⁄₁₆ × 13⁷⁄₁₆ in. (50.2 ×   1972.687.2
   34.1 cm.); *sheet* 20⅞ × 14¹⁄₁₆ in.
   (51.9 × 35.7 cm.)   *Note:* The Metropolitan Museum's
Commercial lithography; black,   poster, dated in pencil "Jan/95," is
   vermilion, and green   missing the last line of text,
Signature BRADLEY (*center*)   printed below the image. The
Published by Narcoti Chemical   text, as supplied by the Library of
   Company, Springfield, Mass.   Congress, reads: "Copies of this
References DFP 162; Bolton, p. 4;   poster will be mailed to any
   Quincy 11; Mass. Mech. 21;   address on receipt of 2 two cent
   Whitehead, p. 8; Century and   stamps. Narcoti Chemical Co.,
   Echo 142; Reims 1146; Wong 25   Springfield, Massachusetts."

18   MAY/THE CHAP-/BOOK

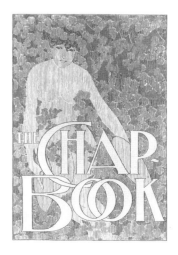

1895
Image 20¹⁄₁₆ × 13⁵⁄₁₆ in. (51 × 33.8   Echo 155; Bradley 23, see 12;
   cm.); *sheet* 22¹⁄₁₆ × 16⅛ in. (56.1   PAFA 23, 171, see 23A; Richmond
   × 41 cm.)   14; Reims 1138; Wong 4
Commercial lithography; vermilion   1984.1202.9 [Lauder]
   and green
Signature BRADLEY (*lower left*)   *Note:* The Metropolitan Museum
Published by Stone and Kimball,   owns a preparatory sketch for the
   Chicago   poster in green and pink wash over
References DFP 154; Mass. Mech. 26;   pencil (1972.586.6).
   Whitehead, p. 8; Century and

19 THE/ECHO/Chicago's/Humorous and Artistic/Fortnightly

1895

Image 20⁷⁄₁₆ × 13³⁄₈ in. (52 × 33.9 cm.); *sheet* 22⁷⁄₁₆ × 13¹⁵⁄₁₆ in. (57.1 × 35.5 cm.)

Commercial lithography; yellow, blue, and orange

Signature WILL H. BRADLEY (*lower left corner*)

Printer RALPH MERRIMAN CO. PRESS (*lower right corner*)

Published by The Echo, Chicago

References DFP 161; Whitehead, p. 8; Century and Echo 139, 140; Bradley 28, see 10, 11; PAFA 28,

167, see 28A; Reims 1143; Wong 24

1984.1202.11 [Lauder]; 36.23.22, 23 [Silve]

Note: A variant version of the poster has the text: "THE/ECHO/CHICAGO'S NEW PAPER :/ IN WHICH WILL APPEAR A SERIES/OF COLORED FRONTISPIECES BY/WILL H. BRADLEY/FORTNIGHTLY HUMOROUS AND·ARTISTIC" (DFP).

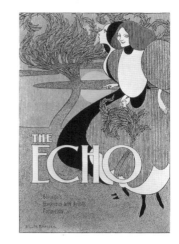

20 THE/CHAP-BOOK

1895

Image 20³⁄₁₆ × 13⁵⁄₈ in. (51.3 × 34.5 cm.); *sheet* 21³⁄₈ × 14¹⁵⁄₁₆ in. (54.3 × 38 cm.)

Commercial lithography; orange, green, and black

Signature WILL H/BRADLEY (*upper right*)

Published by Stone and Kimball, Chicago

References DFP 156; Mass. Mech. 27;

Whitehead, p. 8; Century and Echo 156; Bradley 24, PAFA 24, 170; Richmond 16; Reims 1140; Wong 6

1984.1202.10 [Lauder]; 41.12.92 [Vonnoh]

Note: The fifth poster for *The Chap-Book*, "The Pipes."

21 SPRINGFIELD BICYCLE/CLUB TOURNAMENT/ SPRINGFIELD MASS/SEPT. 11 AND 12, 1895

1895

Image 19¹⁄₈ × 12⁵⁄₁₆ in. (48.6 × 31.3 cm.); *sheet* 19³⁄₈ × 12⁵⁄₈ in. (49.3 × 32 cm.)

Commercial lithography; black and red

Signature WILL H BRADLEY '95 (*lower left*)

Published by Springfield Bicycle Club

References DFP 163; Whitehead, p. 8; Century and Echo 159

1986.1005.1 [Lauder]

Note: Whitehead owned two copies of the poster, one printed on brown paper. Bradley also provided a design for the cover of the tournament booklet. In 1896, he again designed the tournament poster.

22 THE/CHAP/BOOK

1895

Image 19⁷⁄₈ × 13³⁄₈ in. (50.5 × 34 cm.); *sheet* 21³⁄₁₆ × 14³⁄₁₆ in. (53.8 × 36 cm.)

Commercial lithography; red and black

Signature BRADLEY (*lower center*)

Published by Stone and Kimball, Chicago

References DFP 153; see Mass. Mech.

20; Whitehead, p. 8; Century and Echo 157; Bradley 25; PAFA 25; Richmond 15; Reims 1137; Wong 7

57.627.4(13); 41.12.140 [Vonnoh]

Note: "Pegasus," the sixth *Chap-Book* poster, appeared in September.

23 THE CHAP BOOK/THANKSGIVING NO.

1895

Image 19⅝ × 18⁵⁄₁₆ in. (49.9 × 33.8
cm.); *sheet* 20¾ × 18⅞ in. (52.8 ×
35.2 cm.)
Commercial lithography; vermilion
and blue
Signature WILL. . H/BRADLEY.
(*lower left corner*)
Published by Stone and Kimball,
Chicago
References DFP 151; Whitehead, p. 8;
Century and Echo 158; Bradley
26; PAFA 26, 181, see 26A;
Richmond 17; Reims 1141; Wong 2

41.12.85 [Vonnoh]; 1984.1202.7
[Lauder]

Note: First appeared in the Stone and
Kimball advertisement in the
December 1, 1895, issue of *The
Chap-Book* (4.2, p. 107). By
January 1896, it was out of print
(*The Chap-Book* 4.5 [January 15,
1896], p. 262).
Colorplate 33

24 VICTOR/BICYCLES OVERMAN WHEEL CO/ BOSTON NEW YORK DETROIT DENVER/SAN FRANCISCO LOS ANGELES PORTLAND ORE

1895

Image 40³⁄₁₆ × 12¹³⁄₁₆ in. (102.1 ×
32.6 cm.); *sheet* 40⁹⁄₁₆ × 13⅛ in.
(102.8 × 33.4 cm.)
Commercial lithography; yellow,
red, green, and black
Signature WILL H. BRADLEY '95
(*lower center*)
Publisher Copyright, 1896, Overman
Wheel Co., Chicopee Falls, Mass.
(*lower left*)
Printer J. Ottmann/LITH. CO.
PUCK BLDG., N.Y. (*lower left
corner*)
References DFP 164; Bradley 69, 155;
PAFA 108, 163, see 107;
Richmond 29; Reims 1149;

probably Flood 53
1984.1202.12 [Lauder]

Note: Bradley's first poster for
Overman Wheel Co.'s Victor
bicycle was known as "The
Knickerbockers" because of the
young bicyclist's costume. In the
January 1896 exhibition in his
Springfield studio, he exhibited
several progressive proofs of the
poster, which was available to
collectors for one dollar (*Bradley:
His Book* 1.1 [May 1896], p. xxii).
Colorplate 30

25 Fringilla/or Tales-in-Verse/by RICHARD DODDRIDGE/ BLACKMORE M. A. OXON/With Sundry Decorative Pic-/ turings by WILL H BRADLEY/CLEVELAND THE BURROWS/BROTHERS CO MDCCCXCV

1895

Image 18 × 7¼ in. (45.7 × 18.4
cm.); *sheet* 18³⁄₁₆ × 7⁷⁄₁₆ in. (46.3
× 18.9 cm.)
Commercial relief process and
letterpress; black and vermilion on
gray-brown paper
Signature BRADLEY (*middle left*)
Published by The Burrows Brothers
Co., Cleveland

References DFP 159; Whitehead, p. 8;
Bradley 2; PAFA 60, 162, see 59;
Richmond 39; Wong 34
52.625.119 [Dufner]

Note: Richard Doddridge
Blackmore, *Fringilla. or. Tales in
Verse* (Cleveland: The Burrows
Brothers Co., 1895).

26 WHITING'S/LEDGER PAPERS/In their Clear Surface and/in their Perfect Erasing and/Wearing Qualities these/are the Finest Papers made/Ask to have WHITING'S/LEDGERS used in your /next lot of Blank Books

1895
Sheet 19¹³⁄₁₆ × 9³⁄₁₆ in. (50.4 × 23.4 cm.)
Commercial lithography; yellow, vermilion, light green, dark green, and black
Signature BRADLEY (*upper right*)
Published by Whiting Paper Co.
References DFP 168; see Bradley 26; see PAFA 114; Richmond 31; Reims 1151; Wong 30 1984.1202.14 [Lauder]; 52.625.147 [Dufner]

Note: Bradley's poster for Whiting's Ledger Papers was known as "The Acorns" from its elaborate oak-leaf-and-acorn border design. In the January 1895 exhibition in his Springfield studio, Bradley exhibited an unlettered proof now in the Metropolitan Museum's

collection (52.625.147). In the proof, the design continued into the areas where the text was later printed. The poster was available for seventy-five cents (*Bradley: His Book* 1.1 [May 1896], p. xxii). The Columbia University Libraries have a variant of the poster adapted to advertise Whiting's Standard Papers: "WHITING'S/ STANDARD PAPERS/ MANUFACTURED BY/ WHITING PAPER COMPANY/ NEW YORK/HOLYOKE, PHILADELPHIA, CHICAGO,/ BOSTON" (Victor Margolin, *American Poster Renaissance* [New York: Watson-Guptill, 1975], p. 187).

27 VICTOR BICYCLES/OVERMAN WHEEL CO./ Boston   New York   Detroit   Denver/San Francisco   Los Angeles   Portland Ore.

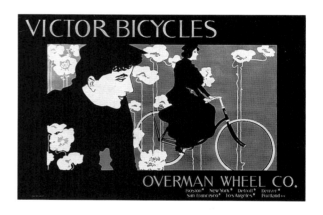

1896
Sheet 27 × 40¾ in. (68.5 × 104.2 cm.)
Commercial lithography; light purple, purple, red, and black
Signature BRADLEY (*upper right corner*)
Published by The Overman Wheel Co.
Printer Forbes Co., Boston (*lower left corner*)
References DFP 165; Richmond 30; Reims 1148; probably Flood 54

1986.1207 [Lauder]

Note: The title for Bradley's second Victor Bicycle poster, "In Purple and White," came from the effect of the colors. The poster was available to collectors for one dollar (*Bradley: His Book* 1.1 [May 1896], p. xxii).
Colorplate 32

28 THE SPRINGFIELD/BREWING/COMPANY'S/EXTRA TIVOLI

1896
Image 31¹³⁄₁₆ × 21³⁄₁₆ in. (80.9 × 53.8 cm.); *sheet* 32¾ × 22⅛ in. (83.2 × 56.2 cm.)
Commercial lithography; gray, yellow, green, pink, vermilion, and black
Signature BRADLEY (*lower right*)
Published by Springfield Brewing Co.
Printer J. OTTMANN LITH. CO., PUCK B'L'D'G. N.Y. (*lower left corner*)

References Bradley 154; see PAFA 110 1984.1202.21 [Lauder]

Note: In an offering of Bradley's posters, "Extra Tivoli" was noted as a five-color lithograph presently on press; the cost, seventy-five cents (*Bradley: His Book* 1.1 [May 1896], p. xxii).
Colorplate 31

29 The Echo/America's foremost Pictorial Fortnightly/is now a
New York Paper/NEW YORK PEOPLE SHOULD READ IT

1896
Sheet 15 1/16 × 12 in. (38.2 ×
  30.5 cm.)
Commercial relief process and
  letterpress; red and black
Signature BRADLEY (*center*)

Published by The Echo, Chicago
References DFP 166; Richmond 19;
  Reims 1142
1984.1029.1 [Williams]

30 Bradley His Book

1896
Image 39 7/8 × 27 in. (101.3 × 68.6
  cm.); *sheet* 41 9/16 × 28 7/8 in. (106.1
  × 73.2 cm.)
Commercial lithography and
  woodcut; yellow, blue, black, and
  red
Unsigned
Published by The Wayside Press,
  Springfield
References DFP 174; see Bradley 156;
  see PAFA 2; Richmond 38;
  Wong 27
1984.1202.16 [Lauder]; 36.23.6
  [Silve]

Note: Bradley had problems with
  "The Kiss," intended as the first
  poster in a series for *Bradley: His
  Book.* The May issue announced
  that the poster would appear
  without additional lettering (i.e.,
  "May") because the first issue of
  the magazine was nearly sold out,
  and that it would be "lithographed

in subdued and delicate tints"
drawn on the stones by Bradley.
The cost was one dollar, but the
publisher reserved the right to
advance the price at any time even
though the poster was "In Press"
(*Bradley: His Book* 1.1 [May 1896],
p. xxii). Due to unexplained
delays, the poster was not
published until that November; it
was described as "engraved on
wood" (*Bradley: His Book* 2.1
[November 1896], p. 30).
Presumably, the printer used stones
for printing the yellow and blue
and wood blocks for the black and
red. The Metropolitan Museum
also owns a small pen-and-ink
drawing of "The Kiss"
(52.625.141), most likely
intended for the November cover
of the periodical.
Colorplate 2

31 BRADLEY/HIS BOOK/PRICE TEN CENTS/FOR SALE
HERE/JUNE

1896
Image 18 13/16 × 7 5/8 in. (47.7 × 19.3
  cm.); *sheet* 19 9/16 × 10 in. (49.7 ×
  25.5 cm.)
Commercial relief process; blue,
  purple, and red
Signature BRADLEY (*lower left*)
Published by The Wayside Press,
  Springfield
References DFP 171; Reims 1132
  (yellow version); Wong 35
1972.687.1; 1984.1202.19
  [Lauder]

Note: Known as "The Queen," this
poster was advertised in the June

issue of *Bradley: His Book* as the
second poster for the magazine, for
fifty cents (*Bradley: His Book* 1.2
[June 1896], p. 65). The Lauder
copy of the poster was printed in
yellow, blue, green, and red—the
same colors as the poster exhibited
at Reims. The Metropolitan
Museum also owns Bradley's
original drawing, in black ink over
graphite on heavy stock, identical
in size to the poster image
(52.625.138).

32 Bradley His Book/For JULY the same being daintily print/ed and titled a WOMAN'S NUMBER/For sale by book venders at 25 cents./Published by the Wayside Press at/the Sign of the Dandelion on the/Town Street Springfield Mass. U.S.A

1896
Image 14 × 8⅜ in. (35 × 21.4 cm.); *sheet* 18⁹⁄₁₆ × 9¼ in. (47.2 × 23.5 cm.)
Commercial relief process and letterpress; black, green, and gold on gray paper
Signature BRADLEY (*lower right*)
Published by The Wayside Press, Springfield
References DFP 172; Reims 1133

1984.1202.15 [Lauder]

Note: The July poster was an enlarged version of the cover design and printed in different colors. The Lauder copy of the poster has the stamp of the Paris dealer Sagot on the verso.
Colorplate 29

33 BRADLEY: HIS BOOK/THIS NUMBER CONTAINS/"BEAUTY & THE BEAST"

1896
Sheet 19¼ × 10¹⁄₁₆ in. (48.9 × 25.6 cm.)
Commercial lithography and letterpress; purple, black, and red
Unsigned

Published by The Wayside Press, Springfield
References DFP 173; Reims 1134
1984.1202.18 [Lauder]

34 Bradley: His Book/CHRISTMAS
1896
Image 39¹¹⁄₁₆ × 26⅝ in. (100.7 × 67.7 cm.); *sheet* 41¹³⁄₁₆ × 28¾ in. (106.3 × 73 cm.)
Woodcut; yellow, green, red, and black
Signature B (*lower right corner*)
Published by The Wayside Press, Springfield
Printer S. L. Busha/Eng. (*lower left corner*)

References DFP 175; Flood 45
1984.1202.17 [Lauder]

Note: Described in the November 1896 issue of *Bradley: His Book* (2.1, n.p.) as the second poster of the series engraved on wood.

35 VICTOR/BICYCLES OVERMAN WHEEL COMPANY/BOSTON NEW YORK DETROIT DENVER/SAN FRANCISCO LOS ANGELES PORTLAND ORE/AGENTI GENERALI PER L'ITALIA/ING. FERRERO, GATTA-OLIVETTI/TORINO

1896
Image 57⁷⁄₁₆ × 36¾ in. (145.8 × 93.4 cm.); *sheet* 62⁹⁄₁₆ × 38¹⁵⁄₁₆ in. (158.9 × 99 cm.)
Commercial lithography with overprinting; dark green, yellow, orange, and black, overprinted in dark green and orange
Unsigned
Published by Overman Wheel Co.

Printer IST. ITAL. D'ARTI GRAFICHE—BERGAMO (Italia) (*lower center*)
References see DFP 176; see Flood, illus. p. 13
1984.1202.13 [Lauder]

Note: This is a two-sheet poster, with the lower sheet listing cities

with Overman Wheel Co. offices. The Italian agent for the Victor bicycle, Gatta-Olivetti of Turin, ordered their imprint to be added in the provided space by a Bergamo firm. The lower sheet measures 12¹³⁄₁₆ × 38¹⁵⁄₁₆ inches (32.6 × 99 cm.). DFP 176 illustrates a Victor Bicycle poster, listing American offices only, that is identical in design to the Metropolitan Museum's poster, although smaller, with a solid background, and printed only in black. Bradley's name appears at lower center, just above the text area. Is the Museum's version by Bradley and was it printed under his supervision? Or was it printed elsewhere, perhaps by a firm in Bergamo?

Claude Fayette Bragdon

36   THE/Chap-Book/PRICE, 5 CENTS.

1895
Image 39⅝ × 22⁵⁄₁₆ in. (100.6 × 56.7 cm.); *sheet* 42¼ × 27⅞ in. (107.2 × 70.9 cm.)
Commercial lithography; red and black
Signature C. F. Bragdon (*lower center*)
Publisher Designed by Claude F. Bragdon. Printed by Stone & Kimball Chicago. (*lower left corner*)
References DFP 183; Whitehead, p. 10; PAFA 245; Richmond 43

1984.1202.22 [Lauder]

Note: Bragdon's first poster for *The Chap-Book*, the ninth and largest of the series, known as "The Sandwich Man." Issued December 1895 (see the sandwich board), the poster was listed in Stone and Kimball's January advertisement for one dollar (*The Chap-Book* 4.5 [January 15, 1896], p. 262).

37   THE/Chap-Book/PRICE FIVE CENTS/Being a MISCELLANY of Curious and/Interesting Songs, Ballads, Tales, His-/tories &c.; adorned with a variety/of pictures and very delightful to/read; newly composed by MANY/CELEBRATED WRITERS; To which/are annex'd a LARGE COLLECTION/of Notices of Books

1896
Image 16¹⁵⁄₁₆ × 12¹⁄₁₆ in. (43 × 30.7 cm.); *sheet* 18³⁄₁₆ × 12⁹⁄₁₆ in. (46.2 × 31.9 cm.)
Commercial lithography; black, red, and yellow
Signature C B (*middle right*); artist's logo on door of carriage
Published by Stone and Kimball, Chicago
References DFP 185; PAFA 246; Richmond 42; Reims 1153

41.12.219 [Vonnoh]; 36.23.9 [Silve]; 57.627.10(14)

Note: "The Carriage" was the second poster design provided by Bragdon to the editors of *The Chap-Book*. It was listed as the tenth *Chap-Book* poster in the Stone and Kimball advertisement in the January 15, 1896, *Chap-Book* (4.5, p. 262); the cost, fifty cents.

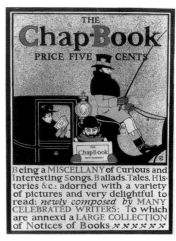

George Reiter Brill

38 PHILADELPHIA/Sunday Press/Contents, September 29, 1895/ [contents]/It pays to use Press Want Ads.

1895
Image 20$\frac{3}{16}$ × 13$\frac{5}{8}$ in. (51.2 × 34.7 cm.); *sheet* 21$\frac{3}{8}$ × 15$\frac{11}{16}$ in. (54.5 × 39.8 cm.)
Commercial relief process and letterpress; brown, red, and green
Signature Brill (*within printer's logo, lower right corner*)
Published by Philadelphia Press
Printer H. I. IRELAND,

PHILADELPHIA (*lower right corner*)
References Whitehead, p. 10; PAFA 208; Reims 1178
41.12.214 [Vonnoh]

Note: The artist also signed this impression in the lower left corner.

39 PHILADELPHIA/Sunday Press/Contents, October 6, 1895/ [contents]/It pays to use Press Want Ads.

1895
Image 20$\frac{1}{8}$ × 13$\frac{9}{16}$ in. (51.2 × 34.7 cm.); *sheet* 21$\frac{15}{16}$ × 15$\frac{11}{16}$ in. (55.7 × 39.9 cm.)
Commercial relief process and letterpress; brown, blue, and red
Signature missing

Published by Philadelphia Press
Printed by H. I. Ireland, Philadelphia
References Whitehead, p. 10; PAFA 209; Reims 1167
41.12.215 [Vonnoh]

40 PHILADELPHIA/Sunday Press/SPECIAL FEATURES FOR NOV. 10, 1895/[contents]/It pays to use Press Want Ads.

1895
Image 20$\frac{1}{8}$ × 13$\frac{5}{8}$ in. (51 × 34.7 cm.); *sheet* 21$\frac{7}{8}$ × 15$\frac{1}{2}$ in. (55.6 × 39.4 cm.)
Commercial relief process and letterpress; yellow, red, and blue
Signature Brill (*within printer's logo, lower right corner*)

Published by Philadelphia Press
Printer H. I. IRELAND, PHILADELPHIA (*lower right corner*)
Reference PAFA 214
41.12.96 [Vonnoh]

41 PHILADELPHIA/SUNDAY PRESS/SPECIAL FEATURES for SUNDAY, JANUARY 12, 1896./[contents]/A SPLENDID ART SOUVENIR FREE TO EVERY READER./IT PAYS TO USE PRESS WANT ADS.

1896
Image 20$\frac{11}{16}$ × 13$\frac{13}{16}$ in. (52.6 × 35.1 cm.); *sheet* 21$\frac{7}{8}$ × 15$\frac{9}{16}$ in. (55.6 × 39.6 cm.)
Commercial relief process and letterpress; brown, red, and black
Signature Brill (*within printer's logo, lower left corner*)

Published by Philadelphia Press
Printer H. I. IRELAND, PHILADELPHIA (*lower left corner*)
References DFP 190; PAFA 223
41.12.97 [Vonnoh]

Frank Gelett Burgess

42 THE/Purple Cow!/VAGARIES REPRINTED FROM/ "THE LARK"/The Purple/Cow!/WM. DOXEY SAN FRANCISCO/ Price, 25 cents

1895
Sheet 12¹¹/₁₆ × 7⅝ in. (32.2 × 19.3 cm.)
Commercial relief process; purple
Signature F G B (*monogram, center left*)
Published by William Doxey, San Francisco

Reference PAFA 466
41.12.220 [Vonnoh]

Note: Gelett Burgess, *The Purple Cow* (San Francisco: William Doxey, 1895).

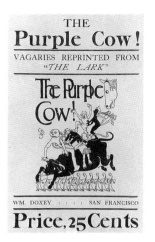

William L. Carqueville

43 LIPPINCOTT'S/DECEMBER

1894
Image 18¼ × 11¹⁵/₁₆ in. (46.3 × 30.3 cm.); *sheet* 19 × 12⁷/₁₆ in. (48.2 × 31.6 cm.)
Commercial lithography; yellow, red, and blue
Signature WILL./CARQUEVILLE. (*lower left corner*)
Published by J. B. Lippincott Co., Philadelphia

Printer SHOBER & CARQUEVILLE LITHO. CO. CHICAGO (*lower right corner*)
References DFP 194; Bolton, p. 4; Quincy 20; Mass. Mech. 41; Whitehead, p. 12; Century and Echo 181; PAFA 257; Reims 1210
41.12.133 [Vonnoh]

44 LIPPINCOTT'S/FOR JANUARY.

1895
Image 18⁷/₁₆ × 12 in. (46.8 × 30.5 cm.); *sheet* 18¹⁵/₁₆ × 12½ in. (48 × 31.7 cm.)
Commercial lithography; yellow, red, and blue
Signature WILL CARQUEVILLE (*lower right corner*)
Published by J. B. Lippincott Co., Philadelphia

References DFP 195; Bolton, p. 4; Quincy 21; Mass. Mech. 42; Whitehead, p. 12; Century and Echo 182; PAFA 262A; Richmond 55; Reims 1200; Flood 61
41.12.134 [Vonnoh]

45 LIPPINCOTT'S/FEBRUARY.

1895
Sheet 19¹/₁₆ × 12⅝ in. (48.4 × 32.1 cm.)
Commercial lithography; yellow, red, and blue
Signature W. L. Carqueville (*middle left*)
Published by J. B. Lippincott Co., Philadelphia

References DFP 196; Bolton, p. 4; Quincy 22; Mass. Mech. 40; Whitehead, p. 12; PAFA 258; Richmond 56; Reims 1201
1984.1202.25 [Lauder]; 41.12.86 [Vonnoh]
Colorplate 6

46   LIPPINCOTT'S/MARCH

1895

Image 18½ × 11¹³⁄₁₆ in. (47.1 ×
  30.1 cm.); *sheet* 19¹⁄₁₆ × 12⅝ in.
  (48.5 × 32.1 cm.)
Commercial lithography; yellow,
  vermilion, and blue
Signature WILL CARQUEVILLE
  (*lower right corner*)
Published by J. B. Lippincott Co.,
  Philadelphia

References DFP 197; Bolton, p. 4;
  Quincy 23; Mass. Mech. 43;
  Whitehead, p. 12; Century and
  Echo 183; PAFA 259; Richmond
  57
1984.1202.26 [Lauder]; 41.12.132
  [Vonnoh]

47   LIPPINCOTT'S/APRIL

1895

Image 18½ × 12¹⁄₁₆ in. (47.1 × 30.5
  cm.); *sheet* 19 × 12⅜ in. (48.2 ×
  31.6 cm.)
Commercial lithography; yellow,
  red, and dark green
Signature WILL CARQUEVILLE
  (*lower right corner*)
Published by J. B. Lippincott Co.,
  Philadelphia

References DFP 198; Bolton, p. 4;
  Quincy 24; Mass. Mech. 44;
  Whitehead, p. 12; Century and
  Echo 184; PAFA 269; Richmond
  58; Reims 1202
1984.1202.27 [Lauder]; 41.12.130
  [Vonnoh]

48   LIPPINCOTT'S/MAY

1895

Image 18⁹⁄₁₆ × 12¹⁄₁₆ in. (47.2 ×
  30.4 cm.); *sheet* 18¹³⁄₁₆ × 12⁵⁄₁₆ in.
  (47.8 × 31.1 cm.)
Commercial lithography; yellow,
  vermilion, light green, and blue
Signature WILL/CARQUEVILLE
  (*lower right corner*)
Published by J. B. Lippincott Co.,
  Philadelphia

References DFP 199; Quincy 25; Mass.
  Mech. 45; Whitehead, p. 12;
  Century and Echo 185; PAFA 262;
  Richmond 59; Reims 1203
1984.1202.28 [Lauder]; 41.12.131
  [Vonnoh]

49   LIPPINCOTT'S/JUNE

1895

Image 18½ × 12⅛ in. (47 × 30.8
  cm.); *sheet* 18⅞ × 12½ in. (48 ×
  31.7 cm.)
Commercial lithography; red, blue,
  and green
Signature W. L Carqueville (*lower
  left corner*)
Published by J. B. Lippincott Co.,
  Philadelphia

References DFP 200; Quincy 26; Mass.
  Mech. 45; Whitehead, p. 12;
  Century and Echo 186; PAFA 264;
  Richmond 60; Reims 1204
1984.1202.29 [Lauder]; 41.12.127
  [Vonnoh]

50 LIPPINCOTT'S/SERIES OF SELECT/NOVELS/ISSUED
MONTHLY.

1895
Image 18½ × 12⅛ in. (47 × 30.7
  cm.); *sheet* 18¾ × 12⁵⁄₁₆ in. (47.6
  × 31.2 cm.)
Commercial lithography; yellow,
  vermilion, and blue
Signature WILL. CARQUEVILLE
  (*lower right corner*)

Published by J. B. Lippincott Co.,
  Philadelphia
References DFP 206; Mass. Mech.
  380; Whitehead, p. 12;
  Richmond 54
1984.1202.24 [Lauder]; 41.12.135
  [Vonnoh]

51 LIPPINCOTT'S/JULY

1895
Image 18½ × 12 in. (47 × 30.5
  cm.); *sheet* 18¾ × 12⁵⁄₁₆ in. (47.7
  × 31.2 cm.)
Color lithography; green, red, and
  blue
Signature WILL CARQUEVILLE
  (*lower right corner*)

Published by J. B. Lippincott Co.,
  Philadelphia
References DFP 201; Mass. Mech. 47;
  Whitehead, p. 12; Century and
  Echo 187; PAFA 268; Richmond
  61; Reims 1205
41.12.125 [Vonnoh]

52 LIPPINCOTT'S/AUGUST

1895
Image 18⁷⁄₁₆ × 12¹⁄₁₆ in. (46.9 ×
  30.7 cm.); *sheet* 18¹³⁄₁₆ × 12¼ in.
  (47.8 × 31.2 cm.)
Commercial lithography; yellow,
  red, and blue
Signature WILL CARQUEVILLE
  (*lower left*)
Published by J. B. Lippincott Co.,
  Philadelphia

References DFP 202; Mass. Mech. 48;
  Whitehead, p. 12; Century and
  Echo, illus. p. 7; PAFA 266;
  Richmond 62; Reims 1206;
  Flood 62
1984.1202.30 [Lauder]; 41.12.129
  [Vonnoh]
Colorplate 7

53 LIPPINCOTT'S/SEPTEMBER

1895
Sheet 18¹⁵⁄₁₆ × 12⁷⁄₁₆ in. (48.1 ×
  31.6 cm.)
Commercial lithography; blue,
  vermilion, and light tan
Signature WILL/CARQUEVILLE
  (*middle left*)

Published by J. B. Lippincott Co.,
  Philadelphia
References DFP 203; Mass. Mech. 49;
  Whitehead, p. 12; Century and
  Echo 188; PAFA 267; Reims 1207
41.12.124 [Vonnoh]

54   LIPPINCOTT'S/OCTOBER

1895

Image 18⁹⁄₁₆ × 12⅛ in. (47.2 × 30.8
   cm.); *sheet* 18¾ × 12⁷⁄₁₆ in. (47.6
   × 31.5 cm.)
Commercial lithography; red,
   brown, light green, and blue
Signature WILL CARQUEVILLE
   (*middle right*)

Published by J. B. Lippincott Co.,
   Philadelphia
References DFP 204; Whitehead,
   p. 12; Century and Echo 189;
   PAFA 263; Reims 1208
1984.1202.31 [Lauder]; 41.12.126
   [Vonnoh]

55   LIPPINCOTT'S/NOVEMBER

1895

Image 18⁹⁄₁₆ × 12³⁄₁₆ in. (47.1 ×
   30.9 cm.); *sheet* 19 × 12⅝ in.
   (48.3 × 32.1 cm.)
Commercial lithography; yellow,
   vermilion, blue, and green
Signature WILL CARQUEVILLE
   (*lower right corner*)
Published by J. B. Lippincott Co.,
   Philadelphia

References DFP 205; Mass. Mech.
   381; Whitehead, p. 12; Century
   and Echo 190; PAFA 265; Reims
   1209; Flood 63
1984.1202.32 [Lauder]; 41.12.128
   [Vonnoh]

56   INTERNATIONAL—/NOVEMBER

1896

Image 18¼ × 12⅛ in. (46.2 × 30.9
   cm.); *sheet* 20³⁄₁₆ × 13¹⁵⁄₁₆ in. (51.4
   × 35.4 cm.)
Commercial lithography; green and
   blue

Signature WILL CARQUEVILLE
   (*lower left corner*)
Published by International, Chicago
Reference DFP 208
1986.1005.3 [Lauder]

57   INTERNATIONAL/APRIL

1897

Image 17⁷⁄₁₆ × 11¹³⁄₁₆ in. (44.2 × 30
   cm.); *sheet* 20¹⁵⁄₁₆ × 13⅞ in. (53.3
   × 35.2 cm.)
Commercial lithography; red and
   blue
Signature WILL CARQUEVILLE
   (*lower right corner*)

Published by International, Chicago
References DFP 210; Flood 60
1986.1005.2 [Lauder]
Colorplate 35

Robert William Chambers

58 THE/RED/REPUBLIC/BY/R W CHAMBERS

1895

Sheet 15¹³⁄₁₆ × 12¹⁄₁₆ in. (40.2 × 30.7 cm.)

Commercial lithography; light green, red, and black

Signature R. W. Chambers (*middle right*)

Published by Burt, New York, *or* G. P. Putnam's Sons, New York

Reference Richmond 64

57.627.10(13)

Note: Robert William Chambers, *The Red Republic. A Romance of the Commune* (New York: Burt, 1895; or New York: G. P. Putnam's Sons, 1895).

Howard Chandler Christy

59 THE/BOOKMAN/FOR/NOVEMBER

1896

Image 16¼ × 14¼ in. (41.2 × 36.2 cm.); *sheet* 17¾ × 15⅛ in. (45.1 × 38.4 cm.)

Commercial lithography; black, green, and pink on yellow-green paper

Signature H. CHRISTY. (*lower left corner*)

Published by The Bookman

References DFP 213; Flood 67

1984.1202.33 [Lauder]

Charles Arthur Cox

60 BEARINGS/FOR/SALE HERE

1896

Image 16³⁄₁₆ × 11 in. (41.1 × 28.1 cm.); *sheet* 18⅛ × 13³⁄₁₆ in. (46 × 33.5 cm.)

Commercial lithography; yellow, red, apple-green, and black

Signature Charles A Cox (*lower left corner*)

Published by Bearings

1984.1202.34 [Lauder]

Note: Cox designed a number of posters for *Bearings*, a magazine catering to fashionable interest in the bicycle. Sometimes his designs included bears—for example, riding on a handlebar or as part of a cloud formation.

Francis Day

61 SCRIBNER'S MA[GAZINE]/OCTOBER

1894

Sheet 17½ × 12⁹⁄₁₆ in. (44.5 × 31.9 cm.)

Commercial relief process; yellow, black, and red

Unsigned

Published by Charles Scribner's Sons, New York

References Bolton, p. 6; Quincy 55; Whitehead, p. 14; Flood 83

41.12.152 [Vonnoh]

De Yongh

62   The/New-York Times/HIGH CLASS FICTION/ Now
Appearing/IN THE/DAILY EDITION/On Consecutive Days./
NO WAITS./A Series of Short Stories/{listing of authors}/
Don't Miss Them.

ca. 1896
Image 27⅛ × 17 in. (69.9 × 43.2
   cm.); *sheet* 30⅛ × 20¹/₁₆ in. (76.5
   × 50.9 cm.)
Commercial lithography and
letterpress; yellow, red, blue, and
black
Signature De Y. (*lower center*)
Published by The New York Times

Printer LIEBLER & MAASS. LITH.
  N.Y. (*lower center*)
Reference PAFA 284
41.12.217 [Vonnoh]

Note: This poster, now restored, was
  in pieces. One section, "Times," is
  still missing.

63   CROWNING OF A CZAR/MAY CENTURY

1896
Sheet 20¹³/₁₆ × 14⅜ in. (52.9 ×
   36.5 cm.)
Commercial lithography; yellow,
light brown, blue, black, and red
Signature de Yongh (*lower right*)
Published by The Century Co., New
  York

Printer LIEBLER & MAASS LITH.
  N.Y. (*lower right corner*)
References Reims 1337; Flood 362
57.627.10(12)

Lafayette Maynard Dixon

64   LO-TO-KAH BY VERNER Z-REED/CONTINENTAL
PUBLISHING CO: NEW YORK/PRICE: $1.00

1897
Image 14³/₁₆ × 13⁷/₁₆ in. (36.1 ×
   34.2 cm.); *sheet* 15⁹/₁₆ × 14¹³/₁₆ in.
   (39.5 × 37.6 cm.)
Commercial relief process; blue,
brown, and black
Signature DIXON 1897/*eagle logo*/
DES. DEL (*lower right corner*)

Published by Continental Publishing
  Co., New York
1986.1005.4 [Lauder]

Note: Verner Zevola Reed, *Lo-To-Kah*
  (New York: Continental
  Publishing Co., 1897).

65   TALES OF THE/SUNLAND BY VERNER-Z-REED/
CONTINENTAL PUBLISHING CO. N-Y./PRICE: $1.25

1897
Image 17⅞ × 12¹/₁₆ in. (45.4 × 30.6
   cm.); *sheet* 19¹³/₁₆ × 13¾ in. (50.4
   × 35 cm.)
Commercial relief process; yellow,
brown, and black
Signature DIXON 1897/*eagle logo*/
DES. DEL (*lower right corner*)

Published by Continental Publishing
  Co., New York
1986.1005.5 [Lauder]

Note: Verner Zevola Reed, *Tales of the
  Sunland* (New York: Continental
  Publishing Co., 1897).

Arthur Wesley Dow

66   Modern Art/EDITED BY J. M. BOWLES/PUBLISHED BY
        L. PRANG & CO.

1895
Image 17⅞ × 13⅝ in. (45.3 × 34.6
  cm.); *sheet* 20¹⁄₁₆ × 15⅜ in. (51 ×
  39.1 cm.)
Commercial lithography; yellow,
  pink, light brown, blue, light
  green, and dark green
Signature Arthur W Dow (*lower left
  corner*)
Published and printed by Louis Prang
  & Co., Boston
References DFP 217; Mass. Mech. 92;
  Whitehead, p. 16; Century and
  Echo 216; PAFA 280; Richmond
  86; Reims 1223; Flood 78
1984.1202.35 [Lauder];
  41.12.187 [Vonnoh]

Note: The consummate skill of the
  Prang firm sensitively reproduced
  Dow's woodcut *Sundown, Ipswich
  River* for *Modern Art*, capturing the
  subtle washes of color that
  characterize his watercolors and his
  Japanese-style woodblock prints.
  Dow's poster was available to
  subscribers to the 1895 set (vol. 3)
  of the magazine at no extra cost,
  and to others for twenty-five cents
  in stamps (see advertisement,
  Modern Art 4.1 [Winter 1896],
  n.p.).
Colorplate 4

Henry Brevoort Eddy

67   Bicycle Number, New York Ledger/NEW YORK/LEDGER/
        PRICE 5¢/Ready Feb. 21st. FOR SALE HERE.

1895
Image 11½ × 13⅞ in. (29.2 × 35.3
  cm.); *sheet* 13⁹⁄₁₆ × 16³⁄₁₆ in. (34.5
  × 41.2 cm.)
Commercial lithography and
  letterpress; yellow, red, blue, and
  black
Signature FROM A DESIGN BY
  H. B. EDDY. (*lower right corner*)
Published by New York Ledger
References Whitehead, p. 16;
  PAFA 296
41.12.93 [Vonnoh]

Note: The *New York Ledger* most
  likely commissioned this design
  from Eddy for the special bicycling
  number of the newspaper, as noted
  in the separately printed text of
  the poster. The *Ledger* later used
  copies of the poster to advertise a
  contest with "$1,000 in Cash
  Prizes to Ledger Readers" (Victor
  Margolin, *American Poster
  Renaissance* [New York: Watson-
  Guptill, 1975], illus. p. 180).

George Wharton Edwards

68 Published by/THE CENTURY CO./THE MAN WHO/
MARRIED/THE MOON/And other Tee Wahn/Folk Tales/
By/CHAS. F. LUMMIS/Illustrated/Price $1.50

1894
Sheet 12 × 19¹⁄₁₆ in. (30.5 ×
48.4 cm.)
Commercial relief process and
letterpress; orange, gray, and dark
blue
Signature GEORGE WHARTON
EDWARDS. INV. (*lower left corner*)
Published by The Century Co., New
York

References see Bolton, p. 6;
Whitehead, p. 16
41.12.150 [Vonnoh]

Note: Charles Fletcher Lummis, *The
Man Who Married the Moon and
Other Pueblo Indian Folk-Stories*
(New York: The Century Co.,
1894).

69 THE CENTURY/FEBRUARY/MIDWINTER/NUMBER/
[contents]/STORIES, DEPARTMENTS, POEMS, ETC./For
Sale Here Published by THE CENTURY CO.

1895
Sheet 17⅛ × 12³⁄₁₆ in. (43.6 ×
31 cm.)
Commercial relief process and
letterpress; yellow, pink, and black
Signature GEORGE WHARTON
EDWARDS fct. (*lower left*)
Published by The Century Co., New
York

References Union League 43; Bolton,
p. 6; Quincy 68; Mass. Mech. 98;
Whitehead, p. 16; Century and
Echo 48; PAFA 290; Richmond 88;
Flood 94
41.12.166 [Vonnoh]

Harvey Ellis

70 HARPER'S/MAGAZINE/CHRISTMAS: 1898

1898
Image 16¹⁄₁₆ × 10¹³⁄₁₆ in. (40.8 ×
27.5 cm.); *sheet* 16⁷⁄₁₆ × 11³⁄₁₆ in.
(41.8 × 28.4 cm.)
Commercial lithography; yellow,
red, blue, and black
Signature HARVEY ELLIS. (*lower left
corner*)

Published by Harper and Brothers,
New York
Reference DFP 222
57.627.10 (8)

Wilson Eyre, Jr.

71 ART CLUB/ARCHITECTURAL/EXHIBITION/OPEN
FROM/FEB 23d TO MARCH 6th/1892/THE EXHIBITION
WILL INCLUDE MANY DRAWINGS/BY JOSEPH
PENNELL, (LOANED BY THE CENTURY/COMPANY),
THE DRAWINGS FOR THE CATHEDRAL/OF ST. JOHN
THE DIVINE, NEW YORK, ETC., ETC.

1892
Sheet 22 × 13¹⁵⁄₁₆ in. (55.7 ×
35.5 cm.)
Commercial relief process and
letterpress; black
Signature W Eyre/92 (*lower right*)
Published by Philadelphia Art Club
Printer GLOBE PRINTING
HOUSE (*lower left corner*)

41.12.165 [Vonnoh]

Note: This design, reduced, appeared
on the cover of the catalogue of the
exhibition.

Charles Farrand

72 LIPPINCOTT'S / FOR / NOVEMBER

1894
Sheet 18⅜ × 12³⁄₁₆ in. (46.8 × 31 cm.)
Commercial relief process; red and black
Unsigned

Published by J. B. Lippincott Co., Philadelphia
Reference Whitehead, p. 18
41.12.151 [Vonnoh]

A. Fay

73 THE NEW YORK HERALD / SUNDAY / AUG. / 29TH

1897
Image 11³⁄₁₆ × 8⅛ in. (28.5 × 20.6 cm.); *sheet* 12½ × 12⁵⁄₁₆ in. (31.7 × 31.3 cm.)
Commercial lithography; yellow, red, and blue

Signature A. FAY (*lower right corner*)
Published by The New York Herald
1984.1202.36 [Lauder]

Charles Dana Gibson

74 The Princess Sonia / A Romance of Girl Art Life in Paris / By Julia Magruder / With Illustrations by Chas. Dana Gibson / Published by / THE CENTURY CO., NEW YORK.

1895
Image 17¹⁄₁₆ × 12 in. (43.4 × 30.5 cm.); *sheet* 19½ × 13⁷⁄₁₆ in. (47 × 34.2 cm.)
Commercial relief process and letterpress; red, light green, and black
Signature C. D. Gibson (*center*)
Published by The Century Co., New York

References DFP 232; Whitehead, p. 20; Century and Echo 100
41.12.193 [Vonnoh]

Note: Julia Magruder, *The Princess Sonia* (New York: The Century Co., 1895).

75 TWO WOMEN AND A FOOL / By H. C. CHATFIELD-TAYLOR, with Pictures / by C. D. GIBSON. Price $1.50 / IN THE SAME SERIES: / A SAWDUST DOLL, By MRS. REGINALD DeKOVEN, $1.25 / AND / A LITTLE SISTER TO THE WILDERNESS, / By LILIAN BELL, $1.25 / Published by Stone & Kimball

1895
Sheet 16¼ × 11⁵⁄₁₆ in. (41.3 × 28.6 cm.)
Commercial relief process and letterpress; black
Signature C. D. Gibson (*below vignette*)
Published by Stone and Kimball, Chicago

References DFP 234; Quincy 80; Mass. Mech. 119; Whitehead, p. 20; Century and Echo 257; PAFA 305
41.12.87 [Vonnoh]

Note: Hobart Chatfield Chatfield-Taylor, *Two Women and a Fool* (Chicago: Stone and Kimball, 1895).

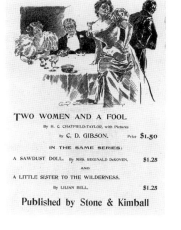

76   C D/GIBSON'S/1ST/LONDON/WITH/PEN & PENCIL/
February/SCRIBNER'S

1897
Sheet 20⅛ × 15 in. (51.2 ×
38.1 cm.)
Commercial relief process; green and
brown
Signature C. D. Gibson (*lower center*)

Published by Charles Scribner's Sons,
New York
References DFP 239; Flood 111
1984.1202.37 [Lauder]

William James Glackens

77   LIPPINCOTT'S/AUGUST/CONTAINS A/COMPLETE/
NOVEL/SWEETHEART MANETTE BY MAURICE
THOMPSON

1894
Image 16 × 11¹³⁄₁₆ in. (40.7 × 30
cm.); *sheet* 17⁷⁄₁₆ × 12⁹⁄₁₆ in. (44.2
× 31.9 cm.)
Commercial lithography; yellow,
vermilion, and black
Signature Wm. J. GLACKENS (*lower
left corner*)

Published by J. B. Lippincott Co.,
Philadelphia
References DFP 241; Mass. Mech. 53;
Whitehead, p. 12
1984.1202.38 [Lauder]

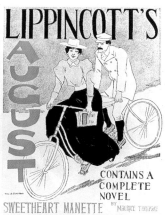

Alice Russell Glenny

78   WOMENS/EDITION/(BUFFALO)/COURIER.

1895
Image 24¼ × 14⁹⁄₁₆ in. (61.7 × 37
cm.); *sheet* 29⁷⁄₁₆ × 20¹¹⁄₁₆ in. (74.8
× 52.5 cm.)
Commercial lithography; pink, light
brown, brown, yellow, green, red,
purple, black, and gold
Signature ARG. (*lower left corner*)
Published by The Buffalo Courier

Printer THE COURIER LITHO.
CO. BUFFALO. N.Y. (*lower right
corner*)
References Quincy 81; Mass. Mech.
124; Whitehead, p. 20; Century
and Echo 261; Richmond 114
57.627.63; 1984.1202.39 [Lauder]
Colorplate 34

Joseph J. Gould, Jr.

79   LIPPINCOTT'S/DECEMBER

1895
Image 12⅜ × 8¼ in. (31.5 × 20.9
cm.); *sheet* 13⁹⁄₁₆ × 9 in. (34.5 ×
22.8 cm.)
Commercial lithography; green and
red
Signature J. J. Gould Jr (*lower right
corner*)
Published by J. B. Lippincott Co.,
Philadelphia
References DFP 243; Whitehead,
p. 20; Century and Echo 273;
PAFA 301; Richmond 106;
Flood 112

41.12.122 [Vonnoh]

Note: The Poster of February 1896
announced that "a new series of
posters for *Lippincott's Magazine*
will attract attention. The work is
by J. J. Gould, Jr." He took over
the series with this poster.
Carqueville, the previous artist for
the series, planned to go to Paris
to pursue his art studies (*The Poster*
1.2 [February 1896], pp. 26, 18).

80 LIPPINCOTT'S/JANUARY

1896

Image 12⅝ × 8³⁄₁₆ in. (32.1 × 20.8
  cm.); *sheet* 13⁹⁄₁₆ × 9⁵⁄₁₆ in. (34.4
  × 23.7 cm.)
Commercial lithography; vermilion,
  gray, and dark blue
Signature J. J. Gould, Jr. (*lower right
  corner*)

Published by J. B. Lippincott Co.,
  Philadelphia
References DFP 244; PAFA 302;
  Richmond 107; Flood 113
1984.1202.40 [Lauder]; 41.12.121
  [Vonnoh]

81 LIPPINCOTT'S/MAY

1896

Image 15¹⁵⁄₁₆ × 10⅞ in. (40.5 ×
  27.6 cm.); *sheet* 16¹⁵⁄₁₆ × 11¹⁵⁄₁₆ in.
  (43.1 × 30.3 cm.)
Commercial lithography; yellow,
  red, and black
Signature J. J Gould Jr. (*lower left
  corner*)

Publisher Copyright 1896 by J. B.
  Lippincott Co. (*lower left corner*)
References DFP 248; Richmond 111;
  Flood 117
1984.1202.41 [Lauder]

82 LIPPINCOTT'S/JUNE

1896

Image 13¹¹⁄₁₆ × 9 in. (34.8 × 22.8
  cm.); *sheet* 16½ × 11⅞ in. (42 ×
  30.1 cm.)
Commercial lithography; yellow,
  green, and red
Signature J. J Gould Jr (*lower left
  corner*)

Publisher Copyright 1896 by J. B.
  Lippincott Co. (*lower left corner*)
References DFP 249; Richmond 112;
  Flood 118
1984.1202.42 [Lauder]

83 LIPPINCOTT'S/JULY

1896

Image 17¹¹⁄₁₆ × 13¹³⁄₁₆ in. (45 × 34.8
  cm.); *sheet* 18⅝ × 14½ in. (47.5 ×
  36.9 cm.)
Commercial lithography; yellow,
  vermilion, and blue
Signature J. J. Gould Jr. (*lower right
  corner*)

Publisher COPYRIGHT 1896 BY
  J B LIPPINCOTT CO. (*lower left
  corner*)
References DFP 250; Flood 119
1984.1202.43 [Lauder]

84   LIPPINCOTT'S/SEPTEMBER

1896

Image 18⁹⁄₁₆ × 13³⁄₁₆ in. (47.2 ×   *Publisher* COPYRIGHT 1896 BY
33.5 cm.); *sheet* 19¹⁵⁄₁₆ × 14⁷⁄₁₆ in.   J. B. LIPPINCOTT CO. (*lower left*
(50.5 × 36.6 cm.)   *corner*)
Commercial lithography; yellow,   *References* DFP 252; Flood 121
red, and blue   1984.1202.44 [Lauder]
Signature J. J. Gould (*lower right*
corner)

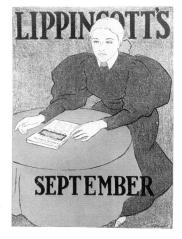

85   LIPPINCOTT'S/OCTOBER

1896

Image 17½ × 13¼ in. (44.4 × 33.7   *Publisher* COPYRIGHT 1896 BY
cm.); *sheet* 18⅛ × 13⅞ in. (46.1 ×   J. B. LIPPINCOTT CO. (*lower left*
35.3 cm.)   *corner*)
Commercial lithography; yellow,   *References* DFP 253; Flood 122
red, and black   1984.1202.45 [Lauder]
Signature J J Gould. (*lower right*
corner)

86   LIPPINCOTT'S/NOVEMBER

1896

Sheet 16½ × 13⅛ in. (42 ×   *Publisher* COPYRIGHT 1896 BY
33.3 cm.)   J B LIPPINCOTT CO. (*lower left*
Commercial lithography; yellow,   *corner*)
red, and blue   *References* DFP 254; Flood 123
Signature J. J. Gould (*lower right*   1984.1202.46 [Lauder]
corner)

87   LIPPINCOTT'S/DECEMBER

1896

Image 15⁹⁄₁₆ × 12¹⁵⁄₁₆ in. (39.6 ×   *Publisher* COPYRIGHT 1896 BY
32.8 cm.); *sheet* 16¾ × 13⅞ in.   J. B. LIPPINCOTT CO. (*lower left*
(42.5 × 35.3 cm.)   *corner*)
Commercial lithography; yellow,   *References* DFP 255; Flood 124
vermilion, and blue   1984.1202.47 [Lauder]
Signature J. J. Gould (*lower right*   Colorplate 9
corner)

88 A NEW NOVEL BY / MARIE CORELLI / AUTHOR OF / BARABBAS / The Sorrows / of Satan / J: B: LIPPINCOTT: CO. / PHILADELPHIA

1896

Image 11⅞ × 8⅝ in. (30.2 × 22 cm.); *sheet* 13 1/16 × 10 1/16 in. (33.1 × 25.5 cm.)

Commercial lithography; red and black

Signature J J Gould Jr (*lower left corner*)

Published by J. B. Lippincott Co., Philadelphia

References DFP 265; Whitehead, p. 20; Century and Echo 272; Richmond 113 41.12.190 [Vonnoh]

Note: Marie Corelli (pseud. of Mary MacKay), *The Sorrows of Satan* (Philadelphia: J. B. Lippincott Co., 1896).

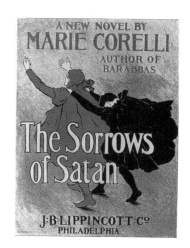

89 LIPPINCOTT'S / FEBRUARY

1897

Sheet 19 × 11 3/16 in. (48.3 × 28.4 cm.)

Commercial lithography; orange, olive brown, and black

Signature J. J. Gould (*upper right corner*)

Publisher COPYRIGHT 1897 BY J B LIPPINCOTT CO (*lower right corner*)

References DFP 258; Flood 126 1984.1202.48 [Lauder]

Colorplate **8**

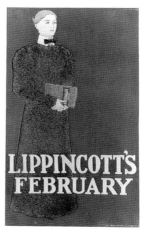

90 LIPPINCOTT'S / FOR MARCH

1897

Image 16⅛ × 13¼ in. (41 × 33.6 cm.); *sheet* 17 3/16 × 14¼ in. (43.6 × 36.1 cm.)

Commercial lithography; yellow, vermilion, and blue

Signature J. J. Gould (*lower left corner*)

Publisher COPYRIGHT 1897 BY J. B. LIPPINCOTT CO. (*lower left corner*)

References DFP 259; Flood 127 1984.1202.49 [Lauder]

91 LIPPINCOTT'S / MAY

1897

Sheet 16⅜ × 11 15/16 in. (41.5 × 30.4 cm.)

Commercial lithography; yellow, blue, and red

Signature J. J. Gould (*lower left corner*)

Published by J. B. Lippincott Co., Philadelphia

Reference DFP 261 1984.1202.50 [Lauder]

1897

Sheet 19³/₁₆ × 11⅞ in. (48 7 ×
  30.2 cm.)
Commercial lithography and
  letterpress; vermilion, green, and
  black
Signature J. J. Gould (*middle right*)

Publisher COPYRIGHT 1897 BY
  J. B. LIPPINCOTT CO (*middle
  left*)
Reference DFP 262
1986.1005.6 [Lauder]

Walter Conant Greenough

93   Sir/Quixote/of the/Moors/by/John/Buchan/Henry Holt & Co.
     Publishers

1895

Image 16⁵/₁₆ × 12 in. (41.5 × 30.5
  cm.); *sheet* 18½ × 14¹/₁₆ in. (47 ×
  35.7 cm.)
Commercial relief process; vermilion
  and blue
Signature W. C. Greenough/1895
  (*lower right corner*)
Published by Henry Holt and Co.,
  New York

References Whitehead, p. 22;
  PAFA 307
41.12.157 [Vonnoh]

Note: John Buchan, *Sir Quixote of the
  Moors* (New York: Henry Holt and
  Co., 1895).

George R. Halm

94   PALMER COX'S FAMOUS/BROWNIE BOOKS/{titles of five
     books}/MORE THAN 100,000 SOLD PRICE $1.50 EACH/
     PUBLISHED BY THE CENTURY CO., NEW YORK

1895

Sheet 10¹/₁₆ × 15⅛ in. (25.6 ×
  38.5 cm.)
Commercial relief process and
  letterpress; brown, yellow, blue,
  and red
Signature GEO./R. HALM (*within
  trefoil, lower right corner*)
Published by The Century Co., New
  York
Printed by The DeVinne Press, New
  York
References Whitehead, pp. 14 (as by
  Cox), 22 (as by Halm); Century
  and Echo 73 (as by Cox)
41.12.173 [Vonnoh]

Note: Palmer Cox, *The Brownies:
  Their Book* (New York: The
  Century Co., ca. 1895); *The*

Brownies Around the World (New
York: The Century Co., 1894);
Another Brownie Book (New York:
The Century Co., 1890); *The
Brownies at Home* (New York: The
Century Co., 1893); *The Brownies
Through the Union* (New York: The
Century Co., ca. 1890, 1895).
Cox's Brownie series was among
the most popular children's books
of the period. For his poster, Halm
used not only several of Cox's
Brownies but also the distinctive
typeface of the covers and title
pages of the series; hence the
discrepancies in the attributions in
the references.

Theodore J. Hampe

95 THE MIDSUMMER NUMBER/August/ST. NICHOLAS

1896

Image 19⅞ × 13¹¹⁄₁₆ in. (50.4 × 34.7 cm.); *sheet* 20¹⁵⁄₁₆ × 14⁷⁄₁₆ in. (53.2 × 36.7 cm.)

Commercial lithography; flesh, light green, dark green, and red

Signature DESIGNED BY THEO. HAMPE. (*lower left corner*)

Publisher COPYRIGHT, 1896, BY THE CENTURY CO. (*lower left corner*)

Printer PRINTED BY G. H. BUEK AND CO. LITH. N.Y. (*lower right corner*)

Reference Whitehead 138

1985.1123.6 [Naef]

Note: Hampe's entry in the *Century* contest received an honorable mention and was probably used for the August *St. Nicholas* poster.

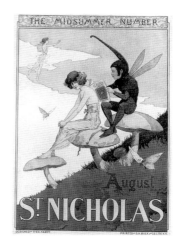

Ernest Haskell

96 TRUTH/XMA'S/'96

1896

Image 18¾ × 12¹³⁄₁₆ in. (47.7 × 32.5 cm.); *sheet* 20 × 14¹⁄₁₆ in. (50.8 × 35.7 cm.)

Commercial lithography; yellow, red, blue, and black

Signature ERNEST/HASKELL/'96 (*middle left*)

Published by Truth, New York

Printer AMERICAN LITHOGRAPHIC CO., BROADWAY N.Y. (*lower right corner*)

1984.1202.51 [Lauder]

Colorplate 38

Frank Hazenplug

97 The/Chap-Book

1895

Image 13⅜ × 7¹⁵⁄₁₆ in. (34 × 20.1 cm.); *sheet* 16⅛ × 10⅞ in. (41 × 27.6 cm.)

Commercial relief process; red and black

Signature F H (*lower right corner*)

Published by Stone and Kimball, Chicago

References DFP 269; Whitehead, p. 22; Century and Echo 285;

PAFA 318; Richmond 118; Reims 1233; Flood 143

1984.1202.53 [Lauder]

Note: Hazenplug's design for *The Chap-Book*'s seventh poster, entitled "The Red Lady," was also used on the cover of the November 1, 1895, issue.

Colorplate 10

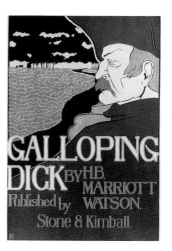

98 GALLOPING/DICK BY H. B./MARRIOTT/WATSON./Published by/Stone & Kimball.

1896

Image 20⅛ × 13¼ in. (51.1 × 33.6 cm.); *sheet* 21¹⁄₁₆ × 14¹⁄₁₆ in. (53.5 × 35.8 cm.)

Commercial lithography; green and vermilion

Signature DESIGNED BY FRANK HAZENPLUG. (*lower left corner*); F H (*lower left corner*)

Publisher PRINTED BY STONE AND KIMBALL CHICAGO.

(*lower right corner*)

References Richmond 119; Reims 1235; Flood 142

1984.1202.56 [Lauder]

Note: Henry Brereton Marriott Watson, *Galloping Dick* (Chicago: Stone and Kimball, 1896).

Colorplate 40

99   The Chap-Book
1896
Image 19¹⁵/₁₆ × 13¹³/₁₆ in. (50.7 ×
35.1 cm.); *sheet* 20½ × 14³/₁₆ in.
(52.2 × 36 cm.)
Commercial lithography; vermilion
and black
Signature DESIGNED BY FRANK
HAZENPLUG (*lower left corner*);
F H (*lower center*)
Publisher PRINTED BY STONE &
KIMBALL CHICAGO (*lower right
corner*)

References DFP 268; Reims 1232
57.627.7(2); 1984.1202.52
[Lauder]

Note: Hazenplug's design for the
twelfth *Chap-Book* poster was
called "The Black Lady." It was
issued in April 1896 and
advertised in the May 1, 1896,
Chap-Book for fifty cents (4.12,
p. ix).

100   THE/CHAP-/BOOK
1896
Image 20³/₈ × 13½ in. (51.8 × 34.3
cm.); *sheet* 21⅛ × 14¹/₁₆ in. (53.8
× 35.8 cm.)
Commercial lithography; green,
yellow, and red
Signature F H. (*middle left*)
Published by Stone and Kimball,
Chicago

Reference Reims 1234
1984.1202.54 [Lauder]; 36.23.10
[Silve]; 57.627.7(1)

Note: Hazenplug's third poster for
The Chap-Book, "The Green Lady,"
was issued May 1896.

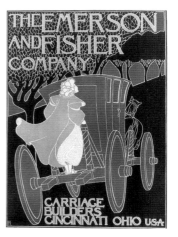

101   THE EMERSON/AND FISHER/COMPANY/CARRIAGE/
BUILDERS/CINCINNATI OHIO U.S.A.
1896
Image 18¼ × 13 in. (46.4 × 33.1
cm.); *sheet* 19¹³/₁₆ × 14 in. (50.3 ×
35.7 cm.)
Commercial lithography; red and
blue
Signature F H. (*lower left corner*)
Printer DESIGNED BY FRANK
HAZENPLUG AND PRINTED
BY STONE & KIMBALL

CHICAGO (*lower left corner*)
Reference DFP 270
1984.1202.55 [Lauder]

Note: The Lauder copy of the poster
is not mounted; on the verso in
blue ink: "PLEASE POST/IN A
CONSPICUOUS PLACE."

Oliver Herford

102   Artful/Anticks/If a cat/may look/at a king/a kitten/may look/
at a prince/By Oliver Herford./The Century Co: Publishers./
Price $1.00

1894
Image 16¼ × 10¹³/₁₆ in. (41.2 ×
27.5 cm.); *sheet* 17½ × 12¹/₁₆ in.
(44.4 × 30.6 cm.)
Commercial relief process and
letterpress; yellow, red, blue, and
black
Unsigned
Published by The Century Co., New
York
References Union League 56; see

Bolton, p. 8; Quincy 103; Mass.
Mech. 157; Whitehead, p. 24;
PAFA 320
41.12.16 [Vonnoh]

Note: Oliver Herford, *Artful Anticks*
(New York: The Century Co.,
1894). The kitten acknowledges
the bow of the Prince of Wales, the
future Edward VII.

Louise Lyons Heustis

103 CHIFFON'S MARRIAGE/BY GYP

1895

Image 9³⁄₁₆ × 9¹⁵⁄₁₆ in. (23.4 × 25.2
cm.); *sheet* 11¹⁄₁₆ × 13¹⁄₁₆ in. (28.2
× 33.2 cm.)
Commercial relief process; yellow
and blue
Signature L. Heustis (*lower left corner*)
Published by E. A. Weeks and Co.,
Chicago
References Whitehead, p. 24;
Century and Echo 295; PAFA 316;
Richmond 121

41.12.186 [Vonnoh]

Note: Gyp (pseud. of Sibylle
Gabrielle Marie Antoinette de
Riquetti de Mirabeau, Comtesse
de Martel de Janville), *Chiffon's
Marriage* (Chicago: E. A. Weeks
and Co., [1895]).

Will Phillip Hooper

104 SLAIN BY THE/DOONES/BY/R. D. BLACKMORE/
DODD, MEAD & COMPANY.

1895

Sheet 16³⁄₄ × 12⁷⁄₈ in. (42.5 ×
32.7 cm.)
Commercial relief process; black and
yellow
Signature Hooper (*lower left corner*)
Published by Dodd, Mead and Co.,
New York
References Whitehead, p. 24;

Century and Echo 289; PAFA 315;
Richmond 124; Flood 154
41.12.182 [Vonnoh]

Note: Richard Doddridge
Blackmore, *Slain by the Doones and
Other Stories* (New York: Dodd,
Mead and Co., 1895).

L. F. Hurd

105 STORIES/OF/THE WAGNER/OPERA/BY/H. A.
GUERBER./DODD MEAD & COMPANY—PUBLISHERS—
NEW YORK.

1895

Image 16³⁄₄ × 11¹⁄₂ in. (42.6 × 29.3
cm.); *sheet* 17 × 11³⁄₄ in. (43.2 ×
29.8 cm.)
Commercial relief process; red and
black on yellow oatmeal paper
Signature HURD (*lower left corner*)
Published by Dodd, Mead and Co.,
New York
References Whitehead, p. 24;

Century and Echo 293; Richmond
128; Flood 145
41.12.189 [Vonnoh]

Note: Helene Adeline Guerber,
Stories of the Wagner Opera (New
York: Dodd, Mead and Co.,
1895).

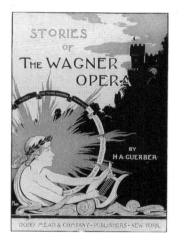

106 THE/BOW/OF ORANGE/RIBBON/A ROMANCE OF
NEW YORK/BY/AMELIA E. BARR/DODD, MEAD &
COMPANY/PUBLISHERS

ca. 1895

Sheet 20¹⁄₂ × 15¹⁄₈ in. (52.1 ×
38.4 cm.)
Commercial lithography; black and
orange
Signature L F Hurd (*lower center*)
Published by Dodd, Mead and Co.,
New York
References Whitehead, p. 24;
Century and Echo 292; PAFA 314;
Flood 147
41.12.216 [Vonnoh]

Note: Amelia Edith Barr, *The Bow of
Orange Ribbon: A Romance of New
York* (New York: Dodd, Mead and
Company, [1886]). The poster
advertised a later edition of the
book. The impression in the
collection of the New York Public
Library has a pencil annotation,
"Sept. 1895."

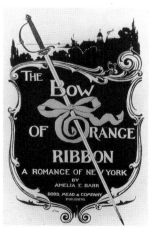

107 The Days of/Auld Lang Syne/BY/IAN MACLAREN/DODD, MEAD & COMPANY PUBLISHERS NEW YORK

1895
Image 16¹³⁄₁₆ × 11½ in. (42.7 × 29.2 cm.); *sheet* 18¼ × 12 in. (46.3 × 30.6 cm.)
Commercial relief process; black, khaki, and purple
Signature L F H (*lower right corner*)
Published by Dodd, Mead and Co., New York

References Whitehead, p. 24; PAFA 311; Richmond 128; Flood 146
41.12.185 [Vonnoh]

Note: Ian Maclaren (pseud. of John Watson), *The Days of Auld Lang Syne* (New York: Dodd, Mead and Co., 1895).

John D. Kelley

108 ST. NICHOLAS/"ST. NICHOLAS OR YOUR LIFE!"/FOR NOVEMBER.

1895
Sheet 20¹³⁄₁₆ × 14⅜ in. (52.9 × 36.5 cm.)
Commercial lithography; light brown, yellow, red, and black
Unsigned
Published by The Century Co., New York

Printer G. H. BUEK & CO. N.Y. LITH. (*lower right corner*)
References Whitehead, p. 26; Century and Echo 125; Richmond 132; Flood 160
41.12.197 [Vonnoh]

William Sargeant Kendall

109 CHARLES DANA GIBSON/IS ONE OF THE ILLUSTRATORS/IN THIS/MONTH'S/SCRIBNERS

1895
Image 15¹¹⁄₁₆ × 11⁹⁄₁₆ in. (39.9 × 29.4 cm.); *sheet* 17⅛ × 12⁹⁄₁₆ in. (43.5 × 31.9 cm.)
Commercial relief process; black, yellow, and red
Signature S K (*middle right*)
Published by Charles Scribner's Sons, New York

References Century and Echo 302; Richmond 129; Flood 161
36.23.19 [Silve]

Note: This poster was for the August issue.

R. W. Lane

110 A Bachelor's/Christmas/BY/Robert Grant/CHARLES SCRIBNER'S SONS,/PUBLISHERS, NEW YORK.

1895
Image 13⅛ × 10⁵⁄₁₆ in. (33.2 × 26.2 cm.); *sheet* 15¼ × 12¹⁵⁄₁₆ in. (38.8 × 31.3 cm.)
Commercial relief process; red, blue, and green
Signature R W L (*middle right*)
Published by Charles Scribner's Sons, New York

References Whitehead, p. 28; Richmond 154
41.12.149 [Vonnoh]

Note: Robert Grant, *The Bachelor's Christmas, and Other Stories* (New York: Charles Scribner's Sons, 1895).

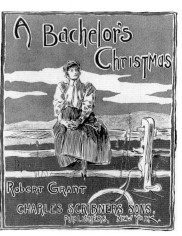

H. M. Lawrence

111 OCTOBER/CENTURY.

1895
Image 17¼ × 10¼ in. (43.8 × 26
  cm.); *sheet* 18¾ × 11¹³⁄₁₆ in. (47.7
  × 30 cm.)
Commercial relief process; blue,
  green, and vermilion
Signature H M L (*lower left*)
Published by The Century Co., New
  York

References DFP 281; Whitehead,
  p. 28; Century and Echo 63;
  Richmond 133; Reims 1128;
  Flood 173
1984.1202.57 [Lauder]; 41.12.154
  [Vonnoh]
Colorplate 39

Joseph Christian Leyendecker

112 THE AUGUST/CENTURY MIDSUMMER HOLIDAY
NUMBER/FIRST PRIZE, CENTURY POSTER CONTEST./
[COPYRIGHT 1896 BY THE CENTURY CO.]/ELIHU
VEDDER,/F. HOPKINSON SMITH,/HENRY J.
HARDENBERGH,/JUDGES.

1896
Image 15 × 14¹⁄₁₆ in. (38.2 × 35.5
  cm.); *sheet* 21⁵⁄₁₆ × 15¹⁵⁄₁₆ in. (54.1
  × 40.4 cm.)
Commercial lithography; yellow,
  green, red, and gold
Signature DESIGNED BY J. C.
  LEYENDECKER. (*lower left corner*)
Published by The Century Co., New
  York
Printer PRINTED FROM

ALUMINUM BY W. B. ORCUTT
  COMPANY, N.Y. (*lower right
  corner*)
References DFP 282; Reims 1239;
  Flood 171
41.12.98 [Vonnoh]; 36.23.5 [Silve];
  57.627.69; 1984.1202.59
  [Lauder]
Colorplate 12

113 August Now Ready/THE INLAND/PRINTER AUGUST/
Price Twenty Cents

1897
Sheet 17 × 10⁵⁄₁₆ in. (43.1 ×
  26.2 cm.)
Commercial relief process; brown on
  brown paper
Signature J. C. Leyendecker/'97
  (*lower right*)
Published by The Inland Printer,
  Chicago
1984.1202.58 [Lauder]

Note: The Inland Printer
  commissioned twelve designs from
  Leyendecker for use as covers and

posters for the magazine during
1897. A descriptive title
accompanied each design; that for
August was "The Sun." *Inland
Printer* exhibited the original
drawings for the twelve designs at
the New York Life Building in
Chicago during January 1898 ("A
Leyendecker Exhibition," *Brush and
Pencil* 1.4 [January 1898], pp.
109, 110).
Colorplate 36

A. W. B. Lincoln

114 DEAD MAN'S COURT/BY/MAURICE H. HERVEY.

1895
Sheet 11¹⁄₁₆ × 14¹⁄₁₆ in. (28.1 × 35.8 cm.)
Commercial lithography; vermilion and black
Signature Lincoln (*lower right corner*)
Published by Frederick A. Stokes Co., New York

References DFP 293; Whitehead, p. 30; Century and Echo 318
41.12.172 [Vonnoh]

Note: Maurice H. Hervey, *Dead Man's Court* (New York: Frederick A. Stokes Co., [1895]).

115 A/White/Baby/by/JAMES WELSH

1895
Image 11¹⁵⁄₁₆ × 8⁷⁄₁₆ in. (30.3 × 21.5 cm.); *sheet* 14⅛ × 11 in. (36.1 × 28 cm.)
Commercial lithography; yellow and blue
Signature Lincoln (*lower right*)
Published by Frederick A. Stokes Co., New York

References Whitehead, p. 30; Richmond 136
41.12.168 [Vonnoh]

Note: James Welsh, *A White Baby* (New York: Frederick A. Stokes Co., [1895]).

Louis Loeb

116 "A Cumberland Vendetta"/A STIRRING THREE-PART STORY OF THE KENTUCKY MOUNTAINS/By JOHN FOX, Jr., author of "A Mountain Europa"/Begins in/THE JUNE/CENTURY/Which contains/[contents]

1894
Image 18¾ × 14 in. (47.7 × 35.6 cm.); *sheet* 19⅞ × 15⅛ in. (50.5 × 38.4 cm.)
Commercial relief process and letterpress; blue, red, and black
Unsigned
Published by The Century Co., New York
References Whitehead, p. 30; Century and Echo 44

41.12.155 [Vonnoh]

Note: The figure of a young rifleman has been isolated from "Why don't ye shoot?," one of Loeb's illustrations for "A Cumberland Vendetta" (*The Century* 48.2 [June 1894], p. 168). The Loeb drawings were engraved by Peter Aitken.

Florence Lundborg

117 What is That/Mother?/THE/LARK/My Child,/FOR/
AUGUST: 5 CTS

1895
Sheet 20⅞ × 15⁷⁄₁₆ in. (53 ×
  39.2 cm.)
Woodcut; brown on light brown
  bamboo paper
Signature F L *(lower left)*
Published by William Doxey, San
  Francisco
References DFP 293; Whitehead,
  p. 30; Century and Echo, illus.
  p. 12; PAFA 344

36.23.12 [Silve]

Note: Lundborg drew the design, but
  Burgess, one of the *Lark* editors,
  cut the block. The paper "is a very
  interesting Bamboo fibre paper
  used in the Chinese drug stores in
  San Francisco" (*The Poster* 1.4
  [April 1896], p. 49).

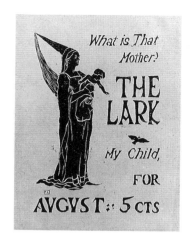

118 THE LARK/NOVEMBER

1895
Sheet 16⅜ × 9⅞ in. (41.5 ×
  25.1 cm.)
Woodcut; green and blue on
  Japanese paper
Signature F L *(lower right corner)*
Published by William Doxey, San
  Francisco
References DFP 296; Whitehead,
  p. 30; Century and Echo, illus.
  p. 12; PAFA 345; Richmond 150

36.23.14 [Silve]; 57.627.6 (2);
  1984.1202.61 [Lauder]

Note: Mt. Tamalpais, one of the
  natural beauties of the Marin
  Peninsula, is the subject.
  Colorplate 5

119 The/LARK/February

1896
Sheet 19⅜ × 11⁷⁄₁₆ in. (49.2 ×
  29.1 cm.)
Woodcut; light green and dark
  green on Japanese paper
Signature F L del Sc. *(lower right
  corner)*
Published by William Doxey, San
  Francisco

References DFP 297; PAFA 490;
  Richmond 151
36.23.15 [Silve]; 1984.1202.62
  [Lauder]

Note: Titled "Robin Hood."

120 The Lark/for May/THE OREAD

1896
Sheet 23¹³⁄₁₆ × 13⅞ in. (60.5 ×
  35.3 cm.)
Woodcut; green and black
Signature F L *(lower left corner)*

Published by William Doxey, San
  Francisco
57.627.6 (3); 36.23.18 [Silve];
  1984.1202.63 [Lauder]

121 THE LARK/AUGUST

1896
Sheet 16¹⁄₁₆ × 12¹⁵⁄₁₆ in. (40.7 × 32.8 cm.)
Woodcut; green, brown, and black
Signature del./F L/sc. (*lower left*)
Published by William Doxey, San Francisco

Reference DFP 298
1984.1202.64 [Lauder]; 36.23.17 [Silve]; 57.627.6(1)

122 THE LARK/NOVEMBER

1896
Sheet 21¹⁄₄ × 14³⁄₈ in. (54.1 × 36.6 cm.)
Woodcut; blue, green, and black
Signature F L/del./Sc. (*lower right corner*)

Published by William Doxey, San Francisco
1984.1202.60 [Lauder]
Colorplate 37

123 FEBRUARY/THE LARK

1897
Sheet 24⁵⁄₁₆ × 12¹⁵⁄₁₆ in. (61.8 × 32.9 cm.)
Woodcut; light brown, brown, and dark brown on brown paper
Signature F L/del/Sc (*middle right*)

Published by William Doxey, San Francisco
1984.1202.65 [Lauder]; 36.23.13 [Silve]

Henry McCarter

124 THE/GREEN/TREE/LIBRARY/FOR SALE HERE/ PUBLISHED BY/STONE & KIMBALL

1894
Image 15⁹⁄₁₆ × 11¹³⁄₁₆ in. (39.5 × 30 cm.); *sheet* 16⁷⁄₁₆ × 12⁹⁄₁₆ in. (41.7 × 31.8 cm.)
Commercial lithography; green, red, and purple
Signature HENRY/McCARTER (*lower left corner*)
Published by Stone and Kimball, Chicago

Printer STROMBERG, ALLEN & CO., PRINTERS, 337–339 DEARBORN ST., CHICAGO. (*lower center*)
References DFP 299; Union League 68; Bolton, p. 9; Quincy 129; Mass. Mech. 186; Whitehead, p. 32; Reims 1241; Flood 195
57.627.10(16)

Blanche McManus

125 The Adventures/OF CAPTAIN HORN/by/FRANK R. STOCKTON/Charles Scribner's Sons Publishers

1895
Sheet 16³/₁₆ × 12 in. (41.2 × 30.5 cm.)
Commercial relief process; yellow, green, and blue
Signature B Mc M (*upper right corner*)
Published by Charles Scribner's Sons, New York
Printer J. E. RHODES. NEW YORK. (*lower right corner*)
References Whitehead, p. 32;

Century and Echo 319; Richmond 156
1986.1005.7 [Lauder]

Note: Frank Richard Stockton, *The Adventures of Captain Horn* (New York: Charles Scribner's Sons, 1895).
Colorplate 11

126 JOSEPH JEFFERSON'S/RIP VAN/WINKLE/ILLUSTRATED/HIS/PLAY/NOW/FIRST/ PUBLISHED/DODD, MEAD & COMPANY. PUBLISHERS NEW YORK

1895
Image 17¹⁵/₁₆ × 11¹⁵/₁₆ in. (45.6 × 30.3 cm.); *sheet* 20⅛ × 13¹⁵/₁₆ in. (51.2 × 35.5 cm.)
Commercial relief process; red and brown on green paper
Signature Blanche/McManus (*lower right*)
Published by Dodd, Mead and Co., New York
References Whitehead, p. 32; Richmond 157; Flood 208

41.12.142 [Vonnoh]

Note: Joseph Jefferson, *Rip Van Winkle, As Played by Joseph Jefferson* (New York: Dodd, Mead and Co., 1895). McManus portrayed Jefferson, one of the most famous actors of the American stage, in his role as Rip Van Winkle. The poster was also printed on yellow paper, according to Whitehead.

127 THE TRUE/MOTHER GOOSE/WITH NOTES AND PICTURES BY/BLANCHE McMANUS/LAMSON WOLFFE & CO BOSTON

ca. 1896
Sheet 21³/₁₆ × 14⁵/₁₆ in. (53.9 × 36.4 cm.)
Commercial relief process; yellow, vermilion, and black
Signature B. McM. (*middle left*)
Publisher COPYRIGHT 1895 BY LAMSON WOLFFE & CO. BOSTON. U.S.A. (*lower right corner*)
Printer HELIOTYPE PTG. CO. BOSTON (*lower left corner*)

References DFP 301; Richmond 158; Reims 1244; Flood 207
1984.1202.66 [Lauder]

Note: Blanche McManus, *The True Mother Goose, Songs for the Nursery; or Mother Goose's Melodies for Children* (Boston: Lamson, Wolffe and Co., 1896). Flood dates the publication of this poster to 1895. The poster may have been issued in advance of the book's publication.

128 "CAPTAINS/COURAGEOUS"/RUDYARD KIPLING'S/AMERICAN NOVEL/The Century Co New York

1897
Image 16⁹/₁₆ × 11½ in. (42 × 29.3 cm.); *sheet* 17¹¹/₁₆ × 12⅛ in. (45 × 32.1 cm.)
Commercial relief process; yellow, red, blue, and black
Signature Blanche McManus (*upper right corner*)
Published by The Century Co., New York

1984.1202.67 [Lauder]

Note: Rudyard Kipling, *Captains Courageous* (New York: The Century Co., 1897).
Colorplate 41

A. J. Moores

129 A New Book/BY RUDYARD KIPLING/THE JUNGLE BOOK/Published by THE CENTURY CO./For Sale Here . . . Price $1.50

1894
Sheet 16¹⁵⁄₁₆ × 12¹⁄₁₆ in. (43 × 30.7 cm.)
Commercial relief process; yellow and black
Unsigned
Published by The Century Co., New York
References Union League 74; Bolton,

p. 10; Quincy 133; Whitehead, p. 34; Century and Echo 95; Flood 190
41.12.179 [Vonnoh]

Note: Rudyard Kipling, *The Jungle Book* (New York: The Century Co., 1894).

130 Across Asia on a Bicycle/THE ADVENTURES OF TWO YOUNG AMERICAN STUDENTS ON A/JOURNEY FROM CONSTANTINOPLE TO PEKING/Published by/THE CENTURY CO./With many illustrations/Price $1.50

1894
Image 10¾ × 15¹⁵⁄₁₆ in. (27.2 × 40.5 cm.); *sheet* 12 × 17 in. (30.5 × 43.1 cm.)
Commercial relief process; orange, light blue, and black
Signature Moores (*lower right corner*)
Published by The Century Co., New York
References Union League 75; see Bolton, p. 10; Quincy 134;

Whitehead, p. 34; Century and Echo 94; Richmond 169; Flood 193
41.12.163 [Vonnoh]

Note: Thomas G. Allen, Jr., and William L. Sachtleben, *Across Asia on a Bicycle* (New York: The Century Co., 1894).

131 CHRIS/AND THE/WONDERFUL/LAMP/A MODERN/ARABIAN NIGHTS/STORY/By/ALBERT STEARNS/Splendidly Illustrated/253 Pages Cloth $1.50/Published by/THE CENTURY CO./NEW YORK

1895
Image 15⅜ × 10⁷⁄₁₆ in. (39 × 26.5 cm.); *sheet* 17 × 12 in. (43.1 × 30.5 cm.)
Commercial relief process and letterpress; vermilion and black
Signature A J M (*lower right corner*)
Published by The Century Co., New York

References Whitehead, p. 34; Century and Echo 90; Richmond 168; Flood 192
41.12.161 [Vonnoh]

Note: Albert Stearns, *Chris and the Wonderful Lamp* (New York: The Century Co., 1895).

Peter Sheaf Hersey Newell

132 LIPPINCOTT'S SERIES/OF SELECT/NOVELS/THE/SPELL/OF/URSULA, BY MRS. ROWLANDS.

1894 (here 1895)
Image 12¹⁄₁₆ × 10 in. (30.6 × 25.4 cm.); *sheet* 13 × 10¹³⁄₁₆ in. (33.1 × 27.4 cm.)
Commercial lithography; yellow, red, and black
Unsigned
Published by J. B. Lippincott Co., Philadelphia
References Bolton, p. 10; Mass. Mech. 207; Whitehead, p. 34; Century and Echo 281
41.12.146 [Vonnoh]

Note: Mrs. Rowlands (pseud. of Effie Adelaide Maria Albanesi), *The Spell of Ursula* (Philadelphia: J. B. Lippincott Co., 1894). This poster, issued in 1894, was reused in 1895 to advertise another book in the series, Bithia Mary Croker's *Mr. Jervis.* Most likely a Lippincott staff artist altered the poster, adding a new title to the book held by the woman.

Maxfield Parrish

133 POSTER SHOW / Pennsylvania / Academy / of the / Fine Arts / Philadelphia
[Separately printed:]
PAINTINGS OF THE GLASGOW SCHOOL. / FOSDICK'S FIRE ETCHINGS. / ACADEMY OF FINE ARTS

1896
Image 30⅝ × 23¾ in. (77.7 × 60.2 cm.); *sheet* 44³⁄₁₆ × 27¹⁵⁄₁₆ in. (112.8 × 71 cm.)
Commercial relief process and letterpress; light brown, brown, dark brown, white, and black; separate text printed in red
Signature Maxfield / Parrish (*lower left corner*)
Publisher not indicated
Printer LEDGER SHOW PRINT. PHILA. (*lower right corner*)
References PAFA 411; Reims 1250; Ludwig 47, p. 213
41.12.218 [Vonnoh]

Note: Parrish's design was used as the catalogue cover and the poster for this exhibition at the Pennsylvania Academy of the Fine Arts, April 1896. A limited number of posters were available to collectors during the exhibition. It is surmised that these posters were pencil-signed

and without the additional text (Jack Rennert, *100 Poster Masterpieces.* Poster Auction V [New York: Phillips Sons and Neale, May 2, 1981], no. 51). According to the introduction to the catalogue, the largest number of posters were pasted up on hoardings around Philadelphia by the American Bill-Posting Co. (*Exhibition of Posters* [Philadelphia: Pennsylvania Academy of the Fine Arts, 1896], p. 4). The exhibitions of the burnt-wood decorations by J. William Fosdick and pictures by artists of the Glasgow School hung concurrently with the posters at the Academy (*The Nineteenth Annual Report, February 3, 1896, to February 1, 1897* [Philadelphia: Pennsylvania Academy of the Fine Arts, 1897], pp. 10, 11).

134 THE CENTURY / Midsummer / Holiday Number. / August. / SECOND PRIZE, CENTURY POSTER CONTEST. / (COPYRIGHT, 1897, BY THE CENTURY CO.) / ELIHU VEDDER, / F. HOPKINSON SMITH, / HENRY J. HARDENBERGH, / JUDGES.

1897 (1896)
Image 18⁹⁄₁₆ × 12 in. (47.1 × 30.6 cm.); *sheet* 19¹⁵⁄₁₆ × 13⁹⁄₁₆ in. (50.5 × 34.5 cm.)
Commercial lithography; yellow, red, blue, and black
Signature Maxfield Parrish (*lower right corner*)
Published by The Century Co., New York

Printer THE THOMAS & WYLIE LITHOGRAPHIC CO. (*lower left corner*)
References DFP 317; Ludwig 52, p. 212
57.627.5(2); 36.23.8 [Silve]; 1984.1202.71 [Vonnoh]
Colorplate 13

135 SCRIBNER'S / FICTION NUM / BER. AUGUST
1897
Image 19½ × 14 (49.5 × 35.6 cm.); *sheet* 19¹³⁄₁₆ × 14⅜ in. (50.3 × 36.5 cm.)
Commercial lithography; light brown, blue, green, dark brown, and black
Signature MAXFIELD / PARRISH / 1897 (*lower right*)

Published by Charles Scribner's Sons, New York
References DFP 316; Ludwig 117, p. 213
1984.1202.69 [Lauder]; 36.23.7 [Silve]; 57.627.5(1)
Colorplate 14

136 Price $1.50/FREE TO/SERVE/E. RAYNER/Boston/
Copeland and Day

1897
Sheet 18⅜ × 12⁹⁄₁₆ in. (46.7 × 31.9 cm.)
Commercial lithography; red and black on mustard-yellow paper
Signature M. P. (*lower right*)
Published by Copeland and Day, Boston
Printer GEO. H. WALKER &

CO. LITH. BOSTON. (*lower left*)
Reference Ludwig 137, p. 213
1984.1202.68 [Lauder]

Note: Emma Rayner, *Free to Serve: A Tale of Colonial New York* (Boston: Copeland and Day, 1897).

137 THE/CHRISTMAS/SCRIBNER'S/[contents]/Special
Christmas/Cover in 9 colors/by Maxfield Parrish

1897
Image 21 × 13³⁄₁₆ in. (53.3 × 33.4 cm.); *sheet* 21⁹⁄₁₆ × 13⅞ in. (54.8 × 35.2 cm.)
Commercial lithography; green, red, and black on mustard-yellow paper
Signature M. P. (*lower center*)

Published by Charles Scribner's Sons, New York
Reference Ludwig 159, p. 213
1984.1202.70 [Lauder]; 57.627.10(7)

William McGregor Paxton

138 THE BOSTON/SUNDAY/HERALD/Ladies Spring Fashions/
March 17

1895
Image 16¹⁄₁₆ × 11¹⁄₁₆ in. (40.8 × 28.1 cm.); *sheet* 19 × 12 in. (48.2 × 30.5 cm.)
Commercial relief process; red and black
Unsigned

Published by Boston Herald
References DFP 680; Bolton, p. 10; Quincy 143; Whitehead, p. 36; Century and Echo 348
1984.1202.139 [Lauder]

Edward Penfield

139 HARPER'S/for/MAY

1893
Sheet 18¾ × 13 in. (47.7 × 33 cm.)
Commercial lithography; blue, yellow, light brown, and red
Unsigned
Published by Harper and Brothers, New York

References DFP 322; Union League 82; Bolton, p. 11; Mass. Mech. 218; Whitehead, p. 36; Century and Echo 326
41.12.59 [Vonnoh]

140 HARPER'S/for/JUNE

1893

Sheet 18⁵⁄₁₆ × 12⁹⁄₁₆ in. (46.5 × 32 cm.)

Commercial lithography; blue, light brown, red, and green on brown paper

Signature EDWARD/PENFIELD (*lower center*)

Published by Harper and Brothers, New York

References DFP 323; Union League 84; Mass. Mech. 219; Whitehead, p. 36

1984.1202.72 [Lauder]

Colorplate 17

141 HARPER'S/AUGUST

1893

Image 18⁷⁄₁₆ × 11⅛ in. (46.8 × 28.3 cm.); *sheet* 19⁵⁄₁₆ × 13½ in. (49.1 × 34.3 cm.)

Commercial lithography; light brown, blue, green, and red-brown

Signature EDWARD/PENFIELD (*lower left corner*)

Published by Harper and Brothers, New York

References DFP 324; Union League 87; Mass. Mech. 221; Whitehead, p. 36

41.12.64 [Vonnoh]

Note: August's gentleman tours the World's Columbian Exhibition in Chicago.

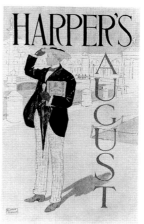

142 HARPER'S/SEPT.

1893

Image 18⁷⁄₁₆ × 12¹⁄₁₆ in. (46.9 × 30.7 cm.); *sheet* 19½ × 13½ in. (49.5 × 34.8 cm.)

Commercial lithography; light brown, red, and blue

Signature EDWARD/PENFIELD (*lower left*)

Published by Harper and Brothers, New York

References DFP 325; Union League 89; Mass. Mech. 222; Whitehead, p. 36

41.12.63 [Vonnoh]

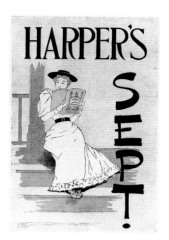

143 HARPER'S/OCTOBER

1893

Sheet 16⅝ × 11⁷⁄₁₆ in. (42.3 × 29 cm.)

Commercial lithography; blue, light brown, yellow, and red

Signature EDWARD/PENFIELD (*lower center*)

Published by Harper and Brothers, New York

References DFP 326; Union League 92; Quincy 157; Mass. Mech. 223; Whitehead, p. 36

41.12.62 [Vonnoh]

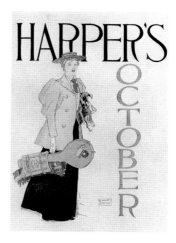

144 HARPER'S/NOVEMBER

1893

Image 17 × 11¹⁵/₁₆ in. (43.2 × 30.4 cm.); *sheet* 19½ × 13½ in. (49.6 × 34.4 cm.)

Commercial lithography; gray, yellow, blue, and red

Signature EDWARD/PENFIELD (*center*)

Published by Harper and Brothers, New York

References DFP 327; Union League 94; Mass. Mech. 224; Whitehead, p. 36

41.12.66 [Vonnoh]

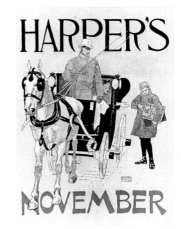

145 HARPER'S/CONTENTS/[contents]/CHRISTMAS NUMBER

1893

Sheet 18½ × 12 in. (47 × 30.4 cm.)

Commercial lithography and letterpress; gray, yellow, red, and black

Signature E. P. (*lower center*)

Published by Harper and Brothers, New York

References Mass. Mech. 225; Whitehead, p. 36; Century and Echo 327

41.12.52 [Vonnoh]

146 HARPER'S/JANUARY

1894

Sheet 17¼ × 11⅞ in. (43.8 × 30.1 cm.)

Commercial lithography; yellow, red, blue, and black

Signature EDWARD PENFIELD (*lower right*)

Published by Harper and Brothers, New York

References DFP 328; Union League 78; Quincy 145; Mass. Mech. 226; Whitehead, p. 36

1984.1202.73 [Lauder]

147 HARPER'S/FEBRUARY

1894

Sheet 16 × 11¼ in. (40.6 × 28.5 cm.)

Commercial lithography; gray, yellow, red, blue, and dark brown

Signature EDWARD PENFIELD (*lower left corner*)

Published by Harper and Brothers, New York

References DFP 329; Union League 79; Quincy 146; Mass. Mech. 227; Whitehead, p. 36

41.12.56 [Vonnoh]

148 HARPER'S/FOR/MARCH

1894

Image 15⅝ × 11¹³⁄₁₆ in. (39.8 × 33 cm.); *sheet* 17¹⁄₁₆ × 13½ in. (44.6 × 34.3 cm.)

Commercial lithography; orange, light brown, and dark brown

Signature EDWARD PENFIELD (*lower right corner*)

Published by Harper and Brothers, New York

References DFP 330; Union League 80; Quincy 147; Mass. Mech. 228; Whitehead, p. 36

41.12.72 [Vonnoh]

149 HARPER'S/MAY

1894

Image 16⅛ × 13 in. (41 × 33 cm.); *sheet* 16¼ × 13³⁄₁₆ in. (41.4 × 33.4 cm.)

Commercial lithography; blue, yellow, and red

Signature EDWARD PENFIELD (*lower right center*)

Published by Harper and Brothers, New York

References DFP 332; Union League 83; Bolton, p. 11; Quincy 148; Mass. Mech. 230; Whitehead, p. 36

1984.1202.74 [Lauder]

150 HARPER'S/JUNE

1894

Image 16⅜ × 12½ in. (41.6 × 31.9 cm.); *sheet* 16⅞ × 13 in. (42.8 × 33 cm.)

Commercial lithography; blue, yellow, and vermilion

Signature EDWARD/PENFIELD (*lower left corner*)

Published by Harper and Brothers, New York

References DFP 333; Union League 85; Bolton, p. 11; Quincy 152; Mass. Mech. 231; Whitehead, p. 36; Century and Echo 328

41.12.67 [Vonnoh]

Note: The couple are rowing on the Harlem River; the High Bridge is in front of them.

151 HARPER'S/JULY

1894

Sheet 18 × 12⅝ in. (45.8 × 32 cm.)

Commercial lithography; light brown, blue, and yellow

Signature EDWARD/PENFIELD (*lower left corner*)

Published by Harper and Brothers, New York

References DFP 334; Bolton, p. 11; Quincy 153; Mass. Mech. 232; Whitehead, p. 36; Century and Echo 329; Reims 1254

1984.1202.75 [Lauder]; 41.12.61 [Vonnoh]

152 HARPER'S/AUGUST

1894

Image 16½ × 12⅜ in. (42 × 31.5 cm.); *sheet* 16¾ × 12⅝ in. (42.5 × 32 cm.)

Commercial lithography; yellow, blue, red, and black

Signature EDWARD/PENFIELD (*lower right corner*)

Published by Harper and Brothers, New York

References DFP 335; Union League 88; Bolton, p. 11; Quincy 154; Mass. Mech. 233; Whitehead, p. 36

57.627.9(8); 41.12.70 [Vonnoh]; 54.582.5 [Dufner]; 1984.1202.76 [Lauder]

Note: Penfield inscribed a copy of this poster (54.582.5) "to/ Will H. Bradley/ from his admiring/ friend/ Edward Penfield/ Sep. 11/94."

153 HARPER'S/SEPTEMBER

1894

Sheet 16⁷⁄₁₆ × 10⅝ in. (41.6 × 27.1 cm.)

Commercial lithography; blue, yellow, and red

Signature EDWARD/PENFIELD (*lower left*)

Published by Harper and Brothers, New York

References DFP 336; Union League 90; Bolton, p. 11; Quincy 154; Mass. Mech. 234; Whitehead, p. 36; Century and Echo 330; Reims 1255

57.627.9(13); 41.12.71 [Vonnoh]; 1984.1202.83 [Lauder]

Note: The poster exists in what may be another state, without the front set of weaving marks on the seat of the rocker (41.12.71).

Colorplate 18

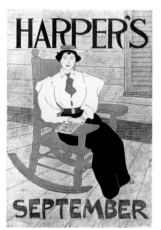

154 HARPER'S/OCTOBER

1894

Image 17⅛ × 12¾ in. (43.4 × 32.3 cm.); *sheet* 17¾ × 13¼ in. (44.9 × 33.7 cm.)

Commercial lithography; blue, yellow, and red

Signature EDWARD/PENFIELD (*lower left corner*)

Published by Harper and Brothers, New York

References DFP 337; Union League 93; Bolton, p. 11; Quincy 156; Mass. Mech. 235; Whitehead, p. 36; Century and Echo 331

41.12.48 [Vonnoh]; 57.627.9(19)

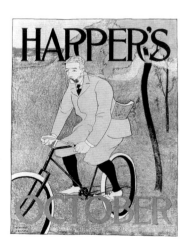

155 HARPER'S/NOVEMBER

1894

Sheet 18 × 12¹¹⁄₁₆ in. (45.7 × 32.1 cm.)

Commercial lithography; blue, yellow, and vermilion

Signature EDWARD/PENFIELD (*lower left corner*)

Published by Harper and Brothers, New York

References DFP 338; Union League 95; Bolton, p. 11; Mass. Mech. 236; Whitehead, p. 36; Century and Echo 332

41.12.69 [Vonnoh]; 57.627.9(39)

156 HARPER'S/CHRISTMAS

1894
Sheet 18³/₁₆ × 12⁵/₁₆ in. (46.2 ×
  31.3 cm.)
Commercial lithography; blue,
  yellow, and red
Signature EDWARD PENFIELD
  (*lower left corner*)
Published by Harper and Brothers,
  New York

References DFP 339; Union League
  96; Bolton, p. 11; Mass. Mech.
  237; Whitehead, p. 36; Century
  and Echo 333; PAFA 369;
  Richmond 179; Reims 1256
  36.23.26 [Silve]; 57.627.9 (38)

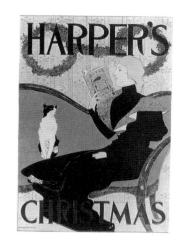

**157 THE FUR-SEAL'S/TOOTH/by/Kirk Munroe/Illustrated by/
W. A. Rogers/Begun in/HARPER'S/YOUNG/PEOPLE/
MARCH 6, 1894**

1894
Sheet 18¹¹/₁₆ × 13¾ in. (47.4 ×
  34.9 cm.)
Commercial lithography; gray, blue,
  yellow, and red
Signature EDWARD PENFIELD
  (*lower left corner*)
Published by Harper and Brothers,
  New York
Reference Quincy 168

41.12.81 [Vonnoh]

Note: Kirk Munroe, *The Fur-Seal's
Tooth: A Story of Alaskan Adventure*
(New York: Harper and Brothers,
1894). The serialized story was
published in book form later in
1894.

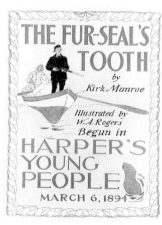

**158 OUR/ENGLISH/COUSINS/BY RICHARD/HARDING/
DAVIS/ILLUSTRATED/HARPER & BROTHERS/NEW
YORK**

1894
Sheet 14⅞ × 17⅞ in. (37.9 ×
  45.3 cm.)
Commercial relief process and
  letterpress; vermilion and black
Signature E. P. (*lower left*)
Published by Harper and Brothers,
  New York

References see Bolton, p. 12; Mass.
  Mech. 262; Whitehead, p. 38
  41.12.50 [Vonnoh]

Note: Richard Harding Davis, *Our
English Cousins* (New York: Harper
and Brothers, 1894).

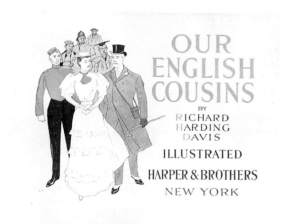

**159 PASTIME/STORIES/BY/THOMAS/NELSON/PAGE/
ILLUSTRATED/HARPER &/BROTHERS/NEW-YORK**

1894
Sheet 16³/₁₆ × 11½ in. (41 ×
  29.2 cm.)
Commercial relief process; black and
  vermilion
Signature EDWARD/PENFIELD
  (*lower left corner*)
Published by Harper and Brothers,
  New York

References see Bolton, p. 12; Mass.
  Mech. 252; Whitehead, p. 38
  41.12.80 [Vonnoh]

Note: Thomas Nelson Page, *Pastime
Stories* (New York: Harper and
Brothers, 1894).

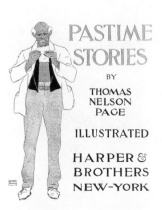

160 VIGNETTES/OF/MANHATTAN/BY/BRANDER/
MATTHEWS/ILLUSTRATED/HARPER/& BROTHERS/
PUBLISHERS

1894
Image 12¹³⁄₁₆ × 9⅜ in. (32.6 × 23.9
cm.); *sheet* 16¹¹⁄₁₆ × 11½ in. (42.4
× 29.2 cm.)
Commercial lithography; yellow,
vermilion, and blue
Signature EDWARD/PENFIELD
(*lower right corner*)
Published by Harper and Brothers,
New York

Reference Whitehead, p. 38
41.12.49 [Vonnoh]

Note: James Brander Matthews,
Vignettes of Manhattan (New York:
Harper and Brothers, 1894).

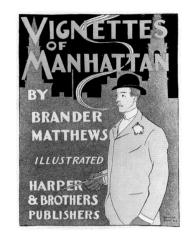

161 HARPER'S/JANUARY

1895
Sheet 18 × 12¹³⁄₁₆ in. (45.7 ×
32.6 cm.)
Commercial lithography; yellow,
red, and blue
Signature EDWARD PENFIELD
(*lower right corner*)
Published by Harper and Brothers,
New York

References DFP 340; Bolton, p. 11;
Quincy 161; Mass. Mech. 238;
Whitehead, p. 36; Century and
Echo 334; PAFA 365; Richmond
180; Reims 1257
1984.1202.77 [Lauder]; 41.12.68
[Vonnoh]; 57.627.9(11)

162 HARPER'S/FEBRUARY

1895
Image 18³⁄₁₆ × 12⅝ in. (46.1 × 32.1
cm.); *sheet* 18⅜ × 12¹⁵⁄₁₆ in. (46.7
× 32.9 cm.)
Commercial lithography; blue,
yellow, and vermilion
Unsigned
Published by Harper and Brothers,
New York

References DFP 341; Bolton, p. 11;
Quincy 162; Mass. Mech. 239;
Whitehead, p. 36; Century and
Echo 335; Richmond 181; Reims
1258; Flood 252
1984.1202.78 [Lauder];
57.627.9(56)

163 HARPER'S/MARCH

1895
Sheet 19¼ × 13⅞ in. (48.9 ×
35.1 cm.)
Commercial lithography; gray, light
green, yellow, red, and blue
Signature EDWARD/PENFIELD
(*lower right*)
Published by Harper and Brothers,
New York

References DFP 342; Bolton, p. 11;
Quincy 163; Mass. Mech. 240;
Whitehead, p. 36; Century and
Echo 336; Richmond 182; Reims
1259; Flood 253
41.12.51 [Vonnoh]; 36.23.29
[Silve]; 57.627.9(46);
1984.1202.79 [Lauder]

164 JOAN of ARC/BY THE/MOST/POPULAR/MAGAZINE/
WRITER/BEGINS IN/APRIL/HARPER'S

1895
Sheet 17⅞ × 12¹¹⁄₁₆ in. (45.4 ×
  32.3 cm.)
Commercial lithography; black,
  yellow, and red
Signature EDWARD/PENFIELD
  (*lower right*)
Published by Harper and Brothers,
  New York
References DFP 343; Bolton, p. 12;
  Quincy 164; Mass. Mech. 241;
  Whitehead, p. 36; Century and

Echo 337; PAFA 366; Richmond
  183; Reims 1260
57.627.9(50); 41.12.60 [Vonnoh]

Note: Mark Twain, one of "the most
  popular magazine writers" of his
  day, wrote the short story "Saint
  Joan of Arc," which was published
  ca. 1897 by Harper and Brothers
  in book form, with illustrations by
  Howard Pyle.

165 HARPER'S/MAY

1895
Sheet 16¹³⁄₁₆ × 13⅜ in. (42.7 ×
  34 cm.)
Commercial lithography; light
  green, blue, yellow, purple, and
  vermilion
Signature EDWARD/PENFIELD
  (*lower right corner*)

Published by Harper and Brothers,
  New York
References DFP 344; Quincy 165;
  Mass. Mech. 242; Whitehead,
  p. 36; Richmond 184;
  Reims 1261
41.12.57 [Vonnoh]; 57.627.9(57)

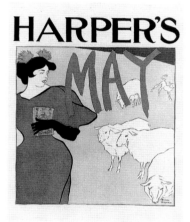

166 HARPER'S/JUNE

1895
Sheet 18¼ × 12¹³⁄₁₆ in. (46.4 ×
  32.6 cm.)
Commercial lithography; light
  green, yellow, red, and blue
Signature EDWARD/PENFIELD
  (*middle left*)
Published by Harper and Brothers,
  New York

References DFP 345; Quincy 166;
  Mass. Mech. 243; Whitehead,
  p. 36; Richmond 185; Reims
  1262; Flood 254
41.12.54 [Vonnoh]; 57.627.9(2);
  1984.1202.80 [Lauder]

167 HARPER'S/The/German/Struggle/for/Liberty/JULY

1895
Sheet 21⅝ × 14³⁄₁₆ in. (55.1 ×
  36 cm.)
Commercial lithography; gray, blue,
  yellow, and red
Unsigned
Published by Harper and Brothers,
  New York

References DFP 346; Mass. Mech.
  244; Whitehead, p. 36; Richmond
  186; Reims 1263; Flood 260
57.627.9(52); 41.12.55 [Vonnoh];
  1984.1202.81 [Lauder]

168 HARPER'S/AUGUST

1895

Sheet 18⅝ × 12 in. (47.4 × 30.4 cm.)

Commercial lithography; light green, brown, purple, red, and black

Unsigned

Published by Harper and Brothers, New York

References DFP 347; Mass. Mech. 245; Whitehead, p. 38; Century and Echo 338; Richmond 187; Reims 1264

36.23.30 [Silve]; 57.627.9(33); 1984.1202.82 [Lauder]

169 HARPER'S/SEPTEMBER/[contents]

1895

Image 13³⁄₁₆ × 9 in. (33.5 × 22.9 cm.); *sheet* 13½ × 9⁵⁄₁₆ in. (34.2 × 23.7 cm.)

Commercial relief process and letterpress; red, blue, and green on light green paper

Signature EDWARD PENFIELD (*lower center*)

Published by Harper and Brothers, New York

References DFP 348; Mass. Mech. 246; Whitehead, p. 38; Richmond 188; Reims 1265

41.12.74 [Vonnoh]; 57.627.9(20)

170 HARPER'S/OCTOBER

1895

Sheet 15³⁄₁₆ × 11¼ in. (38.1 × 28.5 cm.)

Commercial lithography; green, brown, blue, yellow, and red

Signature EDWARD PENFIELD (*lower right corner*)

Published by Harper and Brothers, New York

References DFP 349; Mass. Mech. 247; Whitehead, p. 38; Century and Echo, illus. p. 14; PAFA 363; Richmond 189; Reims 1266

41.12.58 [Vonnoh]; 57.627.9(54)

171 HARPER'S/NOVEMBER

1895

Sheet 16⁵⁄₁₆ × 11¾ in. (41.4 × 29.8 cm.)

Commercial lithography; yellow, blue, and red

Unsigned

Published by Harper and Brothers, New York

References DFP 350; Mass. Mech. 248; Whitehead, p. 38; PAFA 367; Richmond 190; Reims 1267

41.12.73 [Vonnoh]; 1984.1202.84 [Lauder]

Note: In honor of the National Horse Show, Penfield has an elegantly dressed couple inspect one of the entries. According to *The Poster* (1.2 [February 1896], p. 22), the model for the gentleman was the popular young novelist Richard Harding Davis.

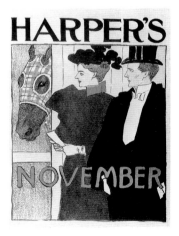

172 [contents]/HARPER'S/CHRISTMAS

1895
Sheet 25½ × 20¼ in. (64.8 ×
  51.5 cm.)
Commercial lithography; yellow,
  red, and blue
Signature EDWARD PENFIELD/
  1895 (*lower left corner*)
Published by Harper and Brothers,
  New York

References DFP 351; Whitehead,
  p. 38; Century and Echo 339;
  PAFA 381; Richmond 191;
  Reims 1268
41.12.47 [Vonnoh]

173 PEOPLE/WE/PASS/Stories of Life/among the Masses/of New
     York City/By/Julian Ralph/Illustrated/Harper & Brothers/
     Publishers

1895
Image 13¹¹⁄₁₆ × 9¹⁵⁄₁₆ in. (34.8 ×
  25.2 cm.); *sheet* 16⁹⁄₁₆ × 11½ in.
  (42.1 × 29.3 cm.)
Commercial relief process and
  letterpress; vermilion and black
Signature EDWARD PENFIELD
  (*upper right corner*)
Published by Harper and Brothers,
  New York
References DFP 368; see Mass. Mech.
  253, Whitehead, p. 38; Century
  and Echo 412; PAFA 394;
  Richmond 174
41.12.79 [Vonnoh]

Note: Julian Ralph, *People We Pass:
Stories of Life Among the Masses of
New York City* (New York: Harper
and Brothers, 1896). In *People We
Pass*, Penfield acknowledged his
debt to Steinlen's humorous
illustrations of Parisian daily life,
which appeared in such magazines
as *Gil Blas*. Penfield lent the
drawing to the exhibition of
posters sponsored by the
Massachusetts Charitable Mechanic
Association (October 2 to
November 30, 1895, Boston).

174 ORIENT/CYCLES/Lead the/Leaders/WALTHAM/M'F'G CO
     [separately printed] Cor. 12th & Walnut Sts.,/
     PHILADELPHIA.

ca. 1895–96
Image 39¹³⁄₁₆ × 26¹⁄₁₆ in. (101.3 ×
  66.3 cm.); *sheet* 42 × 28⅛ in.
  (106.8 × 71.4 cm.)
Commercial lithography with
  letterpress additions; yellow,
  orange-red, gray, and black
Signature EDWARD/PENFIELD
  (*lower left corner*)
Published by Waltham Manufacturing
Co.

Printer J. Ottmann/LITH. CO./
  PUCK B'L'D'G. N.Y. (*lower left
  corner*)
References Richmond 177;
  Reims 1279
1984.1202.121 [Lauder]
Colorplate 15

175 AETNA/DYNAMITE
1895
Image 18¹⁄₁₆ × 13¼ in. (45.8 ×
  33.6 cm.); *sheet* 18⁷⁄₈ × 14³⁄₁₆ in.
  (47.8 × 36 cm.)
Commercial lithography; yellow,
  blue, and red
Signature EDWARD PENFIELD
  (*lower left corner*)

Published by Aetna Powder Company
Printer THE POSTER ART PRESS,
  ART PRINTERS, CHICAGO
  (*lower right corner*)
References Whitehead, p. 38;
  Century and Echo 344
1987.1010 [Lauder]

176 In Washington's Day/By/Woodrow/Wilson/Illustrated/by/
    Howard/Pyle/Begins/in/HARPER'S/JANUARY
1896
Image 17¹⁄₁₆ × 11 in. (43.3 × 28
  cm.); *sheet* 17⁵⁄₁₆ × 11⁵⁄₁₆ in. (43.8
  × 28.7 cm.)
Commercial lithography; gray,
  yellow, vermilion, and blue
Unsigned

Published by Harper and Brothers,
  New York
References DFP 352; PAFA 514;
  Richmond 192; Reims 1269;
  Flood 255
57.627.9(23)

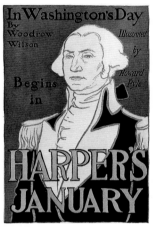

177 HARPER'S/FEBRUARY
1896
Sheet 19¹⁄₁₆ × 10¹³⁄₁₆ in. (48.5 ×
  27.5 cm.)
Commercial lithography; yellow,
  red, blue, and black
Signature EDWARD PENFIELD
  (*lower left corner*)

Published by Harper and Brothers,
  New York
References DFP 353; Richmond 193;
  Reims 1270
1984.1202.85 [Lauder]; 41.12.78
  [Vonnoh]; 57.627.9(17)

178 HARPER'S/MARCH
1896
Sheet 18⁷⁄₁₆ × 10¹⁵⁄₁₆ in. (46.8 ×
  27.9 cm.)
Commercial lithography; brown,
  yellow, red, and blue
Signature EDWARD PENFIELD
  (*upper left corner*)

Published by Harper and Brothers,
  New York
References DFP 354; Richmond 195;
  Reims 1271; Flood 256
1984.1202.86 [Lauder];
  57.627.9(47)

179 HARPER'S / APRIL

1896
Image 17⅝ × 13⅛ in. (44.8 × 33.3
cm.); *sheet* 17⅞ × 13⅜ in. (45.5 ×
34 cm.)
Commercial lithography; gray,
yellow, orange, green, and black
Signature Bull's-head logo (middle left)

Published by Harper and Brothers,
New York
References DFP 355; Richmond 196;
Reims 1272; Flood 257
1984.1202.87 [Lauder];
57.627.9(55)

180 HARPER'S / MAY

1896
Sheet 17¾ × 11⅞ in. (45.1 ×
30.2 cm.)
Commercial lithography; gray,
yellow, vermilion, and black
Signature EDWARD PENFIELD
(lower right corner)
Published by Harper and Brothers,
New York

References DFP 356; Richmond 197;
Reims 1273; Flood 258
1984.1202.88 [Lauder];
57.627.9(37)
Colorplate 43

181 HARPER'S / JUNE

1896
Sheet 18¹³⁄₁₆ × 13¾ in. (47.8 ×
34.9 cm.)
Commercial lithography; gray,
yellow, green, red, and black
Signature EDWARD PENFIELD
(upper left corner)

Published by Harper and Brothers,
New York
References DFP 357; Richmond 198;
Reims 1274; Flood 259
1984.1202.89 [Lauder]; 36.23.31
[Silve]; 57.627.9(25)

182 HARPER'S / JULY

1896
Sheet 18¹¹⁄₁₆ × 13⅞ in. (47.4 ×
35.8 cm.)
Commercial lithography; light
green, red, and blue
Signature Bull's-head logo (lower right)
Published by Harper and Brothers,
New York

References DFP 358; Reims 1275;
Flood 260
1984.1202.90 [Lauder]; 36.23.24
[Silve]; 57.627.9(15)

183 TOM/SAWYER/DETECTIVE/a new story/by/MARK
TWAIN/begins in/this number/HARPER'S/AUGUST

1896
Sheet 18⅝ × 13⅝ in. (47.3 ×
34.7 cm.)
Commercial lithography; gray,
yellow, red, and black
Signature Bull's-head logo/EDWARD/
PENFIELD (*lower left corner*)

Published by Harper and Brothers,
New York
References DFP 359; Reims 1276;
Flood 261
36.23.3 [Silve]; 57.627.9(1);
1984.1202.91 [Lauder]

184 HARPER'S/SEPTEMBER

1896
Sheet 18³⁄₁₆ × 13¹¹⁄₁₆ in. (46.2 ×
34.8 cm.)
Commercial lithography; red,
yellow, blue, and green
Signature Bull's-head logo (*lower right*)
Published by Harper and Brothers,
New York

References DFP 360; Reims 1277;
Flood 262
1984.1202.72 [Lauder]; 36.23.27
[Silve]; 57.627.9(34)

185 HARPER'S/OCTOBER

1896
Sheet 18¼ × 13¹³⁄₁₆ in. (46.4 ×
35.1 cm.)
Commercial lithography; purple,
light green, yellow, red, and blue
Signature EDWARD PENFIELD.
(*lower left corner*)

Published by Harper and Brothers,
New York
References DFP 361; Flood 263
1984.1202.93 [Lauder]; 36.23.34
[Silve]; 57.627.9(53)
Colorplate 19

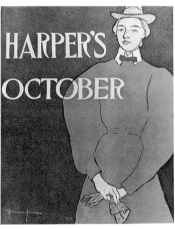

186 HARPER'S/NOVEMBER

1896
Sheet 17¹⁵⁄₁₆ × 13⅝ in. (45.5 ×
34.7 cm.)
Commercial lithography; green,
yellow, red, and black
Signature Bull's-head logo/EDWARD/
PENFIELD (*upper right corner*)

Published by Harper and Brothers,
New York
References DFP 362; Flood 264
1984.1202.94 [Lauder]; 36.23.35,
36 [Silve]; 57.627.9(42)

187 HARPER'S/CHRISTMAS

1896
Sheet 17⁵⁄₁₆ × 12⁷⁄₈ in. (43.9 ×
   32.8 cm.)
Commercial lithography; green,
   yellow, red, and black
Signature EDWARD/PENFIELD/
   bull's-head logo (upper right)

Published by Harper and Brothers,
   New York
References DFP 363; Flood 265
1984.1202.95 [Lauder]; 36.23.28
   [Silve]; 57.627.9(43)

188 THREE GRINGOS IN CENTRAL/AMERICA AND VENEZUELA/BY RICHARD HARDING DAVIS/ ILLUSTRATED/HARPER & BROTHERS. N.Y.

1896
Sheet 17⁷⁄₁₆ × 11⁹⁄₁₆ in. (44.3 ×
   29.4 cm.)
Commercial relief process; yellow,
   green, red, and black
Signature EDWARD PENFIELD
   (middle left)
Published by Harper and Brothers,
   New York
References DFP 369; Richmond 176;
   Reims 1280
1986.1005.8 [Lauder]

Note: Richard Harding Davis, *Three
Gringos in Venezuela and Central
America* (New York: Harper
and Brothers, 1896). William

Clemens praised the "ingenious
and sensational novelty" of
Penfield's *Three Gringos* poster (*The
Poster* 1.5 [May 1896], p. 60). The
drawing, unique in Penfield's
work, indicates a working
knowledge of Gauguin's Tahitian
paintings and drawings, which he
presumably knew through
illustrations in French periodicals,
as yet unidentified. However, the
large areas of flat color are clearly
Penfield's own.
Colorplate 42

189 ON/SNOW/SHOES/TO THE/BARREN/GROUNDS/By/ CASPAR W. WHITNEY/2600 MILES/AFTER/MUSK OXEN/ AND/WOOD BISON/NOW APPEARING/IN/HARPER'S/ MAGAZINE

1896
Image 17¾ × 11¹⁄₁₆ in. (45.1 × 28.1
   cm.); *sheet* 18³⁄₁₆ × 11⁷⁄₁₆ in. (46.2
   × 29.1 cm.)
Commercial lithography; blue, red,
   and brown
Signature EDWARD PENFIELD
   (lower left corner)
Published by Harper and Brothers,
   New York

References DFP 366; PAFA 396;
   Richmond 194; Reims 1278;
   Flood 275
57.627.9(18); 41.12.53 [Vonnoh]

Note: Caspar W. Whitney, *On Snow
Shoes to the Barren Grounds* (New
York: Harper and Brothers, 1896).

190 Ride a/STEARNS/and be/content

1896

Image 53⅞ × 40¼ in. (136.9 ×
  102.3 cm.); *sheet* 55¾ × 42⁵⁄₁₆ in.
  (141.6 × 107.5 cm.)
Commercial lithography; orange,
red, gray, and black
Signature EDWARD PENFIELD
  (*upper right corner*)

Published by Stearns Manufacturing
Company
Printer J. Ottmann/Lith. Co./Puck
B'l'd'g. N.Y. (*lower right corner*)
Reference Flood 273
1984.1202.124 [Lauder]
Colorplate 16

191 [Poster Calendar for 1897, R. H. Russell and Son, New York]

1896

Sheet (A–E) 14 × 10³⁄₁₆ in. (35.5 ×
  25.8 cm.)
Commercial relief process and
lithography; green, yellow, red,
and black (A); green, yellow, blue,
and red (B–E)
Published by R. H. Russell and Son,
New York
References DFP 373; Flood 271
36.23.1 [Silve]; 65.658.40;
  1984.1202.123 [Lauder]

Note: Penfield's 1897 poster calendar
for R. H. Russell and Son was
announced in an advertisement in
Bradley: His Book (2.2 [December
1896], n.p.), at fifty cents. A
special edition of 250 copies,
printed on Imperial Japan paper,

numbered and signed by the artist;
was available for two dollars each;
the Lauder copy is number 82.
Proof sheets of the four calendar
pages, the outlines of the designs,
and the calendars themselves,
printed in black and red, are
included with this copy. It is
initialed, but neither individually
numbered nor signed by the artist
as advertised. The separate sheets
are kept together with a green cord
suitable for hanging from a hook.
The calendar was reissued in 1898
with appropriate changes
(*Illustrated and Descriptive List of the
Publications of R. H. Russell* [New
York, 1897], n.p.).

191A [Cover] POSTER/CALENDAR/1897/Published by/R. H.
Russell & Son/NEW YORK

Signature EDWARD/PENFIELD
  (*upper left corner*)
36.23.1(1) [Silve]; 65.658.40(1);
  1984.1202.123(1) [Lauder]

Note: The Metropolitan Museum also
has a proof of the cover as issued,
on the full sheet of paper and

before mounting on board
(measuring 17⁵⁄₁₆ × 12 in. [44 ×
30.5 cm.]; 1984.1202.122
{Lauder]).
Colorplate 44

191B   1897/JANUARY/FEBRUARY/MARCH

Signature EDWARD/PENFIELD
(lower left corner)

65.658.40(2); 36.23.1(2) [Silve];
1984.1202.123(2,3) [Lauder]

191C   APRIL MAY JUNE

Signature EDWARD/PENFIELD
(middle right)

65.658.40(3); 36.23.1(3) [Silve];
1984.1202.123(4,5) [Lauder]

191D   JULY AUGUST SEPTEMBER

Signature EDWARD/PENFIELD
(lower left corner)

36.23.1(4) [Silve]; 65.658.40(4);
1984.1202.123(6,7) [Lauder]

191E   OCTOBER NOVEMBER DECEMBER

Signature Bull's-head logo/EDWARD/
PENFIELD *(middle right)*

36.23.1(5) [Silve]; 65.658.40(5);
1984.1202.123(8,9) [Lauder]

192 HARPER'S/1897/THE JANUARY NUMBER CONTAINS/
[contents]

1897
Sheet 18⁵/₁₆ × 13⁹/₁₆ in. (46.5 ×
34.4 cm.)
Commercial lithography and
letterpress; yellow, vermilion,
green, brown, and black
Signature EDWARD/PENFIELD/
bull's-head logo (*upper right corner*)

Published by Harper and Brothers,
New York
References DFP 374; Flood 266
57.627.9(16)

193 HARPER'S/FEBRUARY

1897
Sheet 19 × 14 in. (48.3 × 35.5 cm.)
Commercial lithography; gray,
yellow, orange, brown, and black
Signature EDWARD PENFIELD
(*lower right corner*)
Published by Harper and Brothers,
New York

References DFP 375; Flood 267
36.23.2 [Silve]; 57.627.9(24);
1984.1202.96 [Lauder]
Frontispiece

194 HARPER'S/MARCH

1897
Sheet 13¹⁵/₁₆ × 19 in. (35.5 ×
48.2 cm.)
Commercial lithography; yellow,
vermilion, gray, and blue
Signature EDWARD PENFIELD
(*lower left corner*)
Published by Harper and Brothers,
New York
References DFP 376; Flood 268

1984.1202.97 [Lauder];
57.627.9(21)

Note: Penfield adapted a design by
Pierre Bonnard, illustrated and
briefly discussed in *The Studio*
(9.43 [October 1896], pp. 67,
68). Bonnard's four-paneled,
lithographed screen was printed in
1896.

195 HARPER'S/APRIL

1897
Sheet 18³/₈ × 12⁷/₈ in. (46.6 ×
32.7 cm.)
Commercial lithography; gray,
yellow, red, and blue
Signature EDWARD PENFIELD
(*lower left corner*)

Published by Harper and Brothers,
New York
References DFP 377; Flood 269
57.627.9(35); 36.23.25 [Silve];
1984.1202.98 [Lauder]

196 HARPER'S/MAY

1897
Sheet 18⁷⁄₁₆ × 13¼ in. (47.1 × 33.7 cm.)
Color lithography; brown, yellow, red, and blue-black
Signature EDWARD/PENFIELD/ *bull's-head logo* (*upper left corner*)

Published by Harper and Brothers, New York
References DFP 378; Flood 270
57.627.9(40); 36.23.33 [Silve];
1984.1202.99 [Lauder]

197 HARPER'S/JUNE

1897
Sheet 14⁵⁄₁₆ × 18¹¹⁄₁₆ in. (36.4 × 47.5 cm.)
Commercial lithography; yellow, red, blue, and black
Signature EDWARD PENFIELD (*lower right corner*)

Published by Harper and Brothers, New York
Reference DFP 379
1984.1202.100 [Lauder];
57.627.9(28)

198 HARPER'S/JULY

1897
Sheet 14 × 19⅛ in. (35.6 × 48.7 cm.)
Commercial lithography; yellow, red, and black
Signature EDWARD/PENFIELD/ LONDON (*lower right corner*)
Published by Harper and Brothers, New York
Reference DFP 380
1984.1202.101 [Lauder];
57.627.9(5)

Note: In April 1897, Penfield

married Jennie Judd Walker, the daughter of a railroad executive. The honeymoon was spent in Europe, and the bride's father joined them on the voyage. The couple on shipboard here are presumably the artist's bride and father-in-law (David Gibson, *Designed to Persuade: The Graphic Art of Edward Penfield* [Yonkers: The Hudson River Museum, 1984], p. 14).

199 HARPER'S/AUGUST

1897
Sheet 18½ × 13¼ in. (47.1 × 33.7 cm.)
Commercial lithography; yellow, red, blue, and green
Signature EDWARD/PENFIELD (*lower right corner*)

Published by Harper and Brothers, New York
Reference DFP 381
57.627.9(27); 1984.1202.102 [Lauder]

200 HARPER'S/SEPTEMBER

1897
Sheet 13¼ × 18⅜ in. (33.6 ×
  46.8 cm.)
Commercial lithography; yellow,
  brown, vermilion, green, and blue
Signature EDWARD/PENFIELD
  (*upper right corner*)

Published by Harper and Brothers,
  New York
Reference DFP 382
1984.1202.103 [Lauder];
  57.627.9(49)

201 HARPER'S/OCTOBER

1897
Image 19³⁄₁₆ × 14⅛ in. (48.7 × 35.9
  cm.); *sheet* 19⅜ × 14⁵⁄₁₆ in. (49.3
  × 36.4 cm.)
Commercial lithography; brown,
  green, red, and black
Signature EDWARD PENFIELD
  (*lower right corner*)

Published by Harper and Brothers,
  New York
Reference DFP 383
1984.1202.104 [Lauder];
  57.627.9(10)
Colorplate **20**

202 HARPER'S NOVEMBER

1897
Image 13⅞ × 19³⁄₁₆ in. (35.3 × 48.7
  cm.); *sheet* 14¼ × 19⁷⁄₁₆ in. (36.2
  × 49.4 cm.)
Commercial lithography; light
  brown, dark brown, green, and
  black
Signature EDWARD PENFIELD
  (*lower left corner*)

Published by Harper and Brothers,
  New York
Reference DFP 384
57.627.9(3); 36.23.32 [Silve];
  1984.1202.105 [Lauder]

203 HARPER'S/CHRISTMAS

1897
Sheet 18¹³⁄₁₆ × 13³⁄₁₆ in. (47.8 ×
  33.5 cm.)
Commercial lithography; yellow,
  brown, gray, vermilion, and black
Signature EDWARD PENFIELD
  (*lower right corner*)

Published by Harper and Brothers,
  New York
Reference DFP 385
57.627.9(4); 1984.1202.106
  [Lauder]

204 ENGLISH/SOCIETY/GEORGE/DU MAURIER/HARPER &/ BROTHERS/PUBLISHERS/NEW YORK

1897
Sheet 19¹³⁄₁₆ × 12⁷⁄₁₆ in. (50.3 × 31.7 cm.)
Commercial lithography; black
Signature Bull's-head logo (lower left corner)
Published by Harper and Brothers, New York

References DFP 370; Flood 274
1986.1005.9 [Lauder]

Note: George Du Maurier, *English Society* (New York: Harper and Brothers, 1897).

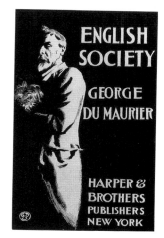

205 THE MARTIAN/BY DU MAURIER/HARPER/& BROTHERS

1897
Sheet 20½ × 12⅞ in. (52 × 32.7 cm.)
Commercial lithography; yellow, green, blue, and brown
Unsigned
Published by Harper and Brothers, New York
Reference DFP 412
1984.1202.119 [Lauder]

Note: George Du Maurier, *The*

Martian, A Novel (New York: Harper and Brothers, 1897). Edgar Breitenbach thought that this poster was unlike the work of Penfield and suggested an attribution to Fred Hyland ("Review: Das frühe Plakat in Europa und den U.S.A., Vol. I," *Art Bulletin* 57.3 [September 1975], p. 458).

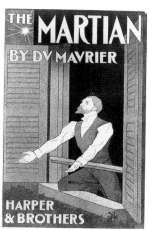

206 HARPER'S/JANUARY/CONTAINS/{contents}

1898
Sheet 18¹³⁄₁₆ × 13¹⁵⁄₁₆ in. (47.8 × 35.4 cm.)
Commercial lithography and letterpress; yellow, vermilion, and black

Signature Bull's-head logo (lower center)
Published by Harper and Brothers, New York
Reference DFP 386
57.627.9(14)

207 HARPER'S/FEBRUARY

1898
Sheet 18¹⁵⁄₁₆ × 13¼ in. (48.6 × 33.6 cm.)
Commercial lithography; orange, green, and black
Signature E P *(upper left corner)*

Published by Harper and Brothers, New York
Reference DFP 387
1984.1202.107 [Lauder];
57.627.9(12)

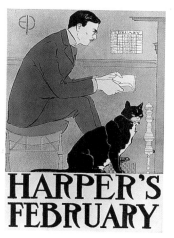

208 STIRRING/TIMES IN/AUSTRIA/DESCRIBED/BY/MARK/
TWAIN/IN/HARPER'S/MARCH

1898
Sheet 15⅝ × 12½ in. (39.7 ×
  31.7 cm.)
Commercial lithography; yellow,
  vermilion, and black
Unsigned

Published by Harper and Brothers,
  New York
Reference DFP 388
57.627.9(31)

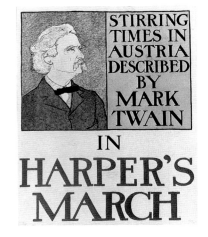

209 HARPER'S/APRIL '98

1898
Image 15⁹⁄₁₆ × 9⅛ in. (39.5 × 23.1
  cm.); *sheet* 16¹⁄₁₆ × 9⅝ in. (40.9 ×
  24.4 cm.)
Commercial lithography; yellow,
  vermilion, blue, and black
Unsigned
Published by Harper and Brothers,
  New York
Reference DFP 389

57.627.9(29); 1984.1202.108
[Lauder]

Note: This design was also used for
  the printed cover of W. G. Van T.
  Sutphen's *The Golficide and Other
  Tales of the Fair Green* (New York:
  Harper and Brothers, 1898).

210 HARPER'S/MAY

1898
Image 15⁹⁄₁₆ × 9¹⁄₁₆ in. (39.6 × 23
  cm.); *sheet* 16⅛ × 9⁹⁄₁₆ in. (41 ×
  24.3 cm.)
Commercial lithography; yellow,
  blue, and vermilion
*Signature Bull's-head logo (lower left
  corner)*

Published by Harper and Brothers,
  New York
Reference DFP 390
57.627.9(7)

211 HARPER'S/JUNE

1898
Image 8¹⁵⁄₁₆ × 15¹¹⁄₁₆ in. (22.8 ×
  39.8 cm.); *sheet* 9⅜ × 16¹⁄₁₆ in.
  (23.8 × 40.8 cm.)
Commercial lithography; blue,
  yellow, and vermilion
*Signature Bull's-head logo (lower left
  corner)*

Published by Harper and Brothers,
  New York
Reference DFP 391
1984.1202.109 [Lauder]

212 HARPER'S/JULY

1898

Image 8¹⁵⁄₁₆ × 14½ in. (22.8 × 36.9 cm.); *sheet* 9⁵⁄₁₆ × 14¾ in. (23.6 × 37.5 cm.)

Commercial lithography; orange, green, and black

Signature Bull's-head logo (lower center, within planter)

Published by Harper and Brothers, New York

Reference DFP 392

57.627.9(26)

213 HARPER'S/AUGUST

1898

Image 12½ × 10 in. (31.7 × 25.5 cm.); *sheet* 12⅞ × 10⅜ in. (32.7 × 26.4 cm.)

Commercial lithography; yellow, red-orange, dark green, and black

Signature Bull's-head logo (upper right corner)

Published by Harper and Brothers, New York

Reference DFP 393

1984.1202.110 [Lauder]; 57.627.9(44)

214 HARPER'S/SEPTEM-/BER

1898

Image 13⅜ × 11⅝ in. (34 × 29.5 cm.); *sheet* 13⅝ × 11¹⁵⁄₁₆ in. (34.7 × 30.5 cm.)

Commercial lithography; yellow, red, and blue

Unsigned

Published by Harper and Brothers, New York

Reference DFP 394

57.627.9(36); 1984.1202.111 [Lauder]

215 HARPER'S/OCTOBER

1898

Sheet 16¹⁵⁄₁₆ × 11¹³⁄₁₆ in. (43 × 30 cm.)

Commercial lithography; yellow, gray, and black

Signature Bull's-head logo (upper right)

Published by Harper and Brothers, New York

Reference DFP 395

1984.1202.112 [Lauder]; 57.627.9(22)

216 HARPER'S/NOV'B'R

1898

Image 11 1/16 × 18 5/16 in. (28 × 46.2 cm.); *sheet* 11 1/2 × 18 5/8 in. (29.2 × 47.3 cm.)

Commercial lithography; yellow, gray-blue, and black

Signature Bull's-head logo (lower left corner)

Published by Harper and Brothers, New York

Reference DFP 396

1984.1202.113 [Lauder]; 57.627.9(51)

217 HARPER'S/JANUARY

1899

Image 11 1/8 × 19 1/16 in. (28.3 × 48.4 cm.); *sheet* 11 1/2 × 19 3/8 in. (29.3 × 49.3 cm.)

Commercial lithography; yellow, blue, vermilion, and black

Signature Bull's-head logo (in horse's harness)

Published by Harper and Brothers, New York

Reference DFP 397

57.627.9(6); 1984.1202.114 [Lauder]

218 The SPANISH/AMERICAN WAR/in its Political Naval/& Military Aspects/By Senator Lodge/Begins in/HARPER'S/FEBRUARY

1899

Image 17 1/4 × 7 15/16 in. (43.9 × 20.2 cm.); *sheet* 17 3/4 × 8 3/8 in. (45.1 × 21.3 cm.)

Commercial lithography; brown, black, and orange

Unsigned

Published by Harper and Brothers, New York

Reference DFP 398

1986.1005.10 [Lauder]

Note: The portrait is of Henry Cabot Lodge (1850–1924), senator from Massachusetts.

219 HARPER'S/MARCH

1899

Image 15 × 10 5/16 in. (38.1 × 26.2 cm.); *sheet* 15 3/8 × 10 11/16 in. (39 × 27.3 cm.)

Commercial lithography; brown, black, green, and red

Unsigned

Published by Harper and Brothers, New York

Reference DFP 399

57.627.9(45); 1984.1202.115 [Lauder]

220 HARPER'S/APRIL

1899
Image 9⅞ × 9¹⁄₁₆ in. (25.2 × 23 cm.); *sheet* 10¹⁄₁₆ × 9³⁄₁₆ in. (25.6 × 23.4 cm.)
Commercial lithography; yellow, gray, green, and black
Signature Bull's-head logo (lower left corner)

Published by Harper and Brothers, New York
Reference DFP 400
57.627.9(30)

221 HARPER'S/MAY

1899
Sheet 10⅝ × 8⁷⁄₁₆ in. (27 × 21.5 cm.)
Commercial lithography; yellow, red-brown, and green
Unsigned

Published by Harper and Brothers, New York
Reference DFP 401
57.627.9(48)

222 HARPER'S/JUNE

1899
Image 12¹¹⁄₁₆ × 9¹⁵⁄₁₆ in. (32.2 × 25.3 cm.); *sheet* 13¹⁄₁₆ × 10¼ in. (33.2 × 26 cm.)
Commercial lithography; yellow, green, red, and black

Unsigned
Published by Harper and Brothers, New York
Reference DFP 402
1984.1202.116 [Lauder]

223 HARPER'S/JULY

1899
Image 9⅝ × 12⁵⁄₁₆ in. (24.4 × 31.2 cm.); *sheet* 9¹⁵⁄₁₆ × 12⅝ in. (25.3 × 32 cm.)
Commercial lithography; yellow, blue, vermilion, and black
Unsigned

Published by Harper and Brothers, New York
Reference DFP 403
57.627.9(32); 1984.1202.117 [Lauder]

224 HARPER'S/AUGUST

1899
Image 11¾ × 10¹⁵⁄₁₆ in. (29.8 ×
27.8 cm.); *sheet* 12⁵⁄₁₆ × 11⁷⁄₁₆ in.
(31.3 × 29 cm.)
Commercial lithography; blue,
black, and red
Unsigned

Published by Harper and Brothers,
New York
Reference DFP 404
1984.1202.118 [Lauder];
57.627.9(41)

**225 The NORTHAMPTON/THE/NORTHAMPTON CYCLE
CO./NORTHAMPTON, MASS.**

ca. 1899
Image 40 × 26³⁄₈ in. (101.5 × 67
cm.); *sheet* 41⁷⁄₁₆ × 28⅛ in. (105.3
× 71.4 cm.)
Commercial lithography; yellow,
brown, red, gray, and black
Signature EDWARD PENFIELD
(*lower right*)

Published by The Northampton Cycle
Co.
Printer J. OTTMANN LITHO.
CO., PUCK B'LD'G. N.Y. (*lower
right corner*)
1984.1202.120 [Lauder]
Colorplate 53

E. Pickert

**226 THE NEW YORK/TIMES/SUNDAY, FEB. 9/32 PAGES OF
GOOD READING, INCLUDING:/[contents]**

1895
Image 27¹⁄₁₆ × 17¹⁄₁₆ in. (68.7 ×
43.4 cm.); *sheet* 30¼ × 19¹⁵⁄₁₆ in.
(76.8 × 50.7 cm.)
Commercial lithography and
letterpress; light brown, yellow,
orange, purple, green, black, and
dark blue
Signature E P/95 (*upper right corner*)
Published by The New York Times
Printer LIEBLER & MAASS. LITH.
N.Y (*lower left corner*)
References Richmond 207; Reims
1126 (as anonymous)
1984.1202.125 [Lauder]

Note: Traditionally this poster has
been ascribed to De Yongh, despite
the "E P" in the upper right
corner. La Forgue, in his chapter
on American posters in *Les Affiches
étrangères illustrées*, illustrated the

poster and gave De Yongh as the
designer. De Yongh provided a
number of poster designs for *The
New York Times*, several in a
mosaic-tile style, including one for
the Easter issue of 1896 (M.
Bauwens et al., *Les Affiches
étrangères illustrées* [Paris: C.
Tallandier, 1897], pp. 177, 180).
The organizers of the benefit
exhibition for Old Dominion
Hospital in Richmond listed
Pickert as the designer (*Poster Show
Benefit Old Dominion Hospital*
[Richmond, 1896], no. 207).
Pickert's name did not appear in
other exhibition catalogues of the
1890s.
Colorplate 21

E. S. Pierce

227   THE BOSTONIAN/FEBRUARY.

ca. 1895
Sheet 13¹⁵⁄₁₆ × 11¹³⁄₁₆ in. (35.4 × 30 cm.)
Commercial lithography; black and red

Signature E S PIERCE (*lower center*)
Published by The Bostonian
1986.1005.11 [Lauder]

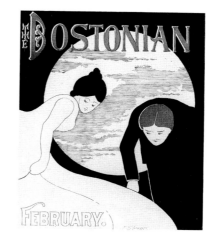

Bruce Porter

228   THE LARK/for May—five cents

1895
Sheet 18⅜ × 12⁵⁄₁₆ in. (46.7 × 31.4 cm.)
Linocut and hand-applied watercolor; yellow and black on light brown paper, with green watercolor
Unsigned
Published by The Lark, San Francisco

References Mass. Mech. 263; Whitehead, p. 38; PAFA 504; Richmond 149
36.23.16 [Silve]

Note: The blocks for Porter's poster were cut by Paul Bernhardt (*The Lark* 1.11 [April 1896]).

Edward Henry Potthast

229   THE JULY NUMBER/JULY/THE CENTURY

1896
Image 20¹⁄₁₆ × 14¹⁄₁₆ in. (51 × 35.7 cm.); *sheet* 20⅞ × 15¹⁄₁₆ in. (53.1 × 38.2 cm.)
Commercial lithography; yellow, purple, brown, green, and red
Signature E P/Designed by EDWARD POTTHAST. (*lower left corner*)
Published by The Century Co., New York

Printer Printed from Aluminum by W. B. ORCUTT COMPANY, N.Y. (*lower right corner*)
References DFP 413; Reims 1281; Flood 249
1984.1202.126 [Lauder]; 57.627.67

Maurice Brazil Prendergast

230 ON THE POINT/JOSEPH KNIGHT COMPANY PUBLISHERS./NATHAN HASKELL DOLE.

1895
Image 13 × 8¹⁄₁₆ in. (33 × 20.5 cm.);
  sheet 16½ × 11¼ in. (41.8 ×
  28.6 cm.)
Commercial relief process; yellow,
  blue, and black
Signature M B P (*lower right corner*)
Published by Joseph Knight Co.,
  Boston
References Whitehead, p. 38;
  Century and Echo, illus. p. 15;
  Richmond 199
1986.1005.12 [Lauder]

Note: Nathan Haskell Dole, *On the*

Point: A Summer Idyll (Boston: Joseph Knight Co., 1895). The contemporary exhibition catalogues cite this poster as the work of H. B. Pennell. However, the initials closely resemble those used by Prendergast on his monotypes and watercolors of the 1890s. He supplied several poster designs for Joseph Knight Co. This design is nearly identical to that of the printed cover of Dole's novel.

Ethel Reed

231 THE BOSTON/SUNDAY/HERALD/[*on paper:*] EVERY LADY WILL READ FASHION SUPPLEMENT MARCH 24

1895
Image 14⁹⁄₁₆ × 10¹⁵⁄₁₆ in. (37.1 ×
  27.8 cm.); *sheet* 18¹⁵⁄₁₆ × 12⅜ in.
  (48.1 × 31.4 cm.)
Commercial relief process; black and
  orange
Signature E. REED (*lower right*)

Published by The Boston Herald
References DFP 433; Bolton, p. 12;
  Quincy 176; Mass. Mech. 270;
  Whitehead, p. 40; Century and
  Echo 351; PAFA 451
1984.1202.135 [Lauder]

232 The Best Guide to Boston/Boston Illustrated/For Sale Here: Price 50 cents

1895
Image 14⅜ × 7¹³⁄₁₆ in. (36.6 × 19.9
  cm.); *sheet* 18⅞ × 12 in. (48.1 ×
  30.4 cm.)
Commercial lithography; green on
  yellow-green paper
Signature ETHEL REED (*lower right
  center*)
Published by The Boston Daily
  Advertiser (?)
References DFP 434; Mass. Mech.
  283; Whitehead, p. 40
1984.1202.136 [Lauder]

Note: Whitehead also listed an impression of this poster on white

paper. In August 1895, Reed's design appeared in altered form, welcoming the triennial conclave of the Knights Templar. A knight on horseback replaced Reed's fashionably dressed young lady; the background of State House dome and Common trees remained the same. The Knights Templar poster, signed by W. F. Hersey, was published by *The Boston Daily Advertiser*, which may therefore have commissioned Reed's original design.

233 UNCLE SAM'S CHURCH/BY/JOHN BELL BOUTON/
LAMSON,/WOLFFE & CO. PUBLISHERS/6. Beacon Street
BOSTON

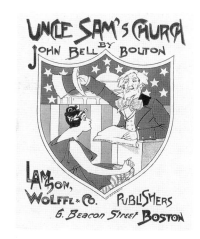

1895
Sheet 18^{15}/$_{16}$ × 15 in. (48.1 ×
38.2 cm.)
Commercial relief process; black,
blue, and red
Signature E. REED (*lower center*)
Publisher COPYRIGHT, 1895, BY
LAMSON, WOLFFE & CO. (*lower
center*)
References DFP 423; see Bolton,

p. 12; Quincy 178; Whitehead,
p. 40; Century and Echo 353;
Richmond 211; Reims 1291;
Flood 292
41.12.188 [Vonnoh]

Note: John Bell Bouton, *Uncle Sam's
Church* (Boston: Lamson, Wolffe
and Co., 1895).

234 ARABELLA AND/ARAMINTA STO-/RIES BY GERTRU-/
DE SMITH WITH/XV PICTURES BY/ETHEL REED/
BOSTON COPE-/LAND AND DAY/PRICE $2.00 NET

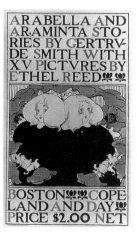

1895
Image 26⅛ × 14½ in. (66.4 × 36.9
cm.); *sheet* 27⅛ × 15^{7}/$_{16}$ in. (69.1
× 39.2 cm.)
Commercial lithography; black, red,
and yellow
Signature ETHEL REED (*lower right*)
Published by Copeland and Day,
Boston
Printer GEO. H. WALKER & CO.
LITH. BOSTON (*lower left corner*)

References Century and Echo 360;
PAFA 452; Flood 289
1984.1202.128 [Lauder]

Note: Gertrude Smith, *The Arabella
and Araminta Stories* (Boston:
Copeland and Day, 1895).
Colorplate 47

235 Albert Morris Bagby's NEW NOVEL/MISS TRÄUMEREI./
LAMSON, WOLFFE, & CO. 6, BEACON ST. BOSTON./
SOLD HERE PRICE $1.50

1895
Image 18⅜ × 12⅜ in. (46.6 × 31.5
cm.); *sheet* 21^{15}/$_{16}$ × 13⅜ in. (55.8
× 34.5 cm.)
Commercial lithography; yellow and
black
Signature ETHEL REED (*lower right
corner*)
Publisher COPYRIGHT, 1895, BY
LAMSON, WOLFFE & CO.
BOSTON. (*lower center*)
References DFP 417; see Bolton,

p. 12; Mass. Mech. 276;
Whitehead, p. 40; Century and
Echo 354; PAFA 447; Richmond
208; Reims 1288; Flood 296
1984.1202.129 [Lauder]; 41.12.83
[Vonnoh]; 57.627.8(1)

Note: Albert Morris Bagby, *Miss
Träumerei, A Weimar Idyll* (Boston:
Lamson, Wolffe and Co., 1895).

236 Behind the Arras/by/Bliss Carman/Lamson, Wolffe, and Co/
Boston and New York.

1895
Image 18^{9}/$_{16}$ × 9⅞ in. (47.1 × 25
cm.); *sheet* 27⅞ × 19^{7}/$_{16}$ in. (70.8
× 49.4 cm.)
Commercial lithography; black and
gold on brown paper
Signature ETHEL REED (*middle
right*)
Publisher COPYRIGHT, 1895, BY
LAMSON, WOLFFE & CO.
BOSTON (*lower right*)
Printer ARMSTRONG & CO.
LITH. BOSTON. (*lower right*)
References DFP 418; see Mass. Mech.
275; Whitehead, p. 40; Century
and Echo, illus. p. 14; PAFA 448;

Richmond 219; Reims 1282;
Flood 297
41.12.222 [Vonnoh];
1984.1202.130 [Lauder]

Note: Bliss Carman, *Behind the Arras,
A Book of the Unseen* (Boston:
Lamson, Wolffe and Co., 1895).
The poster was also printed on
gray paper. The Lauder impression was signed and inscribed
"Number/49" by the artist,
probably as one of a special edition
for poster collectors.

237 THE HOUSE OF THE/TREES and other Poems/BY ETHELWYN WETHERALD/PUBLISHED BY LAMSON, WOLFFE/AND COMPANY, SIX BEACON/STREET, BOSTON NEW YORK:/LIFE BUILDING/SOLD HERE, PRICE, $1.50

1895

Image 12⁵⁄₁₆ × 8 in. (31.2 × 20.4 cm.); *sheet* 18 × 9¹⁵⁄₁₆ in. (45.7 × 23.7 cm.)

Commercial relief process; black and green on light blue paper

Signature E. REED (*lower right*)

Publisher COPYRIGHT, 1895, LAMSON WOLFFE & CO. (*lower center*)

References DFP 419; Mass. Mech. 278; Whitehead, p. 40; Century and Echo 356; Richmond 214; Reims 1285; Flood 295
1986.1005.13 [Lauder]; 41.12.171 (vignette only) [Vonnoh]

Note: Ethelwyn Wetherald, *The House of Trees and Other Poems* (Boston: Lamson, Wolffe and Co., 1895). The poster also appears on white paper, as in the clipped impression in the Museum's collection and in complete form at the New York Public Library. The book was printed at the Everett Press in Boston; the poster was probably printed at the same place (Nancy Finlay, *Artists of the Book in Boston, 1890–1910* [Cambridge: Harvard College Library, 1985], pp. 23–25).

238 Fairy Tales/Mabel F. Blodgett./Lamson, Wolffe & Co./Boston and New York

1895

Sheet 26⁷⁄₁₆ × 18¹⁵⁄₁₆ in. (67.2 × 48.1 cm.)

Commercial lithography; gray, yellow, flesh, brown, black, and red

Signature ETHEL REED (*lower center*)

Publisher Copyright 1895 by Lamson Wolffe & Co./Boston USA (*lower right corner*)

Printer HELIOTYPE PRINTING CO. BOSTON (*lower center*)

References DFP 420; see Mass. Mech. 280; PAFA 450; Richmond 210; Flood 291
1984.1202.131 [Lauder]

Note: Mabel Blodgett, *Fairy Tales* (Boston: Lamson, Wolffe and Co., 1895).

239 Folly or Saintliness/José Echegaray/Lamson Wolffe and Co/Boston and New York

1895

Image 19³⁄₁₆ × 13⁷⁄₈ in. (48.8 × 35.2 cm.); *sheet* 20⅛ × 15¹⁄₁₆ in. (51.1 × 38.2 cm.)

Commercial lithography; white and black on orange paper

Signature ETHEL REED (*lower center*)

Publisher COPYRIGHT 1895 BY LAMSON WOLFFE & CO. BOSTON. U.S.A. (*middle left*)

Printer HELIOTYPE PTG. CO. – BOSTON (*lower right corner*)

References DFP 421; see Mass. Mech. 273; PAFA 445; Richmond 216; Reims 1284; Flood 294
1984.1202.132 [Lauder]; 57.627.8(2)

Note: José Echegaray y Eizaguirre, *Folly or Saintliness* (Boston: Lamson, Wolffe and Co., 1895).

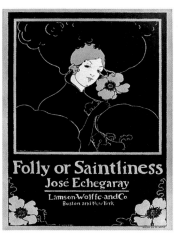

240 Is Polite Society Polite/And Other Essays By/MRS. JULIA WARD HOWE/Lamson, Wolffe, & Co./Boston. Six Beacon St. New York. Life Building

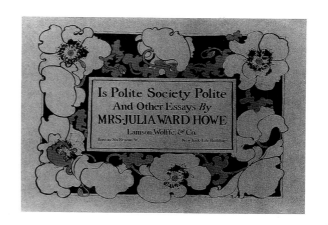

1895
Sheet 17½ × 25 in. (44.5 × 63.6 cm.)
Commercial lithography; black and olive green on red paper
Signature ETHEL REED (*lower center*)
Published by Lamson, Wolffe and Co., Boston
References DFP 422; Mass. Mech. 277; Whitehead, p. 40; Century and Echo 358; PAFA 444; Richmond 209; Reims 1286; Flood 290
1986.1005.14 [Lauder]

Note: Julia Ward Howe, *Is Polite Society Polite? and Other Essays* (Boston: Lamson, Wolffe and Co.,

1895). William Clemens wrote (*The Poster* 1.3 [March 1896], p. 37):

No production by Miss Ethel Reed has been praised more highly than the poster issued by Lamson, Wolffe & Co., to advertise a volume of essays, "Is Polite Society Polite," by Mrs. Julia Ward Howe. This is a purely decorative piece of work, but well drawn and very effective. It is lithographed on imported handmade paper, red in color, and printed in olive green and black. It is truly a work of art.

Colorplate 45

241 THE WHITE WAMPUM/By E. PAULINE JOHNSON/ (Tekahionwake)/LAMSON, WOLFFE & CO/PUBLISHERS & IMPORTERS/6 Beacon St., Boston—Life Building, New-York./SOLD HERE

1895
Sheet 21⅝ × 15¹⁵⁄₁₆ in. (55 × 40.5 cm.)
Commercial relief process; yellow and dark blue on red paper
Signature ETHEL REED (*lower center*)
Published by Lamson, Wolffe and Co., Boston
References DFP 424; see Mass. Mech. 272; Whitehead, p. 40; Century

and Echo 359; PAFA 446; Richmond 218; Reims 1293; Flood 293
41.12.147 [Vonnoh]

Note: Emily Pauline Johnson, *The White Wampum* (Boston: Lamson, Wolffe and Co., 1895). The poster was also printed on brown paper.

242 A VIRGINIA COUSIN &/BAR HARBOR TALES/BY/MRS. BURTON HARRISON/LAMSON WOLFFE & CO BOSTON & NEW YORK/PRICE $1.25

1895
Sheet 24¹¹⁄₁₆ × 17¹³⁄₁₆ in. (62.8 × 43.5 cm.)
Commercial lithography; black and red on pink paper
Unsigned
Published by Lamson, Wolffe and Co., Boston
References DFP 427; see Mass. Mech.

279; Whitehead, p. 40; PAFA 449; Reims 1292
1984.1202.133 [Lauder]

Note: Constance Harrison, *A Virginia Cousin and Bar Harbor Tales* (Boston: Lamson, Wolffe and Co., 1895).

243 Jacques Damour/by Emile Zola/Englished by Wm Foster
Apthorp/Boston/Copeland and Day/Price $1.25 net

1895
Sheet 18½ × 11⅞ in. (47.1 ×
30.1 cm.)
Commercial lithography; blue,
yellow, and red on laid paper with
MBM watermark
Signature ETHEL REED (*lower center*)
Published by Copeland and Day,
Boston

References DFP 428; Whitehead,
p. 40; Century and Echo 355;
Richmond 212; Reims 1287;
Flood 287
1984.1202.134 [Lauder]

Note: Émile Zola, *Jacques Damour*
(Boston: Copeland and Day, 1895).

244 PIERRE/PUVIS/DE CHAVANNES/A SKETCH/LILY LEWIS
ROOD/L. PRANG & COMPANY. BOSTON

1895
Sheet 21 × 15⁷⁄₁₆ in. (53.4
× 39.3 cm.)
Commercial lithography; yellow,
green, and black
Signature ETHEL REED (*lower right
corner*)
Published and printed by Louis Prang
and Co., Boston

References PAFA 453; Richmond 215;
Reims 1290
41.12.194 [Vonnoh]

Note: Lily Lewis Rood, *Pierre Puvis
de Chavannes, A Sketch* (Boston:
Louis Prang and Co., 1895).

245 In Childhood's Country/By Louise Chandler/Moulton
Pictur-/ed by Ethel Reed/Boston: Copeland and/Day
Price $2.00

1896
Sheet 25¹⁄₁₆ × 11³⁄₈ in. (63.7 ×
28.9 cm.)
Commercial lithography; yellow,
pink, blue, and black
Signature ETHEL REED (*upper right
corner*)
Published by Copeland and Day,
Boston
Printer Geo. H. Walker & Co. Lith.
Boston. (*lower right corner*)

References DFP 430; Flood 288
1984.1202.137 [Lauder]

Note: Louise Chandler Moulton, *In
Childhood's Country* (Boston:
Copeland and Day, 1896).
Colorplate 24

246 TIME/AND THE/HOUR
1896
Sheet 18⁵⁄₁₆ × 13⁷⁄₁₆ in. (46.6 ×
34.2 cm.)
Commercial relief process; red and
black on gray oatmeal paper
Signature ETHEL REED (*lower center*)
Published by Time and the Hour,
Boston
1984.1202.138 [Lauder]

Note: This poster was published after

Reed's departure for Europe in May
1896. It was illustrated, printed in
gray and red, in the magazine's Art
Supplement, together with a
related poem by Louise Chandler
Moulton (*Time and the Hour* 1.13
[June 6, 1896], between
pp. 10 and 11).
Colorplate 23

Frederic Remington

247 REMINGTON/in Cuba/for/COLLIER'S WEEKLY

1899

Image 22¹³⁄₁₆ × 16¾ in. (58.1 × 42.6 cm.); *sheet* 24⁵⁄₁₆ × 18 in. (61.4 × 45.7 cm.)

Commercial lithography; buff, black, and vermilion

Signature Frederic Remington/ Havana/Cuba (*lower right corner*)

Published by Collier's Magazine, New York

Printer H. A. THOMAS & WYLIE, LITH. CO. N.Y. (*lower right corner*)

44.36.1 {Card}

Note: Remington's "A First Class Fighting Man" was used by the editors of *Collier's Magazine* as a poster and as a double-page spread in the March 25, 1899, issue. Remington probably drew this image directly on the printing surface before embarking for Cuba, taking some liberty in signing the drawing "Havana/Cuba." He was also in Cuba the previous year; the original sketch may have come from that trip.

Louis John Rhead

248 LUNDBORG'S/PERFUMES

1894

Image 17⁵⁄₁₆ × 11½ in. (43.9 × 29.3 cm.); *sheet* 17⅞ × 12 in. (45.4 × 30.5 cm.)

Commercial lithography; purple, yellow, light green, dark green, and red

Signature LOUIS RHEAD (*lower right*)

Published by Lundborg's Perfumes, New York

Printer COPYRIGHT, 1894, THE GAST LITH. & ENG. CO. N.Y. (*lower left corner*)

References DFP 436; see Mass. Mech. 298; Whitehead, p. 42; Century and Echo 369; Poster-NY 30; Richmond 228; White 29; probably Flood 322

1985.1051.1 {Lauder}

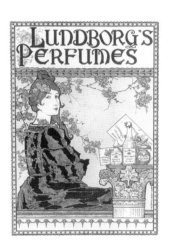

249 CENTURY/MAGAZINE/MIDSUMMER HOLIDAY NUMBER THE CENTURY CO. NEW YORK

1894

Image 13⁷⁄₁₆ × 18⁹⁄₁₆ in. (34.1 × 47.1 cm.); *sheet* 14⁷⁄₁₆ × 19⅝ in. (36.7 × 49.9 cm.)

Commercial lithography; yellow, blue, red, and black

Signature LOUIS/RHEAD (*lower right corner*)

Published by The Century Co., New York

References Bolton, p. 13; Quincy 182; Whitehead, p. 40; Century and Echo 56; Poster-NY 12; PAFA 422; Richmond 230; White 12

1985.1129.4 {Lauder}; 41.12.90 {Vonnoh}

Colorplate 46

250 ST. NICHOLAS/FOR YOUNG/FOLKS/EDITED BY/MARY MAPES DODGE/AUGUST/HOLIDAY NUMBER/NOW READY/THE CENTURY CO. NEW YORK

1894

Image 13¼ × 9⅞ in. (33.6 × 25.1 cm.); *sheet* 14¹⁄₁₆ × 10¾ in. (35.7 × 27.3 cm.)

Commercial lithography; yellow, blue, red, and black

Signature LOUIS RHEAD (*lower right corner*)

Published by The Century Co., New York

References Union League 106 (?); Bolton, p. 13; Whitehead, p. 40; Century and Echo 33; Poster-NY 17; PAFA 440; White 17; Flood 302

41.12.195 {Vonnoh}

251 L. PRANG & CO'S/HOLIDAY/PUBLICATIONS

1895

Image 20¹¹⁄₁₆ × 15⁷⁄₁₆ in. (52.6 ×
39.2 cm.); *sheet* 21¹⁵⁄₁₆ × 16⅛ in.
(55.7 × 41 cm.)
Commercial lithography; yellow-
green, light purple, green, dark
purple, and red
Signature L J/RHEAD (*lower right
corner*)

Published and printed by Louis Prang
and Co., Boston
References DFP 460; Mass. Mech.
307; Whitehead, p. 42; Century
and Echo 375; Poster-NY 34; PAFA
435; Richmond 225; White 33;
Reims 1313; Flood 311
41.12.156 [Vonnoh]

**252 MEADOW-GRASS/BY ALICE BROWN $1.50 NET/
BOSTON/COPELAND AND DAY**

1895

Image 13 × 7⁹⁄₁₆ in. (33.1 × 19.3
cm.); *sheet* 16¹⁵⁄₁₆ × 9⅞ in. (43 ×
25.2 cm.)
Commercial lithography; dark green
and gold on light green paper
Signature RHEAD (*lower right corner*)
Published by Copeland and Day,
Boston
Printer GEO. H. WALKER & CO.
LITH. BOSTON . (*lower right
corner*)
References DFP 444; Mass. Mech.

308, 309; Whitehead, p. 42;
Century and Echo 374; Poster-NY
56; White 57; Flood 307
1984.1202.141 [Lauder]

Note: Alice Brown, *Meadow-Grass:
Tales of New England Life* (Boston:
Copeland and Day, 1895). Rhead's
design, highlighted with gold,
was also printed on the cover of
the book.
Colorplate 26

**253 MEADOW-GRASS/BY ALICE BROWN/PAPER COVERS—
PRICE 50¢/BOSTON/COPELAND AND DAY**

1896

Image 13 × 7⁹⁄₁₆ in. (33.1 × 19.3
cm.); *sheet* 17⁷⁄₁₆ × 10⅛ in. (44.3
× 25.8 cm.)
Color lithography; dark green on
light green paper
Signature RHEAD (*lower right corner*)
Published by Copeland and Day,
Boston
Printer GEO. H. WALKER & CO.

LITH. BOSTON. (*lower right
corner*)
Reference DFP 444 (variant)
57.627.2(4)

Note: This simplified version of the
design, without gold, was used for
the paper-cover edition.

254 The CENTURY/Midsummer/Holiday/Number

1895

Image 15¹⁵⁄₁₆ × 12¹³⁄₁₆ in. (40.5 ×
32.5 cm.); *sheet* 20 × 14³⁄₁₆ in.
(50.7 × 36 cm.)
Commercial lithography; yellow,
light brown, blue, red, and black
Signature LOUIS J. RHEAD (*lower
right*)

Published by The Century Co., New
York
References DFP 447; Whitehead,
p. 40; Century and Echo 29;
Poster-NY 14; Richmond 232;
White 14; Reims 1298
57.627.2(1)

255 Read/The/Sun

1895
Image 42¹³⁄₁₆ × 23⅛ in. (108.8 × 58.7 cm.); *sheet* 45¹⁵⁄₁₆ × 30 in. (116.7 × 76.2 cm.)
Commercial lithography; yellow, red, and dark blue
Signature L. J. R. (*monogram, lower left corner*)
Published by The New York Sun

Printer A. S. Seer & Co/Litho. Print,/ N.Y. (*lower right corner*)
References DFP 439; see Mass. Mech. 290; Whitehead, p. 40; Poster-NY 45; PAFA 413; White 46; Reims 1314; Flood 318
1984.1202.140 [Lauder]

256 IF YOU SEE IT IN/THE SUN/IT'S SO/READ IT

1895
Image 42⅛ × 27³⁄₁₆ in. (106.8 × 69.1 cm.); *sheet* 46⅛ × 31¹⁄₁₆ in. (117.2 × 78.8 cm.)
Commercial lithography; yellow, orange, green, and black
Signature L. J. R. (*monogram, lower left corner*)
Published by The New York Sun
Printer LIEBLER & MAASS LITH. N.Y. (*lower right corner*)

References DFP 440; Mass. Mech. 302; Poster-NY 46; PAFA 415; White 47; Reims 1304; Flood 314
1984.1202.142 [Lauder]

Note: Rhead signed this poster using black ink.

257 ENTIRELY NEW MANAGEMENT·/A CLEAN· TRUTHFUL·WIDE-/AWAKE·HOUSEHOLD·PAPER/ MORNING/JOURNAL/A MODERN NEWSPAPER/AT A MODERN PRICE·/DAILY 1¢–SUNDAY 3¢·

1895
Image 44⁵⁄₁₆ × 58 in. (112.6 × 147.3 cm.); *sheet* 46⁹⁄₁₆ × 58¹¹⁄₁₆ in. (118.3 × 149.1 cm.)
Commercial lithography; yellow, red, light blue, and dark blue
Signature L. J. R. (*monogram, lower right corner*)
Published by The New York Journal
Printer LIEBLER & MAASS. Lith. N.Y. (*lower center*)
References DFP 445; Century and

Echo 378; Poster-NY 50; PAFA 425; White 51; Reims 1307
1986.1005.15 [Lauder]

Note: This is a two-sheet poster: the left sheet 44⁵⁄₁₆ × 29¼ in. (118.6 × 74.2 cm.), and the right sheet 44⁵⁄₁₆ × 30½ in. (118.6 × 77.5 cm.) with a 1¹⁄₁₆ in. (2.2 cm.) overlap.
Colorplate **25**

258 PRANG'S/EASTER/PUBLICATIONS

1895

Image 23¼ × 16⅜ in. (57.2 × 41.7
cm.); *sheet* 23⅞ × 16¹⁵⁄₁₆ in. (60.6
× 43.1 cm.)
Commercial lithography; yellow,
light brown, blue, green, red,
purple, and gold
Signature LOUIS/RHEAD (*lower
right corner*)

Published and printed by Louis Prang
and Co., Boston
References DFP 455; Poster-NY 35;
PAFA 436; Richmond 226; White
34; Reims 1312; Flood 312
1984.1202.146 [Lauder]
Colorplate **50**

259 THE CENTURY/For/XMAS/CONTAINING/[contents]

1895

Image 20⅝ × 13⅝ in. (52.4 × 34.6
cm.); *sheet* 21⅜ × 14½ in. (54.3 ×
36.8 cm.)
Commercial lithography; orange,
red, and dark green
Signature L. J. R. (*lower left corner*)
Publisher COPYRIGHT, 1895, BY
THE CENTURY CO (*lower right
corner*)

Printer G. H. BUEK & CO. N.Y.
LITH. (*lower left corner*)
References DFP 448; Whitehead,
p. 40; Century and Echo 36;
Poster-NY 13; PAFA 433;
Richmond 233; White 13; Reims
1297; Flood 300
41.12.159 [Vonnoh]

260 SCRIBNERS/FOR XMAS

1895

Image 17⅛ × 9³⁄₁₆ in. (43.6 × 24.9
cm.); *sheet* 19⅞ × 14⅛ in. (50.5 ×
35.9 cm.)
Commercial lithography; yellow,
blue, red, and black
Signature LOUIS/RHEAD (*lower
right corner*)
Published by Charles Scribner's Sons,
New York
References DFP 449 (variant);
Whitehead, p. 40; Century and
Echo 377; Poster-NY 42; PAFA
419; Richmond 234; White 41;
Reims 1317 (variant); Flood 306

1984.1202.144 [Lauder],
57.627.2(2)

Note: Scribner's Magazine was also
published in London. For the
convenience of their British
newsagents, text was added to the
top of the poster: "Scribner's
Christmas Number"; and to the
bottom: "Price ONE SHILLING."
An impression of this variant was
in the Reims Exhibition.
Colorplate **52**

261 READ/THE SUN

1895

Image 46¹³⁄₁₆ × 29 in. (118.9 × 73.7
cm.); *sheet* 48¹³⁄₁₆ × 31¼ in. (124
× 79.3 cm.)
Commercial lithography; yellow,
light purple, green, gray, blue,
and red
Signature L. J. R. (*monogram, lower left
corner*)

Published by The New York Sun
Printer LIEBLER & MAASS—
LITH. N.Y— (*lower right corner*)
References DFP 443; Poster-NY 49;
PAFA 417; White 49; Reims 1315;
Flood 317
1984.1202.143 [Lauder]
Colorplate **22**

262 THE JOURNAL/IT WINS/A MODERN PAPER AT A/
MODERN PRICE/DAILY 1 CENT SUNDAY 3 CENTS/1896

1896
Image 45 $^{15}/_{16}$ × 58¾ in. (116.7 ×
149.3 cm.); *sheet* 47 $^{15}/_{16}$ × 60¾ in.
(121.9 × 154.3 cm.)
Commercial lithography; yellow,
red, black, and gold
Signature L. J. R. (*monogram, lower left
corner*)
Published by The New York Journal
Printer LIEBLER & MAASS LITH.
N.Y. (*lower left corner*)
References Poster-NY 52; White 53;
Reims 1305
1984.1202.150 [Lauder]

Note: The right sheet was left blank
for future overprintings of
headlines and features. The left
sheet measures 45 $^{15}/_{16}$ × 30¼ in.
(116.7 × 76.9 cm.); the right
sheet, 45 $^{15}/_{16}$ × 31 $^{3}/_{16}$ in. (116.7 ×

79.2 cm.) with an $^{11}/_{16}$ in. (1.8
cm.) overlap. For many years, the
Metropolitan Museum's copy of the
poster had been folded; during
that period, the black ink offset
like a shadow on the gold areas of
the image. The right section of the
impression, illustrated in *Das
moderne Plakat*, has the following
text: "BEGIN THE/NEW YEAR/BY
TAKING THE/BEST PAPER/IN NEW
YORK./NOTHING CHEAP/ABOUT
THE/JOURNAL/BUT THE PRICE."
The lettering is similar to that on
the Museum's proof (Jean Louis
Sponsel, *Das moderne Plakat*
[Dresden: Gerhard Kühtmann
Verlag, 1897], p. 178).

263 THE/NEW YORK HERALD/SUNDAY/MARCH 22nd/
1896./A NEWSPAPER/MARVEL . . . . . . /Music/Poems/
Pictures/Sermons/The Finest Number EVER ISSUED BY A
NEWSPAPER/Three Eight-Page/ART SECTIONS/REPLETE
WITH SEASONABLE FEATURES./EASTER NUMBER

1896
Image 19 $^{7}/_{16}$ × 12 $^{15}/_{16}$ in. (49.3 ×
32.8 cm.); *sheet* 21 $^{1}/_{16}$ × 13⅞ in.
(53.5 × 35.2 cm.)
Commercial relief process; orange,
green, purple, and blue
Unsigned
Published by The New York Herald
References see DFP 462; PAFA 434;
White 34; Reims 1300
41.12.95 [Vonnoh]

Note: Rhead's design of an angel
amid lilies was accompanied by
two different texts for the *New York*

Herald Easter number. The orange
field in the second version is
curved on top, and "LOUIS RHEAD"
appears in the lower left of the
design. The second text reads:
"EASTER NUMBER/THE NEW YORK
HERALD/SUNDAY, MARCH 22,
1896/IT WILL FAR/SURPASS ALL/
PREVIOUS/SPECIAL/NUMBERS/3/
EIGHT-PAGE/ART SECTIONS/
REPLETE WITH/SEASONABLE/
FEATURES/A NEWSPAPER
MARVEL."

264 Mrs. Burton/Harrison's/GREAT STORY:/"HIS LORDSHIP"/Will Shortly Appear In/THE BOSTON TRANSCRIPT

1896
Image 45⁷/₁₆ × 26⁵/₈ in. (115.4 × 67.6 cm.); *sheet* 47³/₈ × 28½ in. (120.3 × 72.4 cm.)
Commercial lithography; light brown, green, brown, gray, and black
Signature L. J. R. (*monogram, middle right*)
Published by The Boston Transcript
Printer PRINTED BY ALUMINOGRAPHY—THE ELLERY—HOWARD CO., NEW YORK. (*lower right corner*)
References DFP 458 (variant); PAFA 427 (variant); White 38 (variant); Reims 1301 (variant)
1986.1005.16 [Lauder]

Note: Constance Cary Harrison, *The Merry Maid of Arcady, His Lordship, and Other Stories* (Boston: Lamson, Wolffe and Co., 1897). The several variants of this poster raise the problem of the original commission of the design. The brown ink in both the image and

the text may suggest that it originated as an announcement of Harrison's story "His Lordship." She was a popular writer whose stories frequently appeared in newspapers and periodicals before publication in book form. Space was left for each newspaper to add its own name; hence the Metropolitan Museum's poster was used by *The Boston Transcript*, and the poster exhibited at the Pennsylvania Academy in 1896 was used by the *Philadelphia Press*. The design was also used to advertise winter apparel, reserving a lower portion for imprinting the name of the local merchant. The printer provided the general text: "FOR/FASHIONABLE/WINTER/CLOTHING/GO TO." The lettering is similar to that in other Rhead posters.
Colorplate 48

265 THE CENTURY/MAGAZINE/FOR/JUNE

1896
Image 20¹³/₁₆ × 10⁹/₁₆ in. (52.9 × 26.8 cm.); *sheet* 21¹/₁₆ × 10³/₄ in. (53.6 × 27.4 cm.)
Commercial lithography; yellow, blue, red, and purple
Signature LOUIS/RHEAD (*lower left*)
Publisher COPYRIGHT, 1896, BY

THE CENTURY CO. N.Y. (*lower right corner*)
Printer G. H. BUEK & CO. N.Y. LITH. (*lower left corner*)
References DFP 461; Flood 301
1984.1202.147 [Lauder]; 57.627.2(3)

266 CASSELL'S/MAGAZINE/IS/GREATLY ENLARGED/WITH THE/DECEMBER PART/PRICE 6ᴰ WHICH INCLUDES AN ALBUM/OF FREDERICK BARNARD'S SKETCHES.

1896
Image 10¹¹/₁₆ × 13³/₁₆ in. (27.1 × 33.4 cm.); *sheet* 12⁷/₈ × 15 in. (32.1 × 38.1 cm.)
Commercial lithography; yellow-green, red, light blue, and dark blue
Signature L. J. R. 96 (*monogram, lower left corner*)

Publisher and printer CASSELL & COMPANY LIMITED. LITH. LONDON. (*lower right corner*)
Reference DFP 463
1985.1132.1 [Lauder]

267 [Poster Calendar for 1897, L. Prang & Co., Boston]
1896
Sheet 19¼ × 13¾ in. (48.8 ×
 35 cm.)
Commercial lithography
Published and printed by Louis Prang
 and Co., Boston

References DFP 466 (A–E); Flood 310
1986.1005.17 (1–5) [Lauder]

267A [Cover] POSTER CALENDAR/1897

Yellow, pink, light brown, blue,
red, and purple
Signature LOUIS RHEAD (*lower
right*)
Publisher Copyright 1896 by

L. Prang & Co. Boston, U.S.A.
(*lower right corner*)
1986.1005.17(1) [Lauder]
Colorplate 49

267B JANUARY/FEBRUARY/MARCH

Yellow, light pink, dark pink, light
blue, dark blue, yellow-green,
light green, brown, red, and
purple
Signature LOUIS RHEAD (*lower
right corner*)

Publisher Copyright 1896 by
 L. Prang & Co. Boston, U.S.A.
 (*lower left corner*)
1986.1005.17(2) [Lauder]

267C APRIL MAY/JUNE

Light yellow, dark yellow, pink,
gray, blue, green, brown, red, and
purple
Signature LOUIS RHEAD (*lower
right corner*)

Publisher Copyright 1896 by
 L. Prang & Co. Boston. U.S.A.
 (*lower left corner*)
1986.1005.17(3) [Lauder]

267D JULY/AUGUST SEPTEMBER

Yellow, pink, blue, green, brown, red, and purple
Signature LOUIS RHEAD (*lower right corner*)

Publisher Copyright 1896 by L. Prang & Co. Boston. U.S.A. (*lower left corner*)
1986.1005.17(4) [Lauder]

267E OCTOBER NOVEMBER/DECEMBER

Light yellow, dark yellow, pink, gray, blue, light green, brown, red, and purple
Signature LOUIS RHEAD (*lower right corner*)

Publisher Copyright 1896 by L. Prang & Co. Boston. U.S.A. (*lower right corner*)
1986.1005.17(5) [Lauder]

268 THE N.Y. HERALD/XMAS NUMBER/SUNDAY/ DECEMBER 13TH/1896/A SUPERB EDITION/Five Colored Sections/36 ART PAGES 36/X-MAS STORIES/ X-MAS PICTURES/X-MAS MUSIC/X-MAS POEMS

1896
Image 19¹⁵⁄₁₆ × 12³⁄₈ in. (50.5 × 31.4 cm.); *sheet* 20⅝ × 13¹⁄₁₆ in. (52.4 × 33.2 cm.)
Commercial relief process; orange, green, and red

Signature LOUIS RHEAD (*lower right*)
Published by The New York Herald
Reference Flood 313
1984.1202.148 [Lauder]

269 EXPOSITION SPÉCIALE DE SOIXANTE NOUVELLES AFFICHES INÉDITES de/LOUIS RHEAD/SALON DES CENT/31, Rue Bonaparte Paris/DU 20 AVRIL AU 10 MAI 1897

1897
Sheet 23⅞ × 16¹⁄₁₆ in. (60.6 × 40.7 cm.)
Color lithography; green, vermilion, and purple
Signature LOUIS RHEAD. (*lower left corner*)
Publisher and printer Affiches artistiques de la Plume. 31, rue Bonaparte. IMP. CHAIX. PARIS. (Encres Lorilleux) (*lower left corner*)
Reference DFP 468
1985.1051.3 [Lauder]

Note: An exhibition of sixty new posters by Rhead opened at the Salon des Cent on April 20, 1897, and was extended until May 30 (Phillip Dennis Cate, "'La Plume' and Its 'Salon des Cent': Promoters of Posters and Prints in the 1890's," *Print Review* 8 [1978], p. 67). Rhead was the only American artist so honored.
Colorplate 51

270 LE JOURNAL/ de la BEAUTÉ/ 10 Centimes

1897
Image 30⅝ × 58⁷⁄₁₆ in. (77.8 × 148.5 cm.); *sheet* 33³⁄₁₆ × 60¾ in. (84.3 × 154.3 cm.)
Commercial lithography; yellow, light blue, dark blue, and red, overprinted with black and red
Signature L. J. R. (*monogram, lower left corner*)
Publisher Publication artistique de la Société anonyme "LA PLUME" 31, Rue Bonaparte, Paris (*lower left corner*)
Printer IMPRIMERIE CHAIX (Ateliers Chéret) Rue Bergère, 20, PARIS_97_11860-(ENCRES LORILLEUX) (*lower right*)
Reference DFP 454A
1984.1202.145 [Lauder]

Note: Both Mucha and Grasset

received commissions from various Paris publishers for large lithographs that could be incorporated into decorative interior schemes. Such panels were hybrids of posters, wallpapers, or large prints. Rhead received such a commission from the Parisian publisher La Plume for two panels—"Swans" (DFP 454) and "Peacocks"—which show him at his most Art Nouveau. La Plume, which also published *Le Journal de la Beauté*, overprinted an advertisement for the periodical on poorly printed copies of "Peacocks." The panel was thus transformed into a genuine poster.

271 THE QUARTIER LATIN/ A MAGAZINE DEVOTED/ TO THE ARTS– – –

ca. 1898–99
Image 19¾ × 13⅞ in. (50.4 × 35.3 cm.); *sheet* 23¹¹⁄₁₆ × 16⁷⁄₁₆ in. (60.3 × 41.8 cm.)
Commercial lithography; yellow, red, light blue, dark blue, and black
Signature LOUIS RHEAD (*lower right corner*)
Publisher Publication artistique de LA PLUME (*lower right corner*)
Printer Imp. CHAIX PARIS. (*lower left*)

Reference DFP 472
1985.1051.2 [Lauder]

Note: Rhead's design for *The Quartier Latin*, a magazine devoted to the arts and published by the American artistic community of Paris, was praised by Ernest de Crauzet in a listing of new posters, "Les Estampes et les affiches du mois," *L'Estampe et l'affiche* 3.5 (May 15, 1899), p. 123.

Henry Mortika Rosenberg

272 THE/ CENTURY/ FOR SEPTEMBER

1896
Image 20⅛ × 14⅛ in. (51.2 × 35.9 cm.); *sheet* 20¹⁵⁄₁₆ × 14⅝ in. (53.3 × 37.1 cm.)
Commercial lithography; gray, red, light green, and black
Signature H. M. ROSENBERG (*lower left corner*)
Publisher COPYRIGHT, 1896, BY THE CENTURY CO. (*lower left corner*)

Printer G. H. BUEK & CO. LITHOGRAPHERS, N.Y. (*lower right corner*)
References DFP 477; Flood 278
57.627.10(15)

Note: Rosenberg's design received an honorable mention in the *Century* poster competition, 1896.

Julius A. Schweinfurth

273 QUO VADIS/A NARRATIVE OF THE/TIME OF NERO BY/
HENRYK SIENKIEWICZ/PUBLISHED BY LITTLE/
BROWN & CO BOSTON

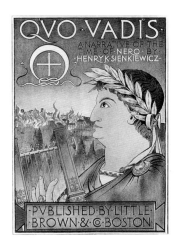

1897
Image 28¹⁄₁₆ × 19¼ in. (71.3 × 49
cm.); *sheet* 28⁷⁄₁₆ × 19¾ in. (72.3
× 50.1 cm.)
Commercial lithography; yellow,
pink, red, gray, blue, green, and
black
Signature J A SCHWEINFURTH
FECIT BOSTON MDCCCXCVII
(*lower edge*)

Published by Little, Brown and Co.,
Boston
57.627.70

Note: Henryk Sienkiewicz, *Quo
Vadis* (Boston: Little, Brown and
Co., 1896; 2nd ed., 1897).

George Frederick Scotson-Clark

274 Outing/NOVEMBER, 1896.
1896
Sheet 11¹⁵⁄₁₆ × 16⅞ in. (30.3 ×
43 cm.)
Commercial lithography; yellow-
green and vermilion
Signature SCOTSON-CLARK *with
sword logo (lower left corner)*

Published by Outing
Reference Flood 75
1984.1202.151 [Lauder]

John Sloan

275 THE AMERICAN ARISTOCRACY/Graphically Depicted/
and/ ITS HOLLOWNESS EXPOSED/in the latest and/Most
Interesting Novel/OF THE SEASON./FOR SALE HERE.
[*on book:*] PRICE, FIFTY CENTS./The Lady/and Her Tree/
A STORY OF SOCIETY/BY CHARLES STOKES WAYNE

1895
Image 7¾ × 5 in. (19.7 × 12.7 cm.);
sheet 11 × 14 in. (28 × 35.5 cm.)
Commercial relief process and
letterpress; yellow and black
Signature John/Sloan (*lower left
corner*)
Published by Vortex Co., Philadelphia
References Whitehead, p. 44;
Morse G
1985.1129.3 [Lauder]

Note: Charles Stokes Wayne, *The
Lady and Her Tree: A Story of Society*
(Philadelphia: Vortex Co., 1895).

The design, here in black
overprinted on a yellow-ink area,
was also used on the cover of the
book. Morse noted a variant,
printed on yellow paper with an
additional text at the bottom:
"221 pages SELLS ON SIGHT heavy
paper" (Peter Morse, *John Sloan's
Prints: A Catalogue Raisonné of the
Etchings, Lithographs, and Posters*
[New Haven: Yale University
Press, 1969], p. 358).

276 Moods/An Illustrated/Quarterly/For The Modern/Published by/The Jenson Press/Philadelphia, U.S.A.

1895

Image 19 × 11⅛ in. (48.3 × 28.2 cm.); *sheet* 20¹/₁₆ × 12⅝ in. (51 × 32.2 cm.)

Commercial relief process; green on light green paper

Signature John/Sloan (*middle left*)

Published by The Jenson Press, Philadelphia

References DFP 478; Whitehead, p. 44; Century and Echo 424; PAFA 458, 459; Richmond 245; Morse H

41.12.164 [Vonnoh]

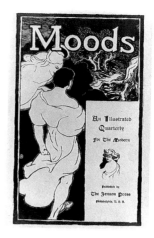

277 THE/ECHO/FOR SALE HERE.

1895

Image 9⅞ × 5¹¹/₁₆ in. (25.1 × 14.5 cm.); *sheet* 18⁷/₁₆ × 8¹/₁₆ in. (46.7 × 20.5 cm.)

Commercial relief process and letterpress; red and black on buff paper

Signature John/Sloan (*lower right*)

Published by The Echo

References Whitehead, p. 44; see Century and Echo 384; Richmond 244; Reims 1323; Morse I

1985.1129.2 [Lauder]

Note: Sloan's poster for *The Echo* was initially advertised in the November 1, 1895, issue of the magazine. At a later date the text was altered: "Fortnightly/Chicago/February 15, 1896." The design was also used for the cover of the February 15, 1896, issue (Morse, p. 360).

278 CINDER-PATH TALES/WILLIAM LINDSEY/BOSTON: COPELAND AND/DAY PRICE $1.00

1896

Image 17¼ × 11³/₁₆ in. (43.9 × 28.3 cm.); *sheet* 23¾ × 13⅝ in. (60.3 × 34.6 cm.)

Commercial lithography; black and white on brown paper

Signature John/Sloan (*lower right*)

Published by Copeland and Day, Boston

Printer George H. Walker & Co., Lith. Boston (*lower right corner*)

References Flood 337; Morse L

1985.1129.1 [Lauder]

Note: William Lindsey, *Cinder-Path Tales* (Boston: Copeland and Day, 1896). The title and design of this poster were also printed on the book cover.

Colorplate 54

Marianna Sloan

279 Women's Edition/The Press–/Thanksgiving Eve/Nov. 27th–1895

1895

Sheet 34¹¹/₁₆ × 20¹/₁₆ in. (88.2 × 51 cm.)

Commercial relief process; yellow, green, and black

Signature MARIANNA SLOAN (*lower left*)

Published by The Philadelphia Press

References Century and Echo 425; PAFA 460; Richmond 243

1986.1005.18 [Lauder]

John Stewardson

280 THE DRAGON OF WANTLEY/HIS TALE: BY OWEN WISTER/ILLUSTRATIONS BY JOHN STEWARDSON

1895
Image 13⁹⁄₁₆ × 10 in. (34.5 × 25.5 cm.); *sheet* 14¹¹⁄₁₆ × 10⅝ in. (37.9 × 27.1 cm.)
Commercial relief process; red and black on oatmeal paper
Unsigned
Published by J. B. Lippincott Co., Philadelphia

References Whitehead, p. 44; Century and Echo 383; PAFA 464A 41.12.181 [Vonnoh]

Note: Owen Wister, *The Dragon of Wantley: His Tale* (Philadelphia: J. B. Lippincott Co., 1895), 2nd ed.

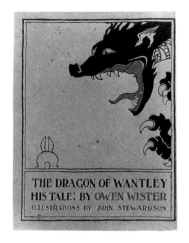

M. Louise Stowell

281 GEO. P. HUMPHREY. AT THE SIGN OF THE "OLD-BOOK MAN"/NUMBER 25 EXCHANGE ST. ROCHESTER. N.Y.

ca. 1896
Image 21¾ × 13¹¹⁄₁₆ in. (55.2 × 34.8 cm.); *sheet* 24¹⁵⁄₁₆ × 16⅞ in. (63.3 × 42.9 cm.)
Commercial lithography; yellow, brown, blue, and black
Signature logo (monogram, lower right corner)

Printer PEERLESS CO. ROCHESTER, N.Y. (*lower right corner*)
Reference Flood 338
57.627.68

John Henry Twachtman

282 THE DAMNATION OF THERON WARE/OR ILLUMINATION/BY HAROLD FREDERIC./PUBLISHED BY STONE & KIMBALL.

1896
Image 20 × 12¹⁄₁₆ in. (50.8 × 30.7 cm.); *sheet* 22 × 14⅛ in. (55.9 × 35.9 cm.)
Commercial lithography; light tan, green, blue, and red
Signature J. H. TWACHTMAN (*middle right*); DESIGNED BY J. H. TWACHTMAN (*lower left corner*)
Published by Stone and Kimball, New York and Chicago

Printer PRINTED BY STONE & KIMBALL, NEW YORK. (*lower right corner*)
Reference DFP 486
57.627.10(22)

Note: Harold Frederic, *The Damnation of Theron Ware* (New York and Chicago: Stone and Kimball, 1896).

Henry Sumner Watson

283 RECREATION/10 CENTS/MARCH

1896

Image 14¾ × 11¹⁄₁₆ in. (37.6 × 28.1 cm.); *sheet* 16½ × 13¹⁵⁄₁₆ in. (41.9 × 35.3 cm.)

Commercial relief process; black

Signature HY. S. WATSON. 96 (*lower right corner*)

Published by Recreation, New York

Reference PAFA 521

41.12.167 [Vonnoh]

Note: Watson provided a series of twelve posters for *Recreation* in 1896, each depicting a different outdoor sport. Designed in a silhouette style and sparked with refreshing humor, Watson's energetic sportsman and his faithful dachshund pursue the sports of the season—in March, ice-boating; in May, fly-fishing; and in August, a refreshing dip in a lake. The posters were available from the magazine's offices at five cents apiece (*The Poster* 1.3 [March 1896], p. 40).

E. B. Wells

284 MRS. CLIFF'S YACHT/FRANK R. STOCKTON/CHARLES SCRIBNER'S SONS

1896

Image 17¹⁵⁄₁₆ × 11¹⁵⁄₁₆ in. (45.6 × 30.3 cm.); *sheet* 18½ × 12⁷⁄₁₆ in. (47 × 31.5 cm.)

Commercial relief process; yellow, black, green, and blue

Signature E. B Wells (*lower left*)

Published by Charles Scribner's Sons, New York

Reference Flood 357

1984.1202.153 [Lauder]

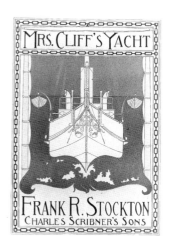

Charles Herbert Woodbury

285 SOCIETY OF PAINTERS IN/WATER COLOR OF HOLLAND./CHASE'S GALLERY/HAMILTON PLACE BOSTON/FIRST ANNUAL EXHIBITION/IN THE/UNITED STATES BEGINNING MARCH 19 '95

1895

Image 19½ × 14¼ in. (49.6 × 36.2 cm.); *sheet* 22¹⁵⁄₁₆ × 17⁷⁄₈ in. (58.3 × 45.5 cm.)

Commercial lithography; orange, blue, and black

Signature C H Woodbury. (*lower left corner*)

Published by Chase's Gallery, Boston

Printer FORBES CO. (*lower right corner*)

References Bolton, p. 14; Quincy 218; Mass. Mech. 352; Whitehead, p. 48; Century and Echo 399

1984.1202.158 [Lauder]

286 BOSTON/PARK/GUIDE/INCLUDING/MUNICIPAL AND/
METROPOLITAN/SYSTEMS/WITH MAPS AND/
ILLUSTRATIONS/PRICE 25 CENTS/BY/SYLVESTER
BAXTER

1895
Image 17⁹/₁₆ × 10¹⁵/₁₆ in. (44.6 ×
37.8 cm.); *sheet* 19¼ × 12¹/₁₆ in.
(48.9 × 30.7 cm.)
Commercial lithography; yellow-
green, purple, brown, and black
Signature CHAS H WOODBURY
(*lower left corner*)
Published by Sylvester Baxter
References DFP 500; Mass. Mech.
353, 356, 357; Whitehead,
p. 48; Century and Echo 398;
Reims 1333

1984.1202.155 [Lauder]

Note: Sylvester Baxter, *Boston Park
Guide . . .* (Boston: Sylvester
Baxter, 1895). A limited edition of
fifty copies on special paper, signed
by the artist and with a stenciled
remarque, was available to
collectors for three dollars each
(Mass. Mech. 353).

287 BY BROOMSTICK/TRAIN/OUR/SUBURBS/AFOOT AND
BY/TROLLEY/Little Journeys About Boston. . ./Reprinted
from the/Boston Evening Transcript/Price, Ten Cents . . .

1895
Image 19⁷/₈ × 9 in. (50.3 × 22.9
cm.); *sheet* 21³/₈ × 10¹⁵/₁₆ in. (54.3
× 27.8 cm.)
Commercial relief process and
letterpress; black and yellow
Signature C H W (*lower left*)
Published by The Boston Evening
Transcript

References Mass. Mech. 354;
Whitehead, p. 48; Century and
Echo 400; PAFA 519
41.12.174 [Vonnoh]

Note: Woodbury's design for the
cover of this collection of reprinted
articles was enlarged for the poster.

288 THE/JULY/CENTURY

1895
Image 17½ × 10³/₈ in. (44.4 × 26.4
cm.); *sheet* 19 × 11¹³/₁₆ in. (48.3 ×
34 cm.)
Commercial lithography; yellow,
blue, and black
Signature Chas H Woodbury (*lower
left corner*)
Published by The Century Co., New
York
References DFP 501; Mass. Mech.
355; Whitehead, p. 48; Century
and Echo 62; PAFA 518; Richmond
258; Reims 1334

1984.1202.156 [Lauder];
57.627.10(17)

Note: W. Lewis Fraser, the head of
the Century Company's art
department, commissioned this
poster after seeing Woodbury's
poster for the Exhibition of the
Society of Painters in Water-Color
of Holland (cat. 285). The subject
chosen for this poster is American
summer festivals (Archives of
American Art, roll 1255).

Colorplate 27

289 TROLLEY TRIPS/ON A/BAY STATE/TRIANGLE
1897
Image 11⁷⁄₁₆ × 16⁵⁄₈ in. (29.1 × 42.3 cm.); *sheet* 11⁹⁄₁₆ × 16¹³⁄₁₆ in. (29.4 × 42.7 cm.)
Commercial relief process; dark blue, light blue, green, and pink
Signature C H Woodbury (*lower right corner*)
Printer Heliotype Printing Co., Boston

1984.1202.157 [Lauder]

Note: The impression of this poster at the New York Public Library has a partially clipped line of copyright with the date, 1897, in the lower left corner.
Colorplate 55

Charles Hubbard Wright

290 THE NEW YORK/SUNDAY/HERALD/MARCH/1ST/The Best of Everything/NEWS . . . HUMOR/IN/ART . . . LITERATURE
1896
Sheet 19⅛ × 12¼ in. (48.5 × 30.8 cm.)
Commercial relief process and letterpress; yellow, red, and black
Signature C H WRIGHT (*lower right*)

Published by The New York Herald
Reference PAFA 527
41.12.143 [Vonnoh]

NOTES ON THE ARTISTS

Edwin Austin Abbey
1852–1911

Abbey's only poster advertised the publication of a group of drawings related to the large mural series "The Quest of the Holy Grail," installed in 1895 in the newly erected Boston Public Library. He was employed in the art department of Harper and Brothers, New York. After 1878, he lived in England, painting and drawing Shakespearean subjects, scenes from earlier British history, and subjects inspired by seventeenth- and eighteenth-century English literature. He was one of the most popular illustrators of the day, and there was a constant flow of commissions for pen-and-ink drawings from American publishers. See *Edwin Austin Abbey (1852–1911)* (New Haven: Yale University Art Gallery, 1974).

W. S. Vanderbilt Allen
Dates unknown

Only one poster by Allen is known, made for *Harper's Weekly*. Allen was probably an illustrator employed by Harper and Brothers.

Barnes
Dates unknown

Barnes designed at least three posters in 1895 for the magazine *To Date* and may have been employed in its art department. Barnes may be an illustrator active in Boston, Hiram Putnam Barnes (born 1857), but nothing at present substantiates this identification.

Elisha Brown Bird
1867–1943

Bird chose not to practice architecture after his graduation from the Massachusetts Institute of Technology; instead, he pursued a career as a commercial designer of advertisements, book plates, and menu covers, as well as book covers, initials, and posters for many New York and Boston

publishers. He designed at least sixteen posters between 1895 and 1897, one of the earliest for the 1895 poster exhibition sponsored by the Massachusetts Charitable Mechanic Association (Cat. 6). There is nothing tentative in the design of his posters, since Bird understood their purpose—whether for such literary magazines as *The Red Letter* (Cat. 10) or *The Chap-Book* (Chicago), or for *The Century*. The March 1896 *Century* poster was well received by American and European critics (Cat. 7). Bird fully espoused the new printing technology and designed accordingly; he preferred to have his work photomechanically reproduced to having it redrawn by staff technicians. See Nancy Finlay, *Artists of the Book in Boston, 1890–1910* (Cambridge, Mass.: Harvard College Library, 1985).

Will H. Bradley
1868–1962

The beautifully refined line, the subtle curvilinear rhythms, and the careful balance of black and white areas characterize twelve cover designs that Bradley provided the editors of Chicago's *Inland Printer* in 1894. These covers were some of the earliest manifestations of Art Nouveau style in American graphic design. Later, cover designs for this magazine of the printing industry were adapted for advertising posters. Bradley trained as a wood engraver in the mid-1880s and turned to pen-and-ink drawing when wood engraving became obsolete. His mature style, well suited for photomechanical reproduction, came to the notice of a new Chicago-based publishing firm, Stone and Kimball, dedicated to fine printing. In 1894, his first poster for their house organ, *The Chap-Book*, appeared to critical acclaim, and six others quickly followed. Along with Penfield's *Harper's* posters, which had appeared the previous year, Bradley's work can be credited with the widespread popularization of the poster in America by mid-decade.

Bradley has often been called the American Aubrey Beardsley. Some critics have claimed that his style is derivative, but more likely the two styles are cases of parallel development, achieving similar goals in graphic design. Bradley's work is not fraught with the immoral innuendos so much a part of Beardsley's work, and shows more influence from the examples of William Morris and the English

Arts and Crafts movement. The finely tuned unity of graphic design, fine printing, and typography naturally appealed to Bradley, who was involved with the printing industry. Late in 1895, he returned to his native Massachusetts and set up his own studio; there, in Springfield, he hoped to pursue the fine printing of books, pamphlets, commercial advertisements, and sales brochures. Even the name of the studio suggests the English model: The Wayside Press at the Sign of the Dandelion.

To promote his ideals, Bradley began to publish his own magazine, *Bradley: His Book*, stressing design, the printing arts, and commercial advertising adhering to his models. Most of the posters issued in conjunction with this magazine, as well as other commissioned work during the Springfield years, showed a marked stylistic change toward design derived from the woodcut. Two of the *Bradley: His Book* posters were woodcuts (Cat. 30, 34); those for Victor bicycles (Cat. 24, 35) adapted the new style to other printing methods. Bradley's career as a poster artist waned with the close of the decade; he increasingly turned his attention to type design, commercial printing, and illustration. In the new century, he worked for American Type Founders, as art editor for *Collier's*, and provided illustrations for *The Century*, *Metropolitan*, and other magazines. See Roberta Waddell Wong, *Will H. Bradley: American Artist and Craftsman (1868–1962)* (New York: The Metropolitan Museum of Art, 1972); and Will H. Bradley, *Will Bradley: His Chap Book* (New York: The Typophiles, 1955).

Claude Fayette Bragdon
1866–1946

Bragdon designed five posters—three for *The Chap-Book* and two for the Rochester *Post Express*. While the latter received critical attention for design, the *Chap-Book* posters displayed a keen understanding of Parisian prototypes, especially the work of Steinlen. While pursuing architectural studies in Paris, he had collected contemporary posters by Chéret, Grasset, Lautrec, and Steinlen. On his return to the United States, he frequently lent his collection to exhibitions, including that to benefit Richmond's Old Dominion Hospital in 1896. His reminiscence of poster collecting in Paris was published in *Poster Lore* (1.1 [January 1896], pp. 20–22), and he was frequently quoted on the subject of posters in the contemporary press. A professional architect, he also designed furniture and theater sets, and wrote several books on design.

George Reiter Brill
1867–1918

After art studies in New York and Philadelphia, Brill pursued a career as an illustrator, providing designs for *Harper's Young People*, the humor magazines *Judge* and *Life*, and numerous books. In 1895 and 1896, he provided designs for nearly one hundred posters for the Sunday editions of the Philadelphia *Press*, the Chicago *Tribune*, the Cleveland *Leader*, and the Topeka *Daily Capital*. All these posters were printed by the Philadelphia lithography firm H. I. Ireland. Presumably Brill was associated with this firm, perhaps on the art staff, during the mid-decade. His name was printed within the printer's own logo on these posters.

Frank Gelett Burgess
1866–1951

Burgess was an author best known for his humorous verse, especially his poem "The Purple Cow." Much of his verse appeared in the humorous literary publication *The Lark*, begun by Burgess and Bruce Porter in 1895 as a counterpoint to such small journals as *The Chap-Book*, which they considered pseudosophisticated. *The Lark* was published by the San Francisco bookseller William Doxey. Burgess also provided *The Lark* with numerous illustrations, drawn in a childlike style. According to a listing of its posters in the April 1896 *Lark*, he cut the block used to print Lundborg's first poster for the magazine (Cat. 117).

William L. Carqueville
1871–1946

Carqueville learned lithography in the family firm of Shober and Carqueville, Chicago. This training stood him in good stead when the Philadelphia firm of J. B. Lippincott Company commissioned a series of monthly magazine posters. Lippincott's competition with the more famous Penfield series for *Harper's* was obvious even then to critics; and today, his posters have been described as imitations of Penfield. Such criticism is unnecessary. If anything, Carqueville's posters of 1894–95 more directly acknowledge the achievements of French contemporaries. He clearly understood commercial color printing and used this knowledge in his designs for *Lippincott's*. He also provided at least three posters, and probably a full complement of twelve, for the magazine *International*. He made stunning use of his printing knowledge in these bold two-color posters. In 1896, he went to Paris to pursue his art studies. On his return to America, he continued working as an illustrator in the Chicago area.

Robert William Chambers
1865–1933

Chambers was an illustrator who became a popular author of historical novels, romances, and horror stories. He provided at least four poster designs for several publishers, including one for a book he wrote (Cat. 58). A design made for the firm of F. Tennyson Neely, New York and Chicago, was used for two different titles—*The King in Yellow* and *Father Stafford*.

Howard Chandler Christy
1873–1952

Today, Christy is remembered as the artist of some of the best-known posters of World War I. His ideal female type, the Christy girl, used in his paintings and drawings, was as popular as the Gibson girl of the 1890s. Christy studied in New York and worked as an illustrator for such major periodicals as *Harper's Weekly*, *Collier's*, and *Scribner's*. His several posters for *The Bookman*, designed between 1896 and 1899, are testimonials to his skill as a draftsman and as an illustrator.

Charles Arthur Cox
Dates unknown

Cox provided at least ten highly imaginative posters for the cycling journal *Bearings* in 1895 and 1896, and another for *Truth* in 1896.

Francis Day
1863–?

After study at the Art Students League, New York, and the Ecole des Beaux-Arts, Paris, Day worked for several New York publishers as an illustrator. He provided designs for several covers and for at least six posters for The Century Company publications, including *St. Nicholas* and *The Century*, from 1892 to 1894. He also designed five posters for *Scribner's* in 1894 and 1895.

DeYongh
Dates unknown

DeYongh is an enigma. Even the compilers of contemporary exhibition catalogues and the authors of poster books disagree on the spelling of the name. All but one of the known posters were for the *New York Times* Sunday editions. Will M. Clemens, editor of *The Poster*, praised DeYongh's striking posters, which used a mosaic scheme in the design (*The Poster* 1.2 [February 1896], p. 19).

Lafayette Maynard Dixon
1875–1946

Dixon, from California, was largely self taught. In 1893, he began a long affiliation with the *Overland Monthly* of San Francisco as an illustrator. His work had a marked fidelity to western life, less romanticized than in the work of Remington. In May 1895, the first of Dixon's *Overland Monthly* posters appeared, and they continued until at least April 1896. In 1897, he illustrated two books by Verner Z. Reed and designed the accompanying posters (Cat. 64, 65). In the next decade, he continued to provide illustrations for various California-based periodicals and newspapers, especially *Sunset* of San Francisco, for which he also designed a number of posters. See Wesley M. Burnside, *Maynard Dixon: Artist of the West* (Provo, Utah: Brigham Young University Press, 1974).

Arthur Wesley Dow
1857–1922

For most modern art historians, Dow has been a footnote to the career of Georgia O'Keeffe, whom he taught. This is unfair to Dow, one of the most important painters and teachers at the turn of the century. Trained in France, he was a painter of conventional landscapes in a Barbizon style until 1891. That year, a book of Hokusai's prints led him to Ernest Fenollosa, curator of Japanese art at Boston's Museum of Fine Arts, from whom he gained a thorough understanding of Japanese composition. His ability to combine

the two traditions brought him critical acclaim and many students.

Dow designed two of the most original and beautifully printed posters of the decade, triumphs of lithographic printing by Boston's Louis Prang and Company. The first, for Prang's *Modern Art* in 1895, reproduced all the nuances of cutting and color in Dow's original woodcut, *Sundown, Ipswich River* (Cat. 66). In 1896, he designed a second, much rarer poster for an exhibition of Japanese prints at a New York gallery. A third poster offered by Fenollosa's New York-based magazine, *Lotos*, was adapted from Dow's design for the magazine's cover. See Frederick C. Moffatt, *Arthur Wesley Dow (1857–1922)* (Washington, D.C.: National Collection of Fine Arts, 1977).

Henry Brevoort Eddy
1872–1935

Eddy had no formal art training. After graduating from Harvard, where he was president of the *Harvard Lampoon*, he returned to New York and worked as an illustrator for several newspapers. In 1896, he noted that in the future the photographer would replace the illustrator, but "one picture by a real artist can tell all that a thousand feet of film can tell. Its succinctness gives it force and beauty." His first of many posters was created for the New York *Ledger* in 1895 (see Cat. 67). The writer Frank Knight noted that it was effective even though badly translated in color. As art editor for *Chips*, Eddy designed a series of posters that attracted considerable attention. See Frank R. Knight, "Henry Brevoort Eddy, Artist," *Bradley: His Book* 1.3 (July 1896), pp. 87–93.

George Wharton Edwards
1869–1950

Edwards was a well-known illustrator and watercolorist who studied in Paris. At least twenty posters are credited to him, most of them for magazines and books published by The Century Company. His title-page designs have a classical elegance now associated with the turn of the century. A title page designed for G. P. Putnam's edition of Washington Irving's *Tales of a Traveller* was adapted for the store placard. Edwards exhibited his watercolors in various exhibitions; he designed the poster for the eighteenth annual exhibition of the American Water Color Society at the National Academy of Design, New York, in 1895.

Wilson Eyre, Jr.
1858–1944

Eyre's houses and gardens define an era of architecture in Philadelphia and its Main Line suburbs. His only known poster was an enlarged version of the cover design for the catalogue of an exhibition of architectural drawings at the Art Club, Philadelphia. He collected posters and lent several to the poster exhibition organized by Parrish and Robert Vonnoh at the Pennsylvania Academy of the Fine Arts, 1896.

Charles Farrand
Dates unknown

Since the only known poster by Farrand is for *Lippincott's* (Cat. 72), he may have worked in the mid-1890s as an illustrator in Philadelphia or have been a student at the Pennsylvania Academy of the Fine Arts.

A. Fay
Dates unknown

This unidentified artist was possibly an illustrator employed by the New York *Herald*.

Charles Dana Gibson
1867–1944

Gibson was one of the most popular illustrators of the 1890s, and the image of the Gibson girl is as familiar today as then. Editors vied to secure his drawings for their magazines because a Gibson design insured an increase in readership. Collections of the drawings also sold well. Technically, the posters ascribed to Gibson were not designed by him; instead, a staff artist would adapt one of the drawings for the poster. At least twelve posters were adapted in this way from Gibson's original pen-and-ink drawings.

William James Glackens
1870–1938

Glackens, like his Philadelphia friends John Sloan, George Luks, and Everett Shinn, is recognized today for his realistic paintings of American urban life. Between 1891 and 1895, he worked as an illustrator-reporter for several Philadelphia newspapers, while attending the Pennsylvania Academy of the Fine Arts at night. Before J. B. Lippincott Company commissioned Carqueville to design the monthly posters for their magazine, the firm used designs by various Philadelphia artists; Glackens designed the August 1894 poster (Cat. 77). In 1895, he went to Paris to continue his art studies, and on his return in late 1896 he settled in New York, where he again worked as an illustrator for various newspapers and magazines. He designed at least one poster for *Scribner's* in 1899. Like Sloan, he gradually decreased his work as an illustrator as he devoted more time to painting. See Nancy E. Allyn, *William Glackens: Illustrator in New York, 1897–1919* (Wilmington: Delaware Art Museum, 1985).

Alice Russell Glenny
1858–1924

Only two posters are known by Glenny: one for the women's edition of the Buffalo *Courier* (Cat. 78), another for the 1897 exhibition of the Buffalo Fine Art Academy and Society of Artists. Both are among the most beautifully printed American posters of the 1890s. These designs have the cool, classical frontality that could be perfectly at home in one of McKim, Mead, and White's classical-revival buildings or at the 1893 World's Columbian Exposition in Chicago. Glenny's drawing is firm and assured, and her feeling for color is unmatched. She trained as a painter in New York and Paris and specialized in murals.

Joseph J. Gould, Jr.
ca. 1880–ca. 1935

The details of Gould's biography have continued to be unclear. He studied in 1894–95 at the Pennsylvania Academy of the Fine Arts. His illustrations appeared in several short-lived Philadelphia journals, including *Moods* and *Footlights*, at mid-decade. In 1895, he began a two-year association with J. B. Lippincott Company, succeeding Carqueville as designer of the monthly series of magazine posters. Critics have unfairly described Gould's posters as derivative of both Carqueville and Penfield. His compositions lacked the static frontal quality of Penfield's figures, implied greater movement through diagonal composition, and relied on planes of nonprimary color. Two other posters for Lippincott are known—one in the "Select Novel" series, and another for Marie Corelli's popular fiction (Cat. 88). Gould continued working as an illustrator and designer in the new century. See *Philadelphia: Three Centuries of American Art* (Philadelphia: Philadelphia Museum of Art, 1976).

Walter Conant Greenough
Dates unknown

Greenough designed at least four posters for New York publishers—one for Henry Holt and Company (Cat. 93) and three for Dodd, Mead and Company—in 1895 and 1896. He was probably trained as an illustrator and may have been on the art staff of Dodd, Mead.

George R. Halm
Dates unknown

Halm provided at least three posters for several New York publishers. His best-known poster was for the series "Ballads of Our Forefathers" (Dodd, Mead, 1895).

Theodore Hampe
Dates unknown

Only one printed poster is known by Hampe: the August 1896 *St. Nicholas* (Cat. 95) records his skill as an illustrator. His entry in *The Century* poster contest received an honorable mention, but no description of it survives.

Ernest Haskell
1876–1925

Haskell is remembered today as one of the important American etchers active in the first quarter of the twentieth century. Like another American printmaker, John Sloan, he began his career as an illustrator for newspapers and magazines in the 1890s. Haskell arrived in New York sometime in 1895 and was soon providing illustrations and many poster designs for the Sunday editions of the *Journal* and the *World*, as well as for *Scribner's* and *Truth*. He seemed to favor two styles. One tended to flat areas of color and idealized subjects (see Cat. 96) closely akin to the work of Penfield and Carqueville; the other was filled with a *joie de vivre* that owed much to Jules Chéret and the French school. By the turn of the century, after a brief period of study at the Académie Julian in Paris, Haskell was successful as a designer of theater posters.

Frank Hazenplug
1873–after 1908

Little is known about Hazenplug prior to 1894, when he entered the employ of Stone and Kimball. He worked closely with Bradley and proved to be an adept co-worker. When Bradley moved to Springfield, Hazenplug took over the elder artist's position in the firm. He has frequently been dismissed as an imitator of Bradley, but this judgment is unfair. While several of his seven posters published by Stone and Kimball shared a kinship with Bradley's posters, Hazenplug's use of color and perspective was his own. The seventh, designed in 1895 for "Living Posters," a benefit for an association of visiting nurses in Chicago, was composed in large, flat areas of color with little dependence on the drawn line.

Oliver Herford
1863–1935

Herford, born in England, studied at the Slade School, London, and at the Académie Julian, Paris, before emigrating to the United States. He worked as a caricaturist and illustrator for the humor magazine *Life* as well as for publishers in New York and Boston. He was also the author of several books, which he illustrated, including *Artful Anticks* (Cat. 102).

Louise Lyons Heustis
ca. 1865–1951

Heustis, a portrait painter and illustrator, studied at the Art Students League, New York, and at the Académie Julian, Paris. She provided illustrations for Harper and Brothers, Charles Scribner's Sons, and The Century Company. She designed at least five posters for books with evocative titles, such as *Stolen Souls*, *I Married a Wife*, and *Chiffon's Marriage* (Cat. 103), published by Frederick A. Stokes Company, New York, in 1895 and 1896.

Will Phillip Hooper
Dates unknown

Hooper, an illustrator, designed four posters for new books issued by four New York publishers. Two of them, *The Prisoner of Zenda* and *Slain by the Doones* (Cat. 104), were fraught with sensational mystery to intrigue a bookseller's customers, much like the popular paperbacks of today. Hooper illustrated Burr McIntosh's *Foot-Ball and Love* of 1895 and designed the accompanying poster.

L. F. Hurd
Dates unknown

Whitehead had seven posters by Hurd in his collection, all for various titles published by Dodd, Mead and Company in 1895. During the following year, Hurd designed two more book posters for two other New York firms, D. Appleton and Company and Frederick A. Stokes Company; both were included in the 1896 benefit exhibition for Old Dominion Hospital, Richmond.

John D. Kelley
Dates unknown

Only one poster is known by Kelley, for The Century Company's *St. Nicholas* (Cat. 108). On the basis of this poster design, it can be presumed that Kelley was an illustrator employed by The Century Company.

William Sargeant Kendall
1869–1938

In 1895, W. Lewis Fraser aptly described Kendall's work as resembling the telegram. His portraits were a "telegraph utterance, short, nervous, incisive, spoken with a dash and go which seem to imply 'I have no time to linger on the curves of those lips, on the turn of that eyebrow, and neither do you. You must take my picture for what it is, a reflex of the time in which I live. I have uttered the essential thought; you may fill in the rest'" ("The Century's American Artists' Series: Sargeant Kendall," *The Century* 50.3 [July 1895], p. 478).

These comments might also describe the effect of Kendall's three posters for *Scribner's*, unique among the hundreds of American posters issued in the 1890s. All three are telegraphic portraits against a stark yellow background, conveying the essential personalities of well-known artists: Charles Dana Gibson, August 1895 (Cat. 109); Robert Blum, January 1896; and Charles Stanley Reinhart, later in 1896. Kendall lettered the posters himself, replacing the conventional masthead of the magazine.

R. W. Lane
Dates unknown

Presumably Lane was an illustrator employed by Charles Scribner's Sons, since the artist's four known posters were for books published by the firm.

H. M. Lawrence
Dates unknown

Lawrence designed at least four posters for *The Century Magazine* and for books published by The Century Company. Presumably he was employed in their art department in 1895. The October 1895 poster for *The Century* (Cat. 111) is unusual in color and design and suggests a possible connection or at least familiarity with various art potteries associated with the American Arts and Crafts movement.

Joseph Christian Leyendecker
1874–1951

Leyendecker's designs for magazine covers for the *Saturday Evening Post* and for advertisements for Arrow shirts, Kuppenheimer suits, and Interwoven socks were an important part of American popular culture in the years before World War II. He was a talented artist who deliberately chose to pursue a commercial career. His earliest poster designs, for two books, were done in 1895 while he was working at the Chicago printing firm of J. Manz and Company. He had been at this firm since 1891, while he also attended evening classes at the Art Institute. In 1896, he won the first prize in *The Century* poster contest (Cat. 112); that same year, he went to Paris to continue his art studies at the Académie Julian. He returned to Chicago after a year. *The Century* competition brought him many commissions during the last years of the decade, including twelve monthly designs for covers and posters from the editors of *The Inland Printer* (see Cat. 113); for *The Chap-Book* in 1899; for *Up to Date*; and for the Chicago firm of Hart, Schaffner, and Marx during the next decade. In 1899, he moved his studio to New York. See Michael Schau, *J. C. Leyendecker* (New York: Watson-Guptill, 1974).

A. W. B. Lincoln
Dates unknown

Lincoln was one of the more prolific designers of posters in the mid-1890s. Most of these small posters, at least twenty-one in number, advertised new titles issued by Frederick A. Stokes Company; he was possibly a member of their art department in 1894 and 1895. He also provided at least nine designs for other book publishers, three for *Pocket Magazine*, and one for *The Century*.

Louis Loeb
1866–1909

After study at the Académie Gérôme, Paris, Loeb worked in New York, where he pursued a career as a painter. He provided many illustrations for New York magazines.

Florence Lundborg
1871–1949

Lundborg, born in California, is remembered today for the seven posters she designed for the humor and literary magazine *The Lark*. Her posters, like the one by Porter for the same magazine (Cat. 228), epitomized the ideals of the Arts and Crafts movement in California. Lundborg studied with two influential leaders of the movement, Arthur F. Mathews and Lucia Mathews, at the Mark Hopkins Institute, San Francisco. In that tradition she cut the wood blocks herself for six of her posters for *The Lark*. Very little is known of her later career. In 1915, she painted three murals for the Tea Room of the Women's Board in the California Building at the Panama-Pacific International Exposition, San Francisco, for which she received a bronze medal. By 1933, she had moved to New York, where she executed murals in two high schools. She illustrated several books and specialized in portrait painting.

Henry McCarter
1865–1943

McCarter studied with Thomas Eakins at the Pennsylvania Academy of the Fine Arts and then went to Paris. On his return, he worked as an illustrator for major New York publishing firms and won prizes for his illustrations at fairs and competitions in the first decades of the new century. His poster for Stone and Kimball's Green Tree Library series (Cat. 124) was unlike any other American poster of the 1890s—boldly conceived in green, red, and purple, echoing the books in this series, which shocked traditional American readers. He designed several posters for magazines, including two for *Scribner's* in 1896 and 1898; one for *The Century*; and, according to Whitehead, one for *McClure's*.

Blanche McManus
1870–?

McManus studied art in Paris. On her return to the United States in 1893, she worked in Chicago as an illustrator and an author. Like many other artists of the decade, she also designed posters, of which eight are known, for almost as many publishers. All but one are for books; two in particular received critical acclaim: *Legends of the Rhine* for A. S. Barnes and Company; and Lamson, Wolffe and Company's *The True Mother Goose* (Cat. 127), of which she herself was the author. Her posters are boldly conceived, with a sure sense of the well-drawn line and a controlled use of contrasting color to create a positive and a negative image. After 1900, she returned to Paris. McManus was married to Francis Miltoun Mansfield; some catalogues use her married name.

A. J. Moores
Dates unknown

Moores designed more than twelve posters for The Century Company while working in their art department—four for *The Century* and *St. Nicholas*, others for various books published from 1894 to 1896.

Peter Sheaf Hersey Newell
1862–1924

The New York artist Newell wrote and illustrated some of the best-known books for children at the turn of the century, including *The Topsys and Turvys* of 1893 and *The Hole Book* of 1908. He was self taught, with only a three-month stint at the Art Students League. His many humorous sketches were quite popular and insured his employment with the editors of *Harper's*, *St. Nicholas*, and other magazines. He provided designs for several posters, including one for *Topsys and Turvys*. See Philip Hofer, "Peter Newell's Pictures and Rhymes," *Colophon* 19 (1934), n.p.

Maxfield Parrish
1870–1966

By the time he finished his studies at the Pennsylvania Academy of the Fine Arts, the painter-illustrator Parrish was already a draftsman and colorist of great individuality. In 1896, he and Robert Vonnoh organized a poster exhibition at the Academy. Parrish designed the catalogue cover and the poster (Cat. 133). His entries in the two major poster contests of 1896 received prizes: second place in *The Century* poster contest (Cat. 134), and first place in the Pope Manufacturing Company's Columbia bicycle poster contest. During the remaining years of the decade, his career as an illustrator flourished. He designed several posters for books and periodicals published by Copeland and Day, R. H. Russell and Company, Harper and Brothers, and Charles Scribner's Sons, among others. Most important, he also received his first commissions for posters and other advertisements from manufacturers of such products as Colgate soap, Adlake cameras, and Hornby's oatmeal. These designs formed another important aspect of his early career. See Coy Ludwig, *Maxfield Parrish* (New York: Watson-Guptill, 1973).

William McGregor Paxton
1869–1941

Paxton, best known for his fashionable portraits and introspective genre scenes with young women in contemporary settings, epitomized the Boston school of painting at the turn of the century. He studied in Boston and Paris, then returned to Boston in 1893 and taught at the Colby Art School. Among his students was Ethel Reed, who made significant contributions to the American poster in the 1890s. Paxton provided several poster designs for the Sunday editions of the Boston *Herald*. See Nancy Finlay, *Artists of the Book in Boston, 1890–1910* (Cambridge, Mass.: Harvard College Library, 1985).

Edward Penfield
1866–1925

Penfield's series of monthly posters for *Harper's* defined and dominated this decade of art posters in America. They were bold, precise, and often witty. The success of the *Harper's* series brought critical acclaim to this young artist. Besides the magazine posters, he designed at least fifteen for books published by Harper and Brothers, two calendars for R. H. Russell and Company, and several commercial posters for manufacturers of bicycles, dynamite, and other products during the 1890s. Penfield resigned his position at *Harper's* in 1901 but continued as an independent artist and illustrator. He supplied cover designs and illustrations for books and for various magazines, such as *Scribner's*, *Collier's*, and *Saturday Evening Post*. After 1901, most of the posters were commissioned by various manufacturers for product advertising—for example, Hart, Schaffner, and Marx clothing. Penfield was one of the best-known illustrators and commercial artists of his day.

It would be tempting to join the critics who dismiss Penfield's posters as simple derivations from French prototypes, especially the work of Steinlen and Lautrec. This attitude does not take into account an important part of Penfield's artistic psyche—he was a superb synthesizer. With great skill he easily adapted the French forcefulness, directness, and extreme simplicity of means, and used them to suit his own artistic needs. As a result, his posters have great individuality. His subjects were also uniquely American types. He used at most one or two figures, often at leisure and casually informal in dress. Penfield's posters' skillfully define an era. See David Gibson, *Designed to Persuade: The Graphic Art of Edward Penfield* (Yonkers, N.Y.: The Hudson River Museum, 1984).

E. Pickert
Dates unknown

Pickert was an enigma even in the 1890s. His two posters for the *New York Times* were published as by DeYongh; the printed initials "E. P." were easily ignored. But he was properly credited in the 1896 catalogue of the benefit poster show for the Old Dominion Hospital, Richmond.

E. S. Pierce
Dates unknown

Pierce worked in Boston, where he designed several posters in 1895 and 1896 for *The Bostonian* and *Miss Blue Stocking*.

Bruce Porter
1865–?

Porter was a co-editor, with Burgess, of *The Lark*. He wrote several articles for the journal, provided some of the illustrations and at least one cover (June 1895), and designed the poster for the opening issue (Cat. 228). He received his formal training as a painter in England and in Paris and was active in San Francisco as a mural painter and as a designer of stained glass.

Edward Henry Potthast
1857–1927

Potthast studied at the Art Academy of Cincinnati as well as at various art centers in Europe. He is remembered as a painter of the summer seashore, but he also designed several posters, including those in 1895 for *The Century Cook Book* and in 1896 for *Metropolitan Magazine*. In 1896, he received an honorable mention in *The Century* poster contest for a design used immediately for the magazine's July 1896 poster (Cat. 229). Poster design was not new to him, since he had worked for the Cincinnati lithographers Strobridge and Company. At least one of their several circus posters—showing a girl balancing on the back of a horse for Barnum and Bailey—bears his printed signature.

Maurice Brazil Prendergast
1859–1924

Prendergast was in his mid-thirties when he returned to Boston after study in Paris. To support himself, he and his brother Charles opened a frame shop in Boston. Like many other artists whose fame as painters came in the next century, he also worked as an illustrator. He provided cover designs, illustrations, and at least four posters for books published by the Boston firms Joseph Knight Company and W. Z. Wilde and Company. His posters combine a graphic boldness with an effective use of line and pattern, showing a familiarity with Japanese prints. His figures, however, are somewhat awkward. Surprisingly, his posters have little connection with his monotypes and watercolors from the 1890s; they lack the expressivity and experimental freedom so essential to those now familiar products of his artistic genius. See Howell Rhys, *Maurice Prendergast 1859–1924* (Cambridge, Mass.: Harvard University Press, 1960); and Eleanor Green, et al., *Maurice Prendergast: Art of Impulse and Color* (College Park, Md.: University of Maryland Art Gallery, 1976).

Ethel Reed
1874–after 1900

In a two-year period, Ethel Reed of Boston emerged from obscurity, blossomed as an artist with an international reputation, and then disappeared completely. Her biography is fairy-tale material. Reed was not only very young but also strikingly beautiful; she was often described in posterlike terms. Many of the women in her posters and illustrations were probably self-portraits. Her engagement, after a passionate whirlwind romance, to another Boston artist, Philip Hale, was publicized in the literary journals and poster magazines. Yet she sailed alone for Europe in May 1896, "to study in the broad school of life." In 1897, she was in London working on her last known poster, for Richard Le Gallienne's *Quest of the Golden Girl*. She was reportedly in Ireland in 1898, resting; then she disappeared.

Sensational though her personal life may have been, Reed had great artistic talent. Her formal training was brief, and to a great measure she was self-taught. Her earliest posters for the Boston Sunday *Herald*, while somewhat self-conscious and tentative, displayed her skill with black-and-white composition. With great rapidity she gained assurance with design and color and a unique style as she continued designing posters for the Sunday *Herald*; Lamson, Wolffe and Company; and Copeland and Day. She designed sixteen posters in 1895 and received favorable notice from European and American critics, especially for Lamson, Wolffe's *Miss Traümerei* (Cat. 235). She favored female figures—if young girls, they are often knowingly naughty—frequently surrounded by either poppies or lilies, which to the fin-de-siècle mind were fraught with secret meanings. During the first five months of 1896, she not only continued working on illustrations for several books but also designed another six (and possibly seven) posters: one each for the Sunday *Herald*, *Time and the Hour* (Cat. 246), and *Pocket Magazine*; two additional posters for books; and one for the fund-raising effort of Chicago's Eugene Field Memorial Committee. In all, Reed designed at least twenty-four posters, many of which rank among the important American posters of the 1890s. It is tempting to speculate on the further development of her extraordinary talents, the path that terminated so suddenly in the late 1890s. See Nancy Finlay, *Artists of the Book in Boston, 1890–1900* (Cambridge, Mass.: Harvard College Library, 1985).

Frederic Remington
1861–1909

Remington's fame and popularity as an artist of the Old West have not waned. Magazines vied to secure his services, whether to illustrate the West or the Cuban campaigns of the Spanish-American War. His sole poster for the New York magazine *Collier's Weekly* (Cat. 247) was most likely drawn directly by him and not photomechanically reproduced. In his 1897 catalogue, Flood listed one other Remington poster, possibly for a book, entitled *Ranch Life and the Hunting Trail*. See Harold McCracken, *Frederic Remington: Artist of the Old West* (Philadelphia: J. B. Lippincott Co., 1947).

Louis John Rhead
1857–1926

Born in England, Rhead came to New York in 1883 as art director for the publisher D. Appleton soon after his studies at London's National Art Training School in South Kensington. During his six years with that firm, he also pursued a private practice, contributing patterns for art needlework and ceramic painting to several ladies' magazines, designing book covers and bindings, and painting. In 1890, his first poster appeared. By the end of the nineties, he had designed as many as one hundred posters and received critical acclaim in America and in Europe. He was the only American to have solo exhibitions of posters in London in 1896 and in Paris at the Salon des Cent in 1897 (Cat. 269). He received commissions from a number of New York publishers, usually for posters to accompany the holiday editions of magazines. At Christmas 1895, his designs appeared simultaneously for *The Century* (Cat. 259), *St. Nicholas*, *The Bookman*, and *Scribner's* (Cat. 260), and for the New York newspaper the *Herald*. The large one- and two-sheet designs for the *Sun* and the *Journal* were among his most effective posters. They were bold and direct, and their impact increased when several were hung together. He also designed a number of posters for commercial products, including Lundborg perfumes (Cat. 248), Pearline washing powders and cleansers, and Packer's soap, as well as two for the printing firm Louis Prang and Company (Cat. 251, 258). His poster activity declined after 1900 as he devoted his talents increasingly to book illustration.

Rhead has been called the American Eugène Grasset. He did emulate the Swiss-French artist and publicly acknowledged an artistic debt. However, this relationship was also one of parallel development. Both artists admired the work of Walter Crane and William Morris, two of the leading English artists of the aesthetic movement, and, like them, worked in all aspects of design. In contrast to the posters of Lautrec and Chéret, however, Grasset's and Rhead's designs reflect the poster's ability to uplift the morality of the viewer. See Gleeson White, "The Posters of Louis Rhead," *The Studio* 8.41 (August 1896), pp. 156–161.

Henry Mortika Rosenberg
1858–1947

Rosenberg's only known poster won an honorable mention in *The Century* poster contest of 1896 (Cat. 272). He was a painter, and eventually he became the director of an art school in Halifax, Nova Scotia.

Julius A. Schweinfurth
1858–1931

Only two posters are known by the Boston architect Schweinfurth: one for the Boston Festival Orchestra, the other for the novel *Quo Vadis* (Cat. 273). He designed the first in 1895, soon after his arrival in Boston from Paris, where he had studied architecture. Mrs. J. A. Schweinfurth lent a number of his posters to the exhibition sponsored by the Massachusetts Charitable Mechanic Association in 1895, according to the accompanying catalogue.

George Frederick Scotson-Clark
1873–?

Scotson-Clark grew up in Brighton, England, where he was a classmate of Beardsley. At the age of eighteen, he emigrated to America, where he worked in New York as a stage and costume designer. He also designed an unknown number of theater posters. From 1895 to 1897, he designed many posters for several New York newspapers, including the *World*, the *Record*, and the *Ledger*. He also worked for Dodd, Mead and Company, supplying several book placards and at least five posters with medievalizing subjects for their magazine, *The Bookman*. Some of his most striking posters were for *Outing* in 1896 and 1897. In 1897, he returned to England, where he continued his career as a designer of theater posters. See Edgar Wenlock, "Some Posters by Scotson-Clark," *The Poster* 2.7 (Jan. 1899), pp. 30–32.

John Sloan
1871–1951

John Sloan was one of the foremost personalities in the world of American art during the first half of the twentieth century. His reputation rests on his many etchings and paintings of the New York urban environment, part of a movement familiarly described as the "Ash Can School." But this work came after his move to New York from Philadelphia in 1904. During the 1890s he worked as an illustrator for various Philadelphia newspapers, including the *Inquirer* and the *Press*. It is unclear how many posters he designed, since only one or two fragments of the long series he created for the Bradley Coal Company of Philadelphia survive. Six other posters are known: one for Apollo Bicycles, another for an auction of caricatures at the Pennsylvania Academy of the Fine Arts, and the remainder for books and magazines (Cat. 275–278). In 1894, *The Chap-Book* published four black-and-white drawings expressive of Sloan's interest in graphic line, based on study of Japanese prints. Their effect is similar to that of his poster for *The Echo* of 1895 (Cat. 277). His posters display a firm control of graphic design that continued throughout his extensive career as an etcher in the new century. See Peter Morse, *John Sloan's Prints: A Catalogue Raisonné of the Etchings, Lithographs, and Posters* (New Haven: Yale University Press, 1969).

Marianna Sloan
1875–1954

Marianna Sloan, the sister of John Sloan, was a landscape and mural painter who studied at the Philadelphia School of Design for Women. Copies of her only poster are quite rare today.

John Stewardson
Dates unknown

Only one poster is known by Stewardson, for a book published by J. B. Lippincott Company (Cat. 280). He may have been a student at the Pennsylvania Academy of the Fine Arts.

M. Louise Stowell
Dates unknown

Stowell, a student at the Art Students League, New York, and of Dow, was active as a painter and illustrator in her native Rochester, New York. She probably designed only one poster. Rochester was a hotbed of poster activity in the mid-1890s, perhaps because Bragdon settled there on his return from Paris, and he actively participated in the local poster mania as designer, author, and collector.

John Henry Twachtman
1853–1902

Twachtman achieved fame as one of the leading American Impressionist painters and in a more minor capacity as an etcher. His only known poster design was commissioned by Stone and Kimball to promote Harold Frederic's *The Damnation of Theron Ware* (Cat. 282). It is clearly a painter's poster and not that of a graphic designer; Twachtman conceived the poster in terms of color and brushwork, not graphic line. In the 1890s, he lived in Cos Cob, Connecticut.

Henry Sumner Watson
1868–1933

After studies at the Pennsylvania Academy of the Fine Arts, Philadelphia, and the Académie Julian, Paris, Watson worked as an illustrator and eventually specialized in scenes of hunting and fishing. He designed about forty posters from 1895 to 1897 for the magazines *Truth*, *Bachelor of Arts*, *Outing*, and *Recreation*.

E. B. Wells
Dates unknown

No biographical information is available on this talented artist.

Charles Herbert Woodbury
1864–1940

Woodbury was a successful landscape painter, watercolorist, and printmaker in Boston. After art studies in Boston, he continued his training in Paris and Holland. His acquaintance with artists in Holland probably led to the commission for his first poster, announcing the exhibition of the Society of Painters in Water-Color of Holland at Chase's Gallery in Boston (Cat. 285). The rich effects of his poster designs were conveyed by the disposition of sharp lines and flat areas of limited color. Like Dow, another native Massachusetts artist, Woodbury founded his sense of design on familiarity with Japanese art, championed by Fenollosa at the Museum of Fine Arts, Boston. Woodbury's six posters received favorable comment from American and European critics.

Charles Hubbard Wright
1870–1939

Wright, a painter and illustrator, designed over thirty posters while on the staff of the New York *Herald* in 1895 and 1896. He also designed at least one other poster, for *The Century* in 1897.

BIBLIOGRAPHY

ADAMS, THEODORE. "A Few Words about the Beginning of a Collection." *Poster Lore* 1.1 (Jan. 1896), pp. 14–17.

ADES, DAWN. *Posters: The Twentieth-Century Poster, Design of the Avant-Garde.* New York: Abbeville Press; Minneapolis, Walker Art Center, 1984.

ALEXANDRE, ARSÈNE; SPIELMANN, M. H.; BUNNER, H. C.; and JACCACI, AUGUST. *The Modern Poster.* New York: Charles Scribner's Sons, 1895.

ALLEN, DOUGLAS. *Frederic Remington and the Spanish-American War.* New York: Crown, 1971.

ALLYN, NANCY E. *William Glackens: Illustrator in New York, 1897–1919.* Wilmington: Delaware Art Museum, 1985.

American Art Nouveau: The Poster Period of John Sloan. Ed. Helen Farr Sloan. Lock Haven, Penn.: Hammermill Paper Co., 1967.

American Publishers' Posters and Books, 1894–98. Houston: University of Houston Library, 1976.

ARNOULD, A. *Catalogue d'affiches artistiques françaises et étrangères.* Paris, 1896.

BADGER, RICHARD GORHAM. "The Development of a Modern Master: Hazenplug." *The Red Letter* 1.3 (Nov. 1896), pp. 56–59.

BAUWENS, MAURICE; HAYASHI, T.; LA FORGUE, JULES; MEIER-GRAEFE, J.; and PENNELL, JOSEPH. *Les Affiches étrangères illustrées.* Paris: C. Tallandier, 1897.

BERALDI, HENRI. *Les Graveurs du XIX siècle* 4. Paris, 1886.

BOLTON, CHARLES KNOWLES. *A Descriptive Catalogue of Posters, Chiefly American, in the Collection of Charles Knowles Bolton with Biographical Notes and Bibliography May MDCCCXCV.* Boston: Winthrop B. Jones, 1895.

————. *The Reign of the Poster.* Boston: Winthrop B. Jones, 1895.

BOLTON, THEODORE. *American Book Illustrators.* New York: R. R. Bowker, 1938.

Books and Artistic Publications: Illustrated and Descriptive List of the Publications of R. H. Russell, 33 Rose Street, New York. New York: R. H. Russell, 1897.

BRADLEY, WILL H. "Edward Penfield, Artist." *Bradley: His Book* 1.1 (May 1896), pp. 6, 7.

———— (?). "Ethel Reed, Artist." *Bradley: His Book* 1.3 (July 1896), pp. 74–76.

————. *Will Bradley: His Chap Book.* Typophile Chap Books 30. New York: The Typophiles, 1955.

Bradley: His Book 1–2.3 (1896–97). Springfield, Mass.: The Wayside Press.

BREITENBACH, EDGAR, and COGSWELL, MARGARET. *The American Poster.* New York: American Federation of Arts, 1967.

BURNSIDE, WESLEY M. *Maynard Dixon: Artist of the West.* Provo, Utah: Brigham Young University Press, 1974.

CACHIN, FRANÇOISE; MOFFETT, CHARLES S.; and BAREAU, JULIET WILSON. *Manet 1832–1883.* New York: The Metropolitan Museum of Art and Harry N. Abrams, 1983.

Catalogue: Being a List of Some Few Posters and Various Other Sketches by Will Bradley . . . Springfield, Mass.: The Wayside Press, 1896.

CATE, PHILLIP DENNIS. "Printing in France, 1850–1900: The Artist and New Technologies." *Gazette of the Grolier Club,* n.s. 5.28–29 (June–Dec. 1978), pp. 57–73.

————, and BOYER, PATRICIA ECKERT. *The Circle of Toulouse-Lautrec: An Exhibition of the Work of the Artist and of His Close Associates.* New Brunswick, N. J.: Jane Voorhees Zimmerli Art Museum, Rutgers University, 1985.

————, and GILL, SUSAN. *Théophile-Alexandre Steinlen.* Salt Lake City: Gibbs M. Smith; and New Brunswick, N. J.: Rutgers University, 1982.

————, and HITCHINGS, SINCLAIR HAMILTON. *The Color Revolution: Color Lithography in France 1890–1900.* Santa Barbara and Salt Lake City: Peregrine Smith, 1978; New Brunswick, N. J.: Rutgers University Art Gallery, 1978.

The Century and Echo Poster Show: Catalogue of Artistic Posters. Chicago, The Echo, 1895.

"A Chat with Miss Ethel Reed." *The Bookman* 2.4 (December 1895), pp. 277–281.

COCHRAN, CHARLES B. "Theatrical Posters in America." *The Poster* 1.2 (July 1898), pp. 62–63.

A Collection of Book Plate Designs by Louis Rhead. Boston: W. Porter Truesdale, 1897.

"A Complete List of Posters Designed by Louis J. Rhead to January 20, 1896." *The Poster* 1.3 (March 1896), pp. 30, 31.

COSMOS CLUB. *An Exhibition of Posters—Mostly American—at the Cosmos Club. Notes and Comments.* Washington, D.C., 1895.

CRICHTON, LAURIE W. *Book Decoration in America, 1890–*

1910: A Guide to an Exhibition. Williamstown, Mass.: Williams College, 1979.

DELSOL, MAURICE. *Paris-Cythère.* Paris, [1895?].

Edwin Austin Abbey (1852–1911). New Haven: Yale University Art Gallery, 1974.

L'Estampe et l'affiche (1897–99). Paris.

FINLAY, NANCY. *Artists of the Book in Boston, 1890–1910.* Cambridge, Mass.: Harvard College Library, 1985.

FLEISSNER, HERBERT. *Kauft Bücher! Verlagsplakate um die Jahrhundertwende.* Die bibliophilen Taschenbücher no. 347. Dortmund: Harenberg Kommunikation, 1982.

FRASER, W. LEWIS. "The Century's American Artist's Series: Sargeant Kendall." *The Century* 50.3 (July 1895), p. 478.

FUSTIER, GUSTAVE. "La Littérature murale." *Le Livre* (Nov. 10, 1884), pp. 337–356.

GIBSON, DAVID. *Designed to Persuade: The Graphic Art of Edward Penfield.* Yonkers, N.Y.: The Hudson River Museum, 1984.

GLUSKER-LEBRAVE, DEBORAH, and DESALMAND, LUCIEN. *Affiches américaines (1890–1900).* Paris: Galier Arenthon, 1983.

GREEN, ELEANOR, et al. *Maurice Prendergast: Art of Impulse and Color.* College Park, Md.: University of Maryland Art Gallery, 1976.

GROLIER CLUB. *Catalogue of an Exhibition of Illustrated Bill-Posters.* New York, 1890.

GRUNWALD CENTER FOR THE GRAPHIC ARTS. *The American Personality: The Artist-Illustrator of Life in the United States 1860–1930.* Los Angeles: University of California Press, 1976.

GULLANS, CHARLES, and ESPEY, JOHN. "American Trade Bindings and Their Designers, 1880–1915." *Collectible Books, Some New Paths.* London and New York: R. R. Bowker, 1979.

———. *A Checklist of Trade Bindings Designed by Margaret Armstrong.* Los Angeles: University of California Library, 1968.

———. *The Decorative Designers 1896–1932.* Los Angeles: University of California Library, 1970.

HAND, MARLA H. "Carloz Schwabe's Poster for the Salon de la Rose + Croix: A Herald of the Ideal in Art." *Art Journal* 44.1 (Spring 1984), pp. 40–45.

HAWKES, ELIZABETH H. *The Poster Decade: American Posters of the 1890s.* Wilmington: Delaware Art Museum, 1977.

HENRIOT, ALEXANDRE. *Catalogue de l'exposition d'affiches artistiques, françaises et étrangères, modernes et rétrospectives.* Reims, 1896; repr. Paris: Union Centrale des Arts Décoratifs, 1980.

HIATT, CHARLES. "On Some Recent Designs by Will H. Bradley, of Chicago." *The Studio* 4.23 (Feb. 1895), pp. 166–168.

——— "Pictorial Book Advertisements in America." *The Poster and Art Collector* 6 (1901). No. 30 (Jan.), pp. 1–5: I, "Some Designs by Maxfield Parrish"; II, "Some Bills by Will Carqueville." No. 31 (Feb.), pp. 65–70: III, "Some Designs by J. J. Gould"; IV, "Some Placards for *The Lark*"; V, "Some Placards by Frank Hazenplug." No. 32 (March), pp. 120–122: VI, "Some Designs by Henry Meyer."

HILLIER, BEVIS. *Posters.* New York: Stein and Day, 1969.

HOFER, PHILIP. "Peter Newell's Pictures and Rhymes." *Colophon* 19 (1934), n.p.

HOLMES, DAVID L. *Autographs*, catalogue 16 (October 1986).

HORNUNG, CLARENCE P., and WONG, ROBERTA WADDELL. *Will Bradley: His Graphic Art.* New York: Dover, 1974.

JOHNSON, ARTHUR WARREN. *Arthur Wesley Dow: Historian-Artist-Teacher.* Ipswich, Mass.: Ipswich Historical Society, 1934.

JUSSIM, ESTELLE. *Slave to Beauty: The Eccentric Life and Controversial Career of F. Holland Day, Photographer, Publisher, Aesthete.* Boston: David R. Godine, 1981.

KEAY, CAROLYN. *American Posters of the Turn of the Century.* New York: St. Martin's Press, 1975.

KEY, MABLE. "The Passing of the Poster." *Brush and Pencil* 4.1 (April 1899), pp. 12–19.

KNIGHT, FRANK R. "Henry Brevoort Eddy, Artist." *Bradley: His Book* 1.3 (July 1896), pp. 87–93.

KOCH, ROBERT. "Artistic Books, Periodicals, and Posters of the 'Gay Nineties.'" *The Art Quarterly* 25.4 (Winter 1962), pp. 371–383.

KOEHLER, SYLVESTER ROSA. *Exhibition Illustrating the Technical Methods of the Reproductive Arts from the XV. Century to the Present Time, with Special Reference to The Photo-Mechanical Processes.* Boston: Museum of Fine Arts, 1892.

KRAMER, SIDNEY. *A History of Stone and Kimball and Herbert S. Stone and Co., with a Bibliography of Their Publications 1893–1905.* Chicago: University of Chicago Press, 1940.

KRAUS, JOE W. *Messrs. Copeland and Day, 69 Cornhill, Boston 1893–1899.* Philadelphia: George S. MacManus, 1979.

LARSON, JUDY L. *American Illustration 1890–1925: Romance, Adventure, and Suspense.* Calgary, Alberta: The Glenbow Museum, 1986.

LATIMER, R. R. "The American Poster." *The Poster* 1.3 (Aug.–Sept. 1898), pp. 115–118.

LEHRER, RUTH FINE, and MOORE, RUSSELL J. *Ernest Haskell (1876–1925): A Retrospective Exhibition.* Brunswick, Me.: Bowdoin College Museum of Art, 1976.

A List of French, English and American Posters . . . the Poster Show Benefit Old Dominion Hospital. . . . Richmond, Va., 1896.

LUDWIG, COY. *Maxfield Parrish.* New York: Watson-Guptill, 1973.

MAINDRON, ERNEST. *Les Affiches illustrées.* Paris: H. Launette, 1886.

Les Maîtres de l'affiche (1896–1900). Paris: Imprimerie Chaix.

MALHOTRA, RUTH; THOM, CHRISTINA; et al. *Das frühe Plakat in Europa und den USA.* Vol. I: *Grossbritannien und Vereinigte Staaten von Nordamerika.* Berlin: Gebr. Mann, 1973.

MARGOLIN, VICTOR. *American Poster Renaissance.* New York: Watson-Guptill, 1975.

MASSACHUSETTS CHARITABLE MECHANIC ASSOCIATION. *Exhibition of Posters, October 2 to November 30 MDCCCXCV.* Boston, 1895.

MATTHEWS, BRANDER. "Books in Paper Covers." *The Century* 50 (1895), pp. 354–361.

McCRACKEN, HAROLD. *Frederic Remington: Artist of the Old West.* Philadelphia: J. B. Lippincott, 1947.

McQUILKIN, A. H. "Will H. Bradley and His Work." *Inland Printer* 14.5 (February 1895), pp. 430–433.

MOFFATT, FREDERICK C. *Arthur Wesley Dow (1857–1922).* Washington, D.C.: National Collection of Fine Arts, 1977.

MORSE, PETER. *John Sloan's Prints: A Catalogue Raisonné of the Etchings, Lithographs, and Posters*. New Haven: Yale University Press, 1969.

OINONEN, RICHARD E. *Oinonen Book Auctions 279, sale no. 71* (Sunday, June 10, 1984). Sunderland, Mass., 1984.

PENNSYLVANIA ACADEMY OF THE FINE ARTS. *Exhibition of Posters*. Philadelphia, 1896.

Philadelphia: Three Centuries of American Art. Philadelphia: Philadelphia Museum of Art, 1976.

PHILLIPS SON AND NEALE, New York. Catalogues: I, *A Century of Posters 1870–1970*, sale no. 242 (Nov. 10, 1979); II, *Poster Classics*, sale no. 290 (May 10, 1980); III, *The World of Posters*, sale no. 326 (Nov. 15, 1980); V, *100 Poster Masterpieces*, sale no. 373 (May 2, 1981).

PICA, VITTORIO. "A Travers les affiches illustrées. I: Etats-Unis." *L'Estampe et l'affiche* 1.6 (Aug. 15, 1897), pp. 164–169.

Das Plakat (1910–21). Berlin.

POLLARD, PERCIVAL. "American Poster Lore." *The Poster* 2.9 (March 1899), pp. 123–127.

———, and PENFIELD, EDWARD. *Posters in Miniature*. New York: R. H. Russell, 1896.

The Poster 1–5 (Jan.–May 1896). New York: Will M. Clemens.

The Poster 1–6 (1898–1901). London.

Poster Lore 1–2.1 (1896). Kansas City, Mo.: Frederic Thoreau Singleton.

Premier Posters, sale no. 1. New York: Poster Auctions International, March 9, 1985.

PRICE, CHARLES MATLACK. *Poster Design*. New York: George W. Bricka, 1913; 2nd ed., 1922.

Publishers' Weekly 1222, 1295 (1895, 1896). New York.

QUADRANGLE CLUB. *Catalogue of an Exhibition of American, French, English, Dutch, and Japanese Posters from the Collection of Mr. Ned Arden Flood*. Chicago, 1897.

QUINCY CITY HOSPITAL. *Art Poster Exhibit in Aid of the Quincy City Hospital . . . May 7 to 10. . . .* Quincy, Mass., 1895.

RANKIN, ELLIS. "March Cover by Will Carqueville." *The Poster* 8.3 (March 1917), pp. 48, 49.

REED, WALT, and REED, ROGER. *The Illustrator in America, 1880–1980: A Century of Illustration*. New York: Madison Square Press for the Society of Illustrators, 1984.

RENNERT, JACK. *100 Years of Bicycle Posters*. New York: Harper and Row, 1973.

RHEAD, LOUIS JOHN. "The Moral Aspect of the Artistic Poster." *The Bookman* 1 (June 1895), pp. 312–314.

RHYS, HOWELL. *Maurice Prendergast 1859–1924*. Cambridge, Mass.: Harvard University Press, 1960.

ROGERS, W. S. *A Book of the Poster*. London: Greening, 1901.

ROSNER, CHARLES. *The Art of the Book Jacket*. London: Victoria and Albert Museum, 1949.

———. *The Growth of the Book Jacket*. Cambridge, Mass.: Sylvan, 1954.

ROWLAND, EARL. "Edward Penfield: An American Master Illustrator." *American Artist* 22.3 (March 1958), pp. 46–51, 60–64.

SCHAU, MICHAEL. *J. C. Leyendecker*. New York: Watson-Guptill, 1974.

SCHOLZ, LYNN. "Louis Rhead's First Career." *The American Fly Fisher* 12.1 (Winter 1985), pp. 18–25.

SCOTSON-CLARK, GEORGE FREDERICK. "The Black Spot in America." *The Poster* 5.28 (Nov. 1900), pp. 84–87.

SHIR-CLIFF, W. H. "Something of Rhead." *Ex Libris* 1.4 (April 1897), pp. 109–113.

SINGER, HANS. "Plakatkunst." *Pan* 1.5 (Feb.–March 1896), pp. 329–336.

SINGLETON, FREDERIC THOREAU. "Concerning the Poster Tendency and Mr. Will H. Bradley." *Poster Lore* 1.1 (Jan. 1896), pp. 10–13.

SOISSONS, S. C. DE. "Ethel Reed and Her Art." *The Poster* 1.5 (Nov. 1898), pp. 199–202.

———. "William H. Bradley and His Art." *The Poster* 1.4 (Oct. 1898), pp. 158–160.

SPARKS, HENRY LAWRENCE. "Edward Penfield." *Das Plakat. Mitteilungen des Vereins der Plakatfreunde* 3.1 (Jan. 1912), pp. 1–4.

SPONSEL, JEAN-LOUIS. *Das moderne Plakat*. Dresden: Gerhard Kühtmann, 1897.

STONE, HERBERT STUART. "Mr. Bradley's Drawings." *The Chap-Book* 2.2 (Dec. 1, 1894), pp. 56–62.

———. "Mr. Penfield's Posters." *The Chap-Book* 1.10 (Oct. 1, 1894), pp. 247–250.

TANSELLE, G. THOMAS. *Book-Jackets, Blurbs and Bibliographers*. London: Bibliographical Society, 1971.

The Turn of a Century, 1885–1910. Art Nouveau-Jugendstil Books. Cambridge: Harvard University Library, 1970.

UNION LEAGUE CLUB. *Some Modern Posters Shown at the Union League Club, February 14–15–16 1895*. New York, 1895.

WEDMORE, FREDERICK. "Art in the Poster." *Art Journal* n.s. 45 (1895), pp. 43–47.

WEILL, ALAIN. *L'Affichomanie: Collectionneurs d'affiches—affiches de collection 1880–1980*. Paris: Musée de l'Affiche, [1980].

WEITENKAMPF, FRANK. *American Graphic Art*. New York: Henry Holt, 1912.

WELLS, CAROLYN. "What a Lark!" *The Colophon* 8 (1931), n.p.

WEMBER, PAUL. *Die Jugend der Plakate, 1887–1917*. Krefeld: Kaiser Wilhelm Museum, 1961.

WENLOCK, EDGAR. "Some Posters by Scotson-Clark." *The Poster* 2.7 (Jan. 1899), pp. 30–32.

WHITE, GLEESON. "The Posters of Louis Rhead." *The Studio* 8.41 (Aug. 1896), pp. 156–161.

WHITEHEAD, WILBUR CHERRIER. *A Memorandum Catalogue and Check List of American Posters in the Collection of Wilbur Cherrier Whitehead*. Cleveland, 1895.

WICK, PETER A. *Toulouse-Lautrec: Book Covers and Brochures*. Cambridge, Mass.: Harvard College Library, 1972.

WONG, ROBERTA WADDELL. *American Posters of the Nineties*. Boston: Boston Public Library et al., 1974.

———. *Will H. Bradley: American Artist and Craftsman (1868–1962)*. New York: The Metropolitan Museum of Art, 1972.

WOODBURY, CHARLES H. "A Note on Posters." *Modern Art* 3.2 (Spring 1895), p. 62.

"The Work of Miss Ethel Reed." *International Studio* 1.4 (June 1897), pp. 230–236.

WUNDERLICH GALLERY. *Catalogue of an Exhibition of Original Designs from Posters by Louis J. Rhead. . . .* New York: Wunderlich Gallery, 1895.

ACKNOWLEDGMENTS

In preparing this catalogue, I received assistance from many colleagues, both in The Metropolitan Museum of Art and in libraries and galleries in New York and elsewhere. The encouragement of Colta Ives and my associates in the Department of Prints and Photographs sustained my efforts over the last year. Helen Otis and her staff of able conservators in Paper Conservation were always happy to assist me in my deliberations on technical questions. I would like to thank the following for all their efforts in helping to amass the information in this catalogue: Beth Alberty; Lynne Ambrosini; Jack Banning; Dorothea Basile; Julia Blaut; Jennifer Casler; Phillip Dennis Cate; Gail Chisholm; Bonnie Clearwater; Katherine Deiss; Nancy Finlay; Sinclair Hitchings; Elena Millie; Robert Nikirk; Martina Norelli; Nadine Orenstein; Robert Rainwater; Jack Rennert; Theresa Salazar; Jonathan Seliger; Helen Farr Sloan; and Roberta Waddell.